READING ACROSS THE DISCIPLINES

SCHOLARSHIP OF TEACHING AND LEARNING

Jennifer Meta Robinson, Whitney M. Schlegel,
and Mary Taylor Huber, *editors*

READING ACROSS THE DISCIPLINES

Edited by
KAREN MANARIN

INDIANA UNIVERSITY PRESS

This book is a publication of

Indiana University Press
Office of Scholarly Publishing
Herman B Wells Library 350
1320 East 10th Street
Bloomington, Indiana 47405 USA

iupress.org

© 2022 by Indiana University Press

All rights reserved

No part of this book may be reproduced or utilized in any form or by any means, electronic or mechanical, including photocopying and recording, or by any information storage and retrieval system, without permission in writing from the publisher. The paper used in this publication meets the minimum requirements of the American National Standard for Information Sciences—Permanence of Paper for Printed Library Materials, ANSI Z39.48-1992.

Manufactured in the United States of America

First printing 2022

Cataloging information is available from the Library of Congress.

ISBN 978-0-253-05871-3 (hardback)
ISBN 978-0-253-05872-0 (paperback)
ISBN 978-0-253-05873-7 (ebook)

CONTENTS

Foreword / Pat Hutchings vii

Reading across the Disciplines: An Introduction / Karen Manarin (Mount Royal University) 1

I. Ways of Reading

1. Exploring Readerly Diversity / Margaret Mackey (University of Alberta) 25

2. Understandings of Reading: Insights from Faculty Development with Reading Apprenticeship / Nelson Graff, Rebecca Kersnar, Dan Shapiro, and Ryne Leuzinger (California State University, Monterey Bay) 44

3. "Mind the Gap": Investigating Faculty Reading Practices / Heather C. Easterling and John Eliason (Gonzaga University) 64

4. Understanding How Students across the Disciplines Read Images / Dana Statton Thompson (Murray State University) 81

5. Student Reading of Documentary and Fiction Film / Elizabeth Marquis (McMaster University) 102

II. Reading in Specific Contexts

6. Reading-to-Write: Rehearsing the Doctoral Literature Review / Rosemary Green (Shenandoah University) 123

7. Embedding Scaffolded Reading Practices into the First-Year University Science Curriculum / Neela Griffiths and Yvonne C. Davila (University of Technology Sydney)   143

8. Reading and Relationships in Organic Chemistry / Brett McCollum (Mount Royal University) and Layne Morsch (University of Illinois Springfield)   166

9. Teaching Analytical Reading in Psychology at Alverno College / Joyce Tang Boyland, Kris Vasquez, Jordan R. Donovan, and Rachel M. Henry (Alverno College)   184

10. Strategies to Promote Reading Compliance and Student Learning in an Introductory Child Development Course / Trent W. Maurer and Catelyn Shipp (Georgia Southern University)   205

11. Read Literature, Read the World: Teaching and Learning the Interpretive Strategies of Literary Studies for Transfer / Angela J. Zito and Jakob T. Zehms (University of Wisconsin–Madison)   219

12. Capturing Confusion: Multidisciplinary Reading as Productive Disruption / Aimee Knupsky and M. Soledad Caballero (Allegheny College)   239

Index   259

FOREWORD

Pat Hutchings

A number of years ago, I was lucky enough to meet Karen Manarin and three of her wonderful colleagues from Mount Royal University—Miriam Carey, Melanie Rathburn, and Glen Ryland. As part of a campus program on the scholarship of teaching and learning, they were in the midst of an extensive study of how students read in different disciplines. In particular, they were interested in what they called "critical reading" and its role in advancing "academic goals and social engagement" as part of the institution's general education program. I was very taken with their project and apparently told them so with sufficient enthusiasm that I was invited to write the foreword for their 2015 volume, *Critical Reading in Higher Education: Academic Goals and Social Engagement*, which I was delighted to do.

A couple of years later, Karen was in touch to say that she was considering a more wide-ranging volume, one that explored the issues around reading from a wider set of angles and in more diverse ways and contexts. That volume, *Reading across the Disciplines*, is of course the one you have in your hands. And once again I find myself writing (with pleasure) the foreword to a wonderful addition to the teaching commons.

The scholarship of teaching and learning, which has contributed so much to that commons, will never run out of issues and topics that call for our attention and careful inquiry. But reading is surely among the most important and the most challenging. It is important because virtually all higher learning depends on the ability to make meaning from texts—be they scientific articles, memoirs, visual images (including film), or the molecular models used in chemistry, all of which figure in this collection. It is challenging because reading is a process that is, for most of us, novices and experts alike, virtually invisible most of the time. As teachers, we ask our students to "read" the assigned essay or scientific article (or whatever). And students tell us they have done so. But what does that mean? What do they do? What do they think they're *supposed* to do?

A personal confession comes to mind here. As a first-year college student, one who had excelled academically at every previous stage of education, I dutifully read the textbook required in the Introduction to Philosophy course I was so excited to take. Indeed, I read it several times, highlighter in hand ... and then proceeded to emerge from the midterm with a lousy C. I soon realized that I had not, in fact, really been reading. I was turning the pages, decoding words. But I was certainly not doing the kind of meaning-making, engaged, critical reading this volume explores. (Happily, I was able to mend my ways thereafter.)

It turns out, as the authors of chapter 7 argue, that we are not born knowing how to be effective critical or engaged readers. Reading, as Sam Wineburg (2001) says about the practice of history as a discipline, is an "unnatural act." Accordingly, it can be hard for those of us who in one way or another make our living (and enjoy our leisure) as readers to remember how hard it is, how complicated a process, and to let students in on what it takes and how it happens. When I needed help with that philosophy text, I was on my own; indeed, I doubt that it would ever have occurred to my professors to talk about how to read in their respective disciplines. Reading was then and, as this volume makes clear, is now still seriously underinstructed. Accordingly, the two main gifts of *Reading across the Disciplines* are, first, to capture what reading entails in all its complexity and variety—the different purposes, processes, and disciplinary frames that readers bring to the practice; and, second, to set out a rich mix of strategies that have been found promising in various contexts—attention to reading within disciplinary contexts, metacognitive strategies, think-alouds, cognitive and reading apprenticeship, decoding the disciplines, defamiliarization, reflective writing about reading, and others.

These interventions are not, it should be said, offered as answers. On the contrary, they are possibilities that faculty are moved to explore because of problems that arise in their own classrooms—and sometimes in their own experience as readers—problems that call out for inquiry and innovation. This brings us to the scholarship of teaching and learning.

As I was writing this foreword, I came across a new essay on the scholarship of teaching and learning by Randy Bass. Many readers of this volume will know Bass's much-cited article from 1999, "The Scholarship of Teaching and Learning: What's the Problem?" In that now-classic piece, he argues that teaching "problems" can be framed as issues for inquiry and exploration rather than indications of failure. Treating teaching problems in the same way we treat research problems—as welcome sites for inquiry—is the signature move made by the scholarship of teaching and learning.

Bass's new essay, written on the twentieth anniversary of the earlier one, is fetchingly entitled "What's the Problem Now?" And that problem is not only new but "wicked": the transformation of higher education "to meet the needs of society, equity, and the future" and, accordingly, seeing "the problem of learning . . . as complexly embedded in social and cultural contexts" (2020, 5). Toward this end, he invokes a concept from the National Science Foundation (2019), "convergence research," which has two characteristics: it is driven by a specific and compelling problem, and it requires deep integration across disciplines.

This strikes me as an apt description of this volume. While never losing sight of the individual student—the reader in front of us in the classroom—*Reading across the Disciplines* shines a light on a big and surely "wicked" problem, it brings together perspectives and findings from a wide range of disciplines and contexts, and its methods are diverse and complementary. And while focused on the realities of the classroom—and what individual teachers may want to try in their own settings—it invites and invokes thinking not only about, say, helping students read that piece of literature (or philosophy text) more critically but, as chapter 11 puts it, fostering abilities to "read the world" in ways that make a difference not only for the individual but for society and our collective future. It's hard to imagine a grander challenge than that—or a smarter road map for meeting that challenge than this collection provides. And who knows, maybe there's yet another volume to come.

References

Bass, Randall. 1999. "The Scholarship of Teaching and Learning: What's the Problem?" *Inventio* 1 (1): 1–10.

———. 2020. "What's the Problem Now?" *To Improve the Academy* 39 (1): 3–30. http://dx.doi.org/10.3998/tia.17063888.0039.102.

Manarin, Karen, Miriam Carey, Melanie Rathburn, and Glen Ryland. 2015. *Critical Reading in Higher Education: Academic Goals and Social Engagement*. Bloomington: Indiana University Press.

National Science Foundation. 2019. "Convergence Research at NSF." https://www.nsf.gov/od/oia/convergence/.

Wineburg, Sam. 2001. *Historical Thinking and Other Unnatural Acts: Charting the Future of Teaching the Past*. Philadelphia: Temple University Press.

READING ACROSS THE DISCIPLINES

READING ACROSS THE DISCIPLINES

An Introduction

KAREN MANARIN

Reading is in crisis—or so the story goes. News releases and popular nonfiction books routinely claim that individuals struggle with basic literacy and that technology is changing how we read and therefore how we think. Many high school graduates don't have the literacy skills necessary for success in postsecondary study (Dion and Maldonado 2013), while those who can read often choose not to. Many college students deliberately avoid courses with heavy reading requirements (Arum and Roksa 2011), although we don't know if that's because they can't read, won't read, or both. Higher-education instructors are all too familiar with this reluctance to read difficult texts, but it has significant consequences for both the individual and society, especially in an age described as "post-truth" where facts seem to be less influential than opinions (Carillo 2018).

At the same time, participation in higher education has expanded dramatically. Greater heterogeneity in age, family history, racial and ethnic background, socioeconomic status, and language of origin brings richness to our classrooms but also brings challenges, as students have different experiences, responsibilities, and assumptions. The classroom itself has also changed dramatically, or at least should have changed based on what we now know about active and collaborative learning. We have an explosion of different forms of resources, including online learning artifacts, supplemental resources offered by textbook publishers, digital images, and a proliferation of communication channels. Information has become easier than ever to access, if not to understand or evaluate. Given this situation, teaching critical reading in higher education has become more important than ever.

Don't Higher-Education Students Already Know How to Read?

The answer really depends on what we mean by reading, and a little later in this introduction, I'll briefly describe some of the elements that go into that wondrous activity. When higher-education faculty complain that their students can't read, most of them are not talking about simple decoding of individual words strung into sentences; they are talking about factors such as comprehension, prior knowledge, implicit beliefs about the role of the reader, and motivation. As Alice Horning (2007, 7) notes,

> Many college teachers will say, if asked, that students are "illiterate." What they seem to mean by this claim is both that they can't read and that they don't read. That is, first, they lack the ability to read in the critically literate sense of being able to go beyond summary of main ideas to analysis, synthesis and evaluation. In addition, though, they are uneducated in reading, lacking experience working with extended texts and the world of ideas from which they arise. In this way, they mean that students are uneducated in ways that derive from reading a wide variety of materials and seeing varied points of view, research, and information relating to ideas or issues.

Examining reading behaviors in required first-year classes, Karen Manarin et al. (2015) found that most students could comprehend required texts at a benchmark level but struggled with evaluation of assumptions; they also did not demonstrate a repertoire of reading strategies for different genres. But as readers, we know that reading a text message is different from reading a newspaper editorial or a novel or a scholarly article. Even when dealing with the same genre, we adjust our reading processes based on purpose, prior knowledge, and context (Linderholm 2006; Kendeou and O'Brien 2016). Behaviors that may be effective for one reading situation may be inadequate for the next. If we accept that reading involves different behaviors in different contexts, it is impossible to leave reading instruction to literacy experts in the primary grades; students need more help negotiating difficult texts, especially as they enter more specialized discourse communities. Whether or not students enter higher-education institutions with adequate reading skills, they need to continue learning to read in higher education as they encounter different disciplinary and professional contexts.

This type of reading is not something that can be covered in a remedial course or general education requirement, because reading skills do not transfer easily between contexts (Maxwell 1997; Paulson and Armstrong 2010). Indeed, the idea of transfer relies on a transmission model of education that many have found inadequate. For example, Greg Mannion et al. (2009) argue that instead of focusing on decontextualized transfer, we should think of reading skills as emergent practices resonating between contexts. A discipline or profession is one such context. John M. Swales (2016, 10) argues that faculty who explicitly focus on "rhetorical principles of organization, on discoursal expectations, on significant linguistic tokens, and on intriguing textual extracts" can help students join disciplinary communities. Since expert readers in a discipline acquire metacognitive awareness and skills necessary to read informational prose in that discipline, "teachers in every discipline can and should help students develop the awarenesses and skills to become expert readers in their field" (Horning 2011, 12).

Teaching reading, then, requires the participation of faculty members across the disciplines and across the levels of higher education. However, faculty members may want to help but feel that they do not have the time or the expertise. After all, they have content to cover, and they weren't trained to teach reading. But they do have the sometimes-tacit knowledge of what it means to read in a particular discipline, and they can make a meaningful difference in how their students read by participating in the scholarship of teaching and learning (SOTL).

What Is SOTL?

SOTL is often conceptualized as the "systematic reflection on teaching and learning made public" (Illinois State University quoted in McKinney 2013, 1). This definition is alarmingly capacious, as it doesn't describe what systematic reflection might look like in different contexts, what assumptions might underlie our conceptions of teaching and learning, or what "going public" might entail. Pat Hutchings, Mary Taylor Huber, and Anthony Ciccone (2011) provide a few more details, noting that "the scholarship of teaching and learning encompasses a broad set of practices that engage teachers in looking closely and critically at student learning in order to improve their own courses and programs, and to share insights with other educators who can evaluate and build on their efforts" (xix). Recognizing the diversity of SOTL work, Peter Felten (2013, 121) argues that SOTL should be "(1) inquiry into student learning, (2) grounded in context, (3) methodologically sound, (4) conducted in partnership with students, and (5) appropriately public."

As a social movement seeking to transform higher education, SOTL is often traced back to Ernest Boyer's (1990) call for teaching as an area of scholarly inquiry, but certainly Boyer wasn't the first to see teaching as a scholarly activity requiring inquiry and reflection. Many disciplines have a long tradition of pedagogical scholarship; chemistry, for example, has had a pedagogical journal since as far back as the 1920s (McKinney 2007). Disciplines and professions often develop signature pedagogies that "implicitly define what counts as knowledge in a field and how things become known. They define how knowledge is analyzed, criticized, accepted, or discarded. They define the functions of expertise in a field, the locus of authority, and the privileges of rank and standing" (Shulman 2005, 54). Exploring these pedagogies then provides insight into not only the transmission and construction of content knowledge but also the assumptions and ethical concerns of the discipline or profession. As Kathleen McKinney (2013, 2) notes, "SOTL began, primarily, as a discipline-based movement that included a few multi-disciplinary conversations. Instructors in a particular discipline looked at a teaching and learning problem in a local setting usually with their own students, in their own classes, and in terms of disciplinary learning."

However, one of the strengths of SOTL, as opposed to purely disciplinary-based pedagogical research, is the possibility of learning across disciplines. Mary Taylor Huber and Sherwyn Morreale (2002) acknowledge that SOTL "draws strength from being situated in a discipline and its particular style. But growth in knowledge also comes at the borders of disciplinary imagination" (2); they argue for the importance of a "trading zone" between disciplinary territories where we could learn from each other (19). Huber and Hutchings (2005) talk about the need to create a "teaching commons" where educators can exchange ideas. David A. Reichard and Kathy Takayama (2013, 170) go so far as to suggest that "cross-disciplinary conversations are a defining feature of SOTL, a signature pedagogy and methodology." Such conversations aren't easy and may be marked by dissonance and superficial politeness (Robinson et al. 2013), but they are important if we are to address serious issues in higher education, issues such as reading. This book provides one opportunity to participate in SOTL by entering this cross-disciplinary conversation about reading. As Nancy Chick (2017, 10) notes, most faculty will not do SOTL as formal scholarship; "however, their role as part of our teaching and learning community is no less important. Many of them are certainly scholarly teachers who care about their teaching and their students' learning and who intentionally strive to improve both." For Dan Bernstein (2010, 4), "the goal of SOTL is to have every teacher treat every course as an opportunity to learn how to create better learning environments and generate richer educational experiences."

In this collection, authors from Australia, Canada, and the United States of America explore reading in undergraduate courses, doctoral seminars, and faculty development activities. By paying attention to the particular classroom and placing those observations in conversation with scholarly literature, some authors create new knowledge about reading in higher education from disciplinary and cross-disciplinary perspectives. Other authors demonstrate how existing research about reading can be applied to specific classroom contexts. Thus, they offer models for faculty members whose own research interests may lie elsewhere but who believe in the importance of reading. This collection seeks to stimulate conversation about what engaged reading looks like in order to create the conditions necessary for a transformation of reading in higher education. However, such a transformation requires more than individual faculty members working on SOTL projects in their particular disciplines. It requires us to consider reading across the disciplines. To set the stage for this conversation, I briefly describe reading, both as a way to decode and as a way to construct meaning; I explore potential sites of reading instruction in higher education; I suggest that we can learn lessons from others, including K-12 debates and writing across the curriculum; and I introduce the chapters of this volume.

What Is Reading?

Reading is a foundational skill for educational success in the K-12 system but usually begins much earlier, as toddlers start to make connections between sounds, images or symbols, and the world (Fresch 2008). However, far from being a simple process that children learn when young and then practice on increasingly complicated texts, reading involves a complex set of cognitive and affective processes by which symbols are used to transmit meaning and through which an individual constructs meaning in a particular context. Reading thus involves both decoding and constructing meaning in particular contexts and for particular purposes. However, we're not sure exactly how symbols come to represent other elements in the process or processes of reading; the complexity of reading is too great for any one model to be sufficient (Tracey and Morrow 2012). Theorists of reading tend to focus on what happens in the brain, the mind, or the sociocultural context (see Dehaene 2010; Willingham 2017; Gee 2015), but of course, all of these elements are at play when an individual reads. Panayiota Kendeou et al. (2014, 11) note that "the cognitive processes of reading comprehension roughly fall into two categories: (1) lower level processes that involve translating the written code into meaningful language units and, (2) higher level processes that involve combining these units into a meaningful and coherent mental representation." Here I only briefly touch on elements of decoding alphabetic text (as opposed to decoding images or logographic characters) before turning to meaning construction. I then address the issue of "reading" images.

Decoding Meaning

How a few marks on a surface (like the ones making up this sentence) come to mean anything is remarkable. Measuring eye movements and watching different parts of the brain activate in response to stimuli provide insight into the mechanics of reading, but they don't really explain how we decode information received, let alone how we construct meaning from that information. We know that oral language development precedes and influences reading. We know that children learn a lot about the role of print culture and reading before they read, in terms of both decoding and meaning-making (Schwanenflugel and Knapp 2016). They need to recognize letters, distinguish between sounds that make up words, understand that print connects in some way to things in the world, recognize grammatical and narrative structures, and so on. As children begin to learn to read, they learn translation rules from letters to sounds and spellings; they learn what words mean and how to combine those words into sentences that are meaningful; they "extract ideas from sentences" (Willingham 2017, 107).

Constructing Meaning

But the reading process required for comprehension doesn't stop there. Daniel T. Willingham (2017) explains that not only do readers extract meaning from a sentence, they coordinate meaning with what has been read before by making connections between ideas (often called a textbase in the research) within a particular context that includes goals for reading; readers thus build a situation model in their minds. Experts will build better situation models because they know what sorts of things in the text are more likely to be important, and they have more background information. Thus, they know what to pay attention to, and they can make more connections (Willingham 2017). They also spend considerably less effort than novices in decoding the text, which makes it more likely that they will persist, particularly if they identify some value in reading the text (Schwanenflugel and Knapp 2016). And experts in a particular field are more likely than novices to attribute value to reading material in that field (Manarin 2019). Expert readers then are not only decoding particular sentences; they are actively constructing meaning as they connect ideas.

Conceptualizing reading as an active process of knowledge construction is more common in some disciplines than in others (as Nelson Graff et al. illustrate in chap. 2 of this collection). Literary and composition scholars, trying to account for multiple interpretations of literary works, have long theorized that meaning depends on writer, text, context, and reader. Wolfgang Iser (1978) posited a theory of aesthetic response relying on interactions between text and reader; in doing so, he identified a disjunction between the real reader facing the text and the implied reader called forth by the text. Louise Rosenblatt ([1978] 1994) claimed that meaning is derived through a series of transactions between reader, text, and context. As Margaret Mackey in chapter 1 of this volume notes, individual differences in readers matter. Rosenblatt ([1978] 1994) also noted that there are many types of reading, distinguished not by type of text but by the reader's focus of attention; she identified a continuum from nonaesthetic, or efferent, reading "where the reader's attention is focused primarily on what will remain as the residue *after* the reading" to aesthetic reading where "the reader's primary concern is with what happens *during* the actual reading event" (23–24). Again, her primary interest here was the literary work, but her exploration of how readers move along the continuum even when reading a single text provides an important reminder that there are many ways of reading successfully for different purposes.

"Reading" Images

Earlier, I claimed that reading involves a complex set of cognitive and affective processes by which symbols are used to transmit meaning and through which an individual constructs meaning in a particular context. This definition of reading applies to visual as well as linguistic texts, and indeed, visual literacy has become a pressing concern in our image-saturated environment because looking seems deceptively natural (to sighted people). As Paul Messaris (1994, 4) notes, "conscious awareness of the process of interpretation and response may be more fugitive in the case of pictures than it is with language or other modes of communication." This lack of awareness not only makes individuals more susceptible to manipulation but also hinders their ability to participate meaningfully in discourses that involve images. Focusing on visual literacy across the disciplines, Deandra Little, Peter Felten, and Chad Berry (2015, 5) argue that "higher education must prepare our students for the practical, professional, and aesthetic challenges of being consumers and producers of visual meaning." I would add that the challenges are also ethical, as current discourse on public issues relies on visual images; critical reading of these images is crucial for a humane and functioning society. In this collection, Elizabeth Marquis (chap. 5) and Dana Statton Thompson (chap. 4) offer some insights into critically reading images in higher education.

Teaching Reading at University: Who, When, and What?

Of course, we can agree that higher-education students should continue to learn how to read texts and images critically and still disagree about how to accomplish this feat. One key issue involves who should teach it and when; a related issue is what type of reading should be taught. Reading instruction can and should occur at multiple sites in higher education.

Developmental Reading Classes

One location of reading instruction is the college developmental classroom. Jodi Patrick Holschuh and Eric J. Paulson (2013), examining the terrain of college developmental reading, note that developmental reading programming serves an important role for some students. Reviewing literature on undergraduate students reading, Heather D. Porter (2018) notes that much more attention has been given to developmental rather than disciplinary reading. Such programming may occur as stand-alone classes, as workshops, or as online modules. Developmental reading programs at universities are traditionally grounded in relatively generic reading and study skills applied to different types of texts. Holschuh and Paulson (2013) note that focusing on decontextualized skills does not provide students with the strategic knowledge of how or when to apply those skills in other contexts; they call for academic development of reading throughout university. Of course, most university students are not in developmental reading classes, the literacy experts at postsecondary institutions tend to be isolated from the other disciplines, and most students get whatever reading instruction they get through the regular curriculum from their composition classes.

Freshman Composition Classes

On the one hand, the writing classroom as a site of reading instruction makes sense. After all, since the 1980s, reading and writing have been conceptualized as complementary (but not identical) cognitive and social processes (Langer and Flihan 2000). Steve Graham and Michael Hebert's (2010) meta-analysis of reading research identifies the important role that writing can play in developing reading skills. On the other hand, it's important to remember that writing instruction in the modern university is shaped by historical debates about English studies (Harl 2013). Writing, as an area of study, displaced the reading of literature in composition classes. So while faculty in other areas often assume that students learn how to read in a required composition class, composition instructors may not see reading as a primary goal, or, as Angela J. Zito and Jakob T. Zehms note in chapter 11 of this collection, they may not have thought through how literary interpretive strategies transfer to other contexts.

Reading skills learned in the composition class may or may not transfer to other contexts. Larry Mikulecky, Peggy Albers, and Michelle Peers (1994) demonstrate that literacy transfer between contexts does not happen automatically or easily even when the contexts are closely related. When the contexts are more dissimilar—say, a required first-year composition course and an upper-level course in a student's major—transfer is even more difficult. Surveying first-year writing instructors across the United States, Ellen C. Carillo (2015, 34) found two primary goals: "1. To use rhetorical reading to connect the course's reading to the writing students will complete; 2. To prepare students for classes beyond first-year composition." But the first goal does not necessarily support the second, not without explicit teaching for transfer. Carillo, drawing on scholarship of learning transfer, notes that students must be able to generalize an abstract principle to a new context in order for transfer to occur; helping students develop knowledge about reading, then, may help them read in other courses. This reading-about-reading approach, analogous in some ways to the writing-about-writing approach promoted by Elizabeth Wardle and Doug Downs (2010), may help students develop the metacognitive awareness to facilitate transfer of reading (and writing).

Disciplinary Classes

However, developing metacognitive awareness about reading in first-year composition is not enough by itself. Disciplinary faculty must help students recognize the many different ways of reading necessary for success in that discipline; after all, they know the needs and assumptions of those particular discourse communities in a way that the developmental reading instructor or first-year writing instructor cannot. The chapters in the second half of this collection focus on reading in specific disciplinary and interdisciplinary contexts. A growing number of teachers and scholars in different disciplines are realizing that reading needs to be supported throughout the undergraduate curriculum and even into postgraduate studies (see Rosemary Green, chap. 6 in this collection; see also McMinn et al. 2009).

A crucial site of reading instruction, then, is the disciplinary classroom, but disciplinary instructors may not even be consciously aware of the processes they use to read disciplinary texts, let alone know how to teach these processes. One might expect that literature instructors would have well-articulated protocols for teaching and supporting reading given the discipline's primary focus on texts; however, as Paul T. Corrigan (2018, 417) notes, "Scholarship on the teaching of writing far surpasses scholarship on the teaching of literature in virtually every way we might consider." Kate Douglas et al. (2016, 258) note that professors often rely on modelling close reading skills, but "we cannot demonstrate for our students what occurs outside the classroom, the activities and skills that inform the act of interpretation we model"; they argue for coaching rather than modeling reading skills to build reading resilience. Offering a lesson plan that breaks down the steps of close reading, Nancy L. Chick, Holly Hassel, and Aeron Haynie (2009, 401) talk about the "need to make our values more explicit for students who are not yet experts." In *Literary Learning: Teaching the English Major*, Sherry Lee Linkon (2011) tries to make literary thinking visible, identifying the attitudes and values that underlie our ways of reading and our ways of creating arguments about texts. She argues for a type of cognitive apprenticeship, where instructors articulate what students need to learn (in terms of both content and strategic knowledge), facilitate multiple opportunities for practice, and provide individualized coaching.

From what some consider the other end of the disciplinary spectrum, those disciplines that make up STEM (science, technology, engineering, and mathematics), there is also interest in cognitive apprenticeship (Lyons et al. 2017; Kolikant et al. 2006; Collins, Brown, and Newman 1987). Allan Collins and John Seely Brown developed the idea of cognitive apprenticeship in terms of computer-based learning environments, but the concept reaches beyond that particular context. Modeling, coaching, and scaffolding are "the core of cognitive apprenticeship, designed to help students acquire an integrated set of cognitive and metacognitive skills through processes of observation and guided and supported practice"; articulation and reflection help students develop the metacognitive abilities necessary for generalization and transfer, while exploration involves pushing students into problem solving and, perhaps even more importantly, problem identification on their own (Collins, Brown, and Newman 1987, 16). Given the highly technical and conceptually difficult material science students must read, there are concerted efforts to help students read primary scientific articles as well as the symbolic notation that makes the communication of scientific discoveries possible. See Neela Griffiths and Yvonne C. Davila (chap. 7) and Brett McCollum and Layne Morsch (chap. 8) in this collection for examples of how reading is taught using an embedded approach that explicitly makes literacy practices of STEM disciplines visible.

Faculty Development Opportunities

Of course, faculty being able to make these practices visible involves faculty being consciously aware of how they read in their disciplines. Faculty may have expert blind spots, where "educators with advanced subject-matter knowledge of a scholarly discipline tend to use the powerful organizing principles, formalisms, and methods of analysis that serve as the foundation of that discipline as guiding principles for their students' conceptual development and instruction, rather than being guided by knowledge of the learning needs and developmental profiles of novices" (Nathan and Petrosino 2003, 906). So a necessary fourth site of reading instruction in higher education is faculty development opportunities, whether in person or through books like this one. Graff et al. in this collection suggest that faculty often encounter "threshold concepts" (Meyer and Land 2003) when engaging in faculty development about reading. As Joan Middendorf and Leah Shopkow (2018, 15) note, "Each of the disciplines has its own ways of reading that instructors practice without thinking about them. Students don't know about these methods because they are never told about them; consequently, they make mistakes." Discussion across disciplines through faculty development opportunities helps bring a particular discipline's epistemologies, assumptions, and practices into focus: "it is easier to see the shapes of disciplines in comparison to each other" (Middendorf and Shopkow 2018, 7). The disciplines are thus "decoded" as faculty begin to recognize where their mental operations diverge from those of students (Pace 2017). Heather C. Easterling and John Eliason in chapter 3 of this collection explore what happens when faculty "mind the gap" between their reading practices and their students.

Reading processes are shaped by the epistemological values of the discipline, but metacognitive reflection on reading is necessarily transdisciplinary. Defining something involves placing it in a category and explaining how it is different from other elements in that category. By explaining how we read in a particular context, we denaturalize the act of reading; we open the possibility of other ways of reading in other contexts; we make our assumptions about genre translucent, rather than invisible and difficult to interrogate; and we allow the possibility of other people entering the conversation from other perspectives (Manarin 2017). We need to learn from each other, including lessons from K-12.

Lessons from K-12: Content Area Reading, Disciplinary Literacy, or Both

Content area reading, an educational movement that gained popularity in the last decades of the twentieth century, focuses on promoting reading strategies in content areas across the K-12 curriculum. It recognizes that students learn to read but that they also read to learn and often need help understanding dense content-area texts—hence the catchphrase "Every teacher is a teacher of reading" (Stewart-Dore 2013, 48). It promotes reading strategies in content areas across the curriculum through multiple professional development texts written by literacy experts for content area teachers. Visual literacy professional development also follows similar patterns. Although content area reading increased the visibility of reading across the K-12 curriculum, many instructors argued that the "outside-in" approach of generic strategies applied to their particular contexts was limited—some felt that teaching reading strategies took time away from content; others felt that literacy experts discounted their disciplinary expertise and that the generic strategies didn't help students develop "the capacity to think, read, and write like an insider or expert" (Brozo et al. 2013, 354–355).

In contrast to content area reading, where generic strategies are used to help novice readers make sense of disciplinary texts, disciplinary literacy seeks to understand and make explicit how disciplinary experts approach texts where even what counts as text differs between disciplines (Moje et al. 2011). Timothy Shanahan and Cynthia Shanahan (2008, 50) link the reading patterns demonstrated by disciplinary experts to "the intellectual values of a discipline and the methods by which scholarship is created in each of the fields": the historian, the chemist, and the mathematician read differently, not just because the content is different but because their epistemologies differ. Elizabeth Birr Moje (2008, 100) urges us to think of a discipline not as a repository of content or information but as "a space in which knowledge is produced or constructed." Disciplinary literacy involves becoming aware of how to participate in the discourse community of the discipline. As Moje (2008, 99) argues, "producing knowledge in a discipline requires fluency in making and interrogating knowledge claims, which in turn require fluency in a wide range of ways of constructing and communicating knowledge. Literacy thus becomes an essential aspect of disciplinary practice, rather than a set of strategies or tools brought in to the disciplines to improve reading and writing of subject-matter texts." Content area reading, then, focuses more on consuming knowledge;

disciplinary literacy has, at its core, the goal of learning how to produce knowledge. A key benefit—perhaps the key benefit—of disciplinary literacy is motivational: the focus shifts from how someone reads to why someone reads, and that motivation is tied to identity (Shanahan and Shanahan 2014).

Recently, some have tried to bring together the strands of content area reading and disciplinary literacy. William G. Brozo et al. (2013) argue that both disciplinary experts and literacy experts have much to learn from each other. They suggest that perhaps learning to read like a professional in a particular discipline is less important than becoming aware that disciplines are discourse communities, a sort of meta-awareness of reading. Judith Dunkerly-Bean and Thomas William Bean (2016), examining content area reading and disciplinary literacy as competing discourses, note that while content area reading is anchored in pedagogical approach, disciplinary literacy emphasizes the primacy and the isolation of the discipline. They argue for the need to bring the movements together, to make connections across disciplines, and to promote interdisciplinary learning.

Turning to higher-education contexts, then, we recognize the need for the pedagogical approaches and metacognition fostered by content area reading. Graff et al. (chap. 2), for example, describe faculty members' experiences with the Reading Apprenticeship program, originally developed to support content area reading in the K-12 system (Schoenbach, Greenleaf, and Murphy 2017), while Joyce Tang Boyland et al. (chap. 9) focus on hierarchical structures in text to improve comprehension. We also recognize the power of comparing reading strategies across disciplines. For example, Aimee Knupsky and M. Soledad Caballero in chapter 12 of this volume discuss how defamiliarization can improve reading skills. However, we also need deeper dives into disciplinary strategies promoted by disciplinary experts. To achieve this vision, we might look to lessons from writing across the curriculum.

Lessons from Writing across the Curriculum

We know that a single composition course taken in first year is not enough to develop all the writing skills necessary for success, which is why, for over fifty years, writing across the curriculum (WAC) has been promoted as a way to improve writing and thinking. George D. Kuh (2008) identifies writing-intensive courses across the curriculum as a high-impact practice, and WAC has gained traction in a number of institutions (Thaiss and Porter 2010). Of course, WAC faces challenges: it is resource intensive, faculty across the disciplines may feel they lack the expertise, and there are internal tensions between domain-neutral and discipline-specific proponents (writing in the disciplines or WID). However, WAC may offer a way to think about reading. Alice S. Horning, Deborah-Lee Gollnitz, and Cynthia R. Haller's collection *What Is College Reading?* (2017) foregrounds this idea of reading across the curriculum. Recognizing that much research into reading is "preaching to the choir" when focused on English studies, Horning (2017, 6) calls for "more consistent attention to reading instruction across the curriculum." Mary Lou Odom (2013) explicitly advocates WAC courses as sites of reading instruction, in part because of the connections between writing and reading.

Reading across the Disciplines

However, reading instruction across the curriculum need not always be tied to WAC or look the same; indeed, it requires a multipronged approach, as demonstrated by the diversity of chapters in this collection. For example, Boyland et al. create a reading course housed in a particular discipline, while Griffiths and Davila explore online modules available to many disciplines. Other chapters emphasize reading comprehension in disciplinary courses, and for those disciplinary instructors who feel constrained by the amount of content to be covered, Trent W. Maurer and Catelyn Shipp in chapter 10 of this volume present a case where increased attention to reading provides a way to manage an overwhelming amount of content.

The authors in this collection speak from their experience teaching STEM, humanities, professional, and social science disciplines, but they also offer insights across disciplinary contexts, as characteristics of learning often transcend disciplinary boundaries. Thus, readers are likely to find meaningful elements in multiple chapters. For example, we assume that chemists will read the chapter about reading in undergraduate organic chemistry classes, but McCollum and Morsch's insights into the power of relationships to foster deep reading are applicable to many disciplines and many levels. As we read beyond our normal disciplines, however, it is important to remember that disciplines have their own discursive styles that may be unfamiliar to us. Huber and Morreale (2002, 20) called for work "in which authors present their own field's sounds and silences to a polyglot audience, [in order to] contribute to a common language for trading ideas, enlarging our pedagogical imaginations, and strengthening our scholarly work." Sometimes this work involves making explicit our disciplinary assumptions about what reading is: the chemical formula, the online text, the digital image, the documentary film, and the scholarly article require different types of reading bound up in our desire to know the world. SOTL provides this transdisciplinary opportunity to learn from each other while recognizing and valuing the situated nature of learning in our classrooms, institutions, and disciplines. We encourage readers to explore both sections of this collection: "Ways of Reading" and "Reading in Specific Contexts."

The first half of the collection explores different ways of reading and opens with the chapter "Exploring Readerly Diversity," by Margaret Mackey; in it, she explores readers' behaviors and preferences when reading in recreational contexts. These preferences often become the default approach to text, and so metacognitive awareness of readerly variation is a powerful tool for both instructors and students who want to explore ways to make their reading processes more effective when reading for different purposes.

The next two chapters emphasize the metacognitive development of faculty members learning about reading. In "Understandings of Reading: Insights from Faculty Development with Reading Apprenticeship," Nelson Graff, Rebecca Kersnar, Dan Shapiro, and Ryne Leuzinger theorize several threshold concepts for faculty teaching reading, identifying a paradigm shift among faculty who move from providing answers to helping students become self-regulated learners through metacognition. Heather C. Easterling and John Eliason examine the disciplinary literacies of faculty colleagues in "'Mind the Gap': Investigating Faculty Reading Practices." Through a social-constructivist framework, they seek not to define what expert reading looks like in different disciplines but to encourage faculty to reflect on and articulate their disciplinary reading practices, suggesting a decoding-the-disciplines approach to improve teaching.

Our definitions of reading are expanded with two chapters on types of visual literacy. Reading an image or film involves recognizing, decoding, and comprehending symbols to construct meaning in specific contexts. In "Understanding How Students across the Disciplines Read Images," Dana Statton Thompson expands our discussion of literacy to include digital images. She explores the criteria that students use independent of instruction to evaluate images before proposing a method for instruction that can be adapted to many different disciplines. In "Student Reading of Documentary and Fiction Film," Elizabeth Marquis uses think-alouds to explore how students read both documentary and fiction film texts in academic settings. The range of reported strategies demonstrates the importance of framing prompts or explicit instruction to support critical reading. Given the wide use of images and film texts in various disciplines, these two chapters provide nuanced explorations of what is happening when students critically engage with visual texts.

The second half of the collection, "Reading in Specific Contexts," opens with a chapter about reading for the literature review, a genre that may be the signature pedagogy of the doctorate. Rosemary Green explores how to help graduate students make this transition from reading to acquire to reading to produce in "Reading-to-Write: Rehearsing the Doctoral Literature Review." Green's doctor of musical arts students develop metacognitive awareness, learn disciplinary conventions, and gain confidence to enter the discipline as scholars.

The next two chapters focus on STEM contexts but have insights about scaffolded reading assignments and the power of peer relationships that reach far beyond the science classroom. Neela Griffiths and Yvonne Davila introduce first-year students to scientific discourse in "Embedding Scaffolded Reading Practices into the First-Year University Science Curriculum"; they develop and evaluate online modules in terms of student confidence and understanding. In the chapter "Reading and Relationships in Organic Chemistry," Brett McCollum and Layne Morsch describe efforts to support science communication by motivating reading habits and minimizing the development of scientifically incorrect local dialects, or interlanguages. They focus on reading for communication.

The next two chapters, based in social science classrooms, explore issues common in many disciplines—a difficult transition from generic communication courses to specialized discourse and content-heavy courses where the instructor doesn't have time to cover it all—but their approaches differ dramatically. Responding to student requests for more help with reading, psychology faculty members at Alverno College developed a separate course in analytical reading; Joyce Tang Boyland, Kris Vasquez, Jordan R. Donovan, and Rachel M. Henry describe their approach. As coauthors of "Strategies to Promote Reading Compliance and Student Learning in an Introductory Child Development Course," Trent Maurer and Catelyn Shipp provide instructor and student perspectives on a series of interventions in a content-heavy course that had to cover even more content because of restructuring; this case study demonstrates how existing research can support and transform student learning even under less-than-ideal conditions.

This collection ends with two chapters that explore reading in and across specific contexts. In "Read Literature, Read the World: Teaching and Learning the Interpretive Strategies of Literary Studies for Transfer," Angela Zito and Jakob Zehms explore student artifacts created in a composition course for evidence of transfer across course foci. They argue for greater awareness of disciplinary reading practices as disciplinary rather than assuming they are universal. In the final chapter, "Capturing Confusion: Multidisciplinary Reading as Productive Disruption," Aimee C. Knupsky and M. Soledad Caballero describe how reading across disciplines in a team-taught course creates an experience of affective disruption, or defamiliarization, that foregrounds the processes of reading. Using the Association of American Colleges and Universities Reading VALUE Rubric, Knupsky and Caballero trace changes in reading skills. They argue that in reading both literary and psychological texts about emotion, students engage in "metaconversations about why we read, how we read, and the power we can wield when we read."

This is a crucial conversation for stakeholders across the higher-education system. Taken together, the chapters in this collection work toward two goals. We want to encourage deep reading across the disciplines, where deep reading is "an active generative process of intellectual inquiry based around reading and sustained engagement with complex, ill-defined problems" (Sullivan 2017, 145). But we also want to work toward a postsecondary system that supports reading of many types across the disciplines. Together we need to consider what reading makes possible, not just for the academy but for society, and decide whether it is worth the trouble. We believe it is. Maryanne Wolf (2018, 200–201) claims that

> the most important contribution of the invention of written language to the species is a democratic foundation for critical, inferential reasoning and reflective capacities. This is the basis of a collective conscience. If we in the twenty-first century are to preserve a vital collective conscience, we must ensure that all members of our society are able to read and think both deeply and well. We will fail as a society if we do not educate our children and re-educate all of our citizenry to the responsibility of each citizen to process information vigilantly, critically, and wisely across media. And we will fail as a society as surely as societies of the twentieth century if we do not recognize and acknowledge the capacity for reflective reasoning in those who disagree with us.

We must nourish reading across the disciplines, not only for the future of the disciplines but for our collective futures.

Acknowledgments

I would like to thank the Mount Royal University Board of Governors, the generous peer reviewers and editors, and all of the wonderful scholars who contributed their work to this collection.

References

Arum, Richard, and Josipa Roksa. 2011. *Academically Adrift: Limited Learning on College Campuses.* Chicago: University of Chicago Press.

Bernstein, Daniel. 2010. "Finding Your Place in the Scholarship of Teaching and Learning." *International Journal for the Scholarship of Teaching and Learning* 4 (2): 4. https://doi.org/10.20429/ijSOTL.2010.040204.

Boyer, Ernest L. 1990. *Scholarship Reconsidered: Priorities of the Professoriate.* San Francisco: Jossey-Bass.

Brozo, William G., Gary Moorman, Carla Meyer, and Trevor Stewart. 2013. "Content Area Reading and Disciplinary Literacy: A Case for the Radical Center." *Journal of Adolescent and Adult Literacy* 56 (5): 353–357. http://www.jstor.org/stable/41827831.

Carillo, Ellen C. 2015. *Securing a Place for Reading in Composition: The Importance of Teaching for Transfer.* Logan: Utah State University Press.

———. 2018. *Teaching Readers in Post-truth America.* Logan: Utah State University Press.

Chick, Nancy L. 2017. "Does Reading SOTL Matter? Difficult Questions of Impact." *InSight: A Journal of Scholarly Teaching* 12:9–13.

Chick, Nancy L., Holly Hassel, and Aeron Haynie. 2009. "Pressing an Ear against the Hive: Reading Literature for Complexity." *Pedagogy* 9 (3): 399–432.

Collins, Allan, John Seely Brown, and Susan E. Newman. 1987. *Cognitive Apprenticeship: Teaching the Craft of Reading, Writing, and Mathematics.* Champaign: University of Illinois at Urbana-Champaign, Center for the Study of Reading. http://hdl.handle.net/2027/uiug.30112106611384.

Corrigan, Paul T. 2018. "The State of Scholarship on Teaching Literature." *Pedagogy* 18 (3): 415–432.

Dehaene, Stanislas. 2010. *Reading in the Brain: The New Science of How We Read.* New York: Penguin.

Dion, Nicholas, and Vicky Maldonado. 2013. *Making the Grade: Troubling Trends in Post-secondary Literacy.* Toronto: Higher Education Quality Council of Ontario.

Douglas, Kate, Tully Barnett, Anna Poletti, Judith Seaboyer, and Roseanne Kennedy. 2016. "Building Reading Resilience: Re-thinking Reading for the Literary Studies Classroom." *Higher Education Research and Development* 35 (2): 254–266. https://doi.org/10.1080/07294360.2015.1087475.

Dunkerly-Bean, Judith, and Thomas William Bean. 2016. "Missing the 'Savoir' for the 'Connaissance': Disciplinary and Content Area Literacy as Regimes of Truth." *Journal of Literacy Research* 48 (4): 448–475.

Felten, Peter. 2013. "Principles of Good Practice in SOTL." *Teaching and Learning Inquiry* 1 (1): 121–125.

Fresch, Mary Jo, ed. 2008. *An Essential History of Current Reading Practices.* Newark, NJ: International Reading Association.

Gee, James Paul. 2015. *Social Linguistics and Literacies: Ideologies in Discourses.* 5th ed. New York: Routledge.

Graham, Steve, and Michael Hebert. 2010. *Writing to Read: Evidence for How Writing Can Improve Reading.* Washington, DC: Alliance for Excellent Education.

Harl, Allison L. 2013. "A Historical and Theoretical Review of the Literature: Reading and Writing Connections." In *Reconnecting Reading and Writing*, edited by Alice S. Horning and Elizabeth W. Kraemer, 26–54. Anderson, SC: Parlor.

Holschuh, Jodi Patrick, and Eric J. Paulson. 2013. *The Terrain of College Developmental Reading.* College Reading and Learning Association. https://www.crla.net/images/whitepaper/TheTerrainofCollege91913.pdf.

Horning, Alice S. 2007. "Reading across the Curriculum as Key to Student Success." *Across the Disciplines* 4. https://wac.colostate.edu/atd/articles/horning2007.cfm.%20Accessed%209%20May%202012.

———. 2011. "Where to Put the Manicules: A Theory of Expert Reading." *Across the Disciplines* 8 (2). https://wac.colostate.edu/docs/atd/articles/horning2011.pdf.

———. 2017. Introduction to *What Is College Reading?*, edited by Alice S. Horning, Deborah-Lee Gollnitz, and Cynthia R. Haller, 3–18. Fort Collins, CO: WAC Clearinghouse.

Horning, Alice S., Deborah-Lee Gollnitz, and Cynthia R. Haller, eds. 2017. *What Is College Reading?* Fort Collins, CO: WAC Clearinghouse.

Huber, Mary Taylor, and Pat Hutchings. 2005. *The Advancement of Learning: Building the Teaching Commons*. San Francisco: Jossey-Bass.

Huber, Mary Taylor, and Sherwyn P. Morreale, eds. 2002. *Disciplinary Styles in the Scholarship of Teaching and Learning: Exploring Common Ground*. Washington, DC: American Association for Higher Education.

Hutchings, Pat, Mary Taylor Huber, and Anthony Ciccone. 2011. *The Scholarship of Teaching and Learning Reconsidered: Institutional Integration and Impact*. San Francisco: Jossey-Bass.

Iser, Wolfgang. 1978. *The Act of Reading: A Theory of Aesthetic Response*. Baltimore: Johns Hopkins University Press.

Kendeou, Panayiota, Paul van Den Broek, Anne Helder, and Josefine Karlsson. 2014. "A Cognitive View of Reading Comprehension: Implications for Reading Difficulties." *Learning Disabilities Research and Practice* 29 (1): 10–16. https://doi.org/10.1111/ldrp.12025.

Kendeou, Panayiota, and Edward J. O' Brien. 2016. "Prior Knowledge: Acquisition and Revision." In *Handbook of Individual Differences in Reading: Text and Context*, edited by Peter Afflerbach, 151–163. New York: Routledge.

Kolikant, Yifat Ben-David, David W. Gatchell, Penny L. Hirsch, and Robert A. Linsenmeier. 2006. "A Cognitive-Apprenticeship-Inspired Instructional Approach for Teaching Scientific Writing and Reading." *Journal of College Science Teaching* 36 (3): 20–25.

Kuh, George D. 2008. *High-Impact Educational Practices: What They Are, Who Has Access to Them, and Why They Matter*. Washington, DC: AAC&U.

Langer, Judith A., and Sheila Flihan. 2000. "Writing and Reading Relationships: Constructive Tasks." In *Perspectives on Writing: Research/Theory/Practice*, edited by Roselmina Indrisano and James R. Squire, 112–139. Newark, NJ: International Reading Association.

Linderholm, Tracy. 2006. "Reading with Purpose." *Journal of College Reading and Learning* 36:70–80.

Linkon, Sherry Lee. 2011. *Literary Learning: Teaching the English Major*. Bloomington: Indiana University Press.

Little, Deandra, Peter Felten, and Chad Berry, eds. 2015. *Looking and Learning: Visual Literacy across the Disciplines*. New Directions in Teaching and Learning, no. 141. San Francisco: Jossey-Bass.

Lyons, Kayley, Jacqueline McLaughlin, Julia Khanova, and Mary Roth. 2017. "Cognitive Apprenticeship in Health Sciences Education: A Qualitative Review." *Advances in Health Sciences Education* 22 (3): 723–739. https://doi.org/10.1007/s10459-016-9707-4.

Manarin, Karen. 2017. "Reading the Stories of Teaching and Learning—ISSOTL 2016 Opening Keynote." *Teaching and Learning Inquiry* 5 (1). https://doi.org/10.20343/teachlearninqu.5.1.13.

———. 2019. "Why Read?" *Higher Education Research and Development* 38 (1): 11–23.

Manarin, Karen, Miriam Carey, Melanie Rathburn, and Glen Ryland. 2015. *Critical Reading in Higher Education: Academic Goals and Social Engagement*. Bloomington: Indiana University Press.

Mannion, Greg, Kate Miller, Ian Gibb, and Ronnie Goodman. 2009. "Reading, Writing, Resonating: Striking Chords across the Contexts of Students' Everyday and College Lives." *Pedagogy, Culture and Society* 17 (3): 323–339.

Maxwell, Martha. 1997. *The Dismal Status of Required Developmental Reading Programs: Roots, Causes and Solutions*. ERIC No. ED 415 5. https://files.eric.ed.gov/fulltext/ED415501.pdf.

McKinney, Kathleen. 2007. *Enhancing Learning through the Scholarship of Teaching and Learning: The Challenges and Joys of Juggling*. San Francisco: Jossey-Bass.

———, ed. 2013. *The Scholarship of Teaching and Learning in and across the Disciplines*. Bloomington: Indiana University Press.

McMinn, Mark R., Anna Tabor, Bobby L. Trihub, Laura Taylor, and Amy W. Dominguez. 2009. "Reading in Graduate School: A Survey of Doctoral Students in Clinical Psychology." *Faculty Publications—Grad School of Clinical Psychology* (George Fox University), Paper 168. http://digitalcommons.georgefox.edu/gscp_fac/168.

Messaris, Paul. 1994. *Visual "Literacy": Image, Mind, and Reality*. Boulder, CO: Westview.

Meyer, Jan H. F., and Ray Land. 2003. "Threshold Concepts and Troublesome Knowledge: Linkages to Ways of Thinking and Practising within the Disciplines." In *Improving Student Learning: Improving Student Learning Theory and Practice—Ten Years On*, edited by C. Rust, 1–16. Oxford: Oxford Centre for Staff and Learning Development.

Middendorf, Joan, and Leah Shopkow. 2018. *Overcoming Student Learning Bottlenecks: Decode the Critical Thinking of Your Discipline*. Sterling, VA: Stylus.

Mikulecky, Larry, Peggy Albers, and Michelle Peers. 1994. *Literacy Transfer: A Review of the Literature*. National Center on Adult Literacy Technical Report TR94-05.

Moje, Elizabeth Birr. 2008. "Foregrounding the Disciplines in Secondary Literacy Teaching and Learning: A Call for Change." *Journal of Adolescent and Adult Literacy* 52 (2): 96–107. https://doi.org/10.1598/JAAL.52.2.1.

Moje, Elizabeth Birr, Darin Stockdill, Katherine Kim, and Hyun-ju Kim. 2011. "The Role of Text in Disciplinary Learning." In *Handbook of Reading Research*, vol. 4, edited by Michael L. Kamil, P. David Pearson, Elizabeth Birr Moje, and Peter P. Afflerbach, 453–486. New York: Routledge.

Nathan, Mitchell J., and Anthony Petrosino. 2003. "Expert Blind Spot among Preservice Teachers." *American Educational Research Journal* 40 (4): 905–928. https://doi.org/10.3102/00028312040004905.

Odom, Mary Lou. 2013. "Not Just for Writing Anymore: What WAC Can Teach Us about Reading to Learn." *Across the Disciplines* 10 (4). https://wac.colostate.edu/docs/atd/reading/odom.pdf.

Pace, David. 2017. *The Decoding the Disciplines Paradigm*. Bloomington: Indiana University Press.

Paulson, Eric J., and Sonya L. Armstrong. 2010. "Postsecondary Literacy: Coherence in Theory, Terminology, and Teacher Preparation." *Journal of Developmental Education* 33 (3): 4–15.

Porter, Heather D. 2018. "Constructing an Understanding of Undergraduate Disciplinary Reading: An Analysis of Contemporary Scholarship." *Journal of College Reading and Learning* 48 (1): 25–46. https://doi.org/10.1080/10790195.2017.1362970.

Reichard, David A., and Kathy Takayama. 2013. "Exploring Student Learning in Unfamiliar Territory: A Humanist and a Scientist Compare Notes." In *The Scholarship of Teaching and Learning in and across the Disciplines*, edited by Kathleen McKinney, 169–185. Bloomington: Indiana University Press.

Robinson, Jennifer Meta, Melissa Gresalfi, Tyler Booth Christensen, April K. Sievert, Katherine Dowell Kearns, and Miriam E. Zolan. 2013. "Talking across the Disciplines: Building Communicative Competence in a Multidisciplinary Graduate-Student Seminar on Inquiry in Teaching and Learning." In *The Scholarship of Teaching and Learning in and across the Disciplines*, edited by Kathleen McKinney, 186–199. Bloomington: Indiana University Press.

Rosenblatt, Louise M. (1978) 1994. *The Reader, the Text, the Poem: The Transactional Theory of the Literary Work*. Carbondale: Southern Illinois University Press.

Schoenbach, Ruth, Cynthia Greenleaf, and Lynn Murphy. 2017. *Leading for Literacy*. San Francisco: Wiley.

Schwanenflugel, Paula J., and Nancy Flanagan Knapp. 2016. *The Psychology of Reading: Theory and Applications*. New York: Guilford.

Shanahan, Timothy, and Cynthia Shanahan. 2008. "Teaching Disciplinary Literacy to Adolescents: Rethinking Content-Area Literacy." *Harvard Educational Review* 78 (1): 40–59. https://doi.org/10.17763/haer.78.1.v62444321p602101.

———. 2014. "The Implications of Disciplinary Literacy." *Journal of Adolescent and Adult Literacy* 57 (8): 628–631. https://doi.org/10.1002/jaal.297.

Shulman, Lee S. 2005. "Signature Pedagogies in the Professions." *Daedalus* 134 (3): 52–59.

Stewart-Dore, Nea. 2013. "Coda: From Content Area Reading to Disciplinary Literacy." *Literacy Learning: The Middle Years* 21 (1): 48–50.

Sullivan, Patrick. 2017. "'Deep Reading' as a Threshold Concept in Composition Studies." In *Deep Reading: Teaching Reading in the Writing Classroom*, edited by Patrick Sullivan, Howard Tinberg, and Sheridan Blau, 143–171. Urbana, IL: National Council of Teachers of English.

Swales, John M. 2016. "Reflections on the Concept of Discourse Community." *ASp* 69:7–19. http://journals.openedition.org/asp/4774.

Thaiss, Chris, and Tara Porter. 2010. "The State of WAC/WID in 2010: Methods and Results of the U.S. Survey of the International WAC/WID Mapping Project." *College Composition and Communication* 61 (3): 534–570. www.jstor.org/stable/40593339.

Tracey, Diane H., and Lesley Mandel Morrow. 2012. *Lenses on Reading: An Introduction to Theories and Models*. 3rd ed. New York: Guilford.

Wardle, Elizabeth, and Doug Downs. 2010. *Writing about Writing: A College Reader*. Boston: Bedford/St. Martin's.

Willingham, Daniel T. 2017. *The Reading Mind: A Cognitive Approach to Understanding How the Mind Reads*. San Francisco: Jossey-Bass.

Wolf, Maryanne. 2018. *Reader Come Home: The Reading Brain in a Digital World*. New York: HarperCollins.

I. WAYS OF READING

1

EXPLORING READERLY DIVERSITY

MARGARET MACKEY

In 1999, I taught a new graduate course, Contemporary Theories and Practices of Reading, for the first time. The student population included master's students in library and information studies, working teachers studying part-time for a master's degree in education, and two auditors—practicing librarians who advised readers every day on their choices of reading material. One day the teachers arrived in a group, chatting intently and with some exasperation about pupils in their school classes. Heide Blackmore, an auditing librarian, listened with evident discomfort and finally asked, "Did you ever meet a reader that you didn't want to change?"

The teachers considered this fascinating question respectfully and eventually concluded that "changing readers" is actually part of their job description, something they are contractually obliged to do. There is nothing inherently improper about working to make readers better at any given task. This thoughtful response led to an extensive discussion about the professional responsibilities of public librarians in terms of any possible duty to change the readers they serve. Our conversation raised important questions about the significance of respecting readers on their own terms. It also provided me with a question that has sharpened my research thinking ever since: What can we learn when we simply ask what readers do when reading by and for themselves, as opposed to investigating what tactics will most effectively change them into readers who are more successful in terms decided by the researcher? Both activities are worthwhile, but they result in different kinds of findings.

This chapter explores the territory of that divide. I investigate how readers behave when left to themselves to read for pleasure and how an improved understanding of variations in behaviors involved in recreational reading can enrich our awareness of many other kinds of reading, including the kinds of reading addressed by the scholarship of teaching and learning (SOTL). Generally, I discuss readers' private behaviors and preferences when reading for themselves in leisure contexts. I believe this approach offers one kind of answer to the challenge of Stephen Bloch-Schulman et al. (2016, 4): "SoTL scholars must pursue questions that uncover, articulate, and interrogate learning in a wider range of ways and spaces."

In this chapter, I explore some ways in which diversity manifests itself, in a model derived from the hundreds of readers I have researched and taught, connecting wherever possible to implications for disciplinary reading and learning. I address tacit conditions of reading such as optimal situation, mental imagery, temporal preferences, tolerance of risk, interest in large or finite reading worlds, and overall commitment to reading, concepts that are frequently taken for granted but that inflect reading behaviors beyond the recreational. I also investigate issues of stance that vary with purpose.

Exploring leisure reading may seem counterintuitive in a book about reading for learning and teaching. I argue that even if the mandate is to change readers for the better, commencing that effort with a subtler understanding of—and respect for—their autonomous recreational reading will improve the effectiveness of the efforts. As Nancy L. Chick (2013, 30) says, "novices will start with what they know." She is talking about new teachers, but her observation applies to students as well. For most skilled readers, leisure reading represents the core matrix out of which other, more specialized capacities develop. A greater self-awareness about one's own proclivities can not only enhance recreational reading but also supply a toolkit for refining other reading skills. Strengthening metacognitive muscles is a valuable form of exercise; as Pat Hutchings (2005) says, "we know that learners who are self-conscious about that process tend to be more successful." For those wishing to improve student reading strategies, a complex awareness of reader variation can be a valuable starting point— for students and instructors alike.

READERLY VARIATION

Many aspects of reading are distinctively individual, even when the text is held constant. We don't know what other people do inside the privacy of their own minds, so we extrapolate from our own behaviors. When we share our idiosyncratic mental tendencies, we are frequently astonished at the variation: "People ... overestimate the extent to which others think the way they do," says Robert J. Sternberg (1997, 18). Lawrence W. Barsalou (2008, 623) agrees: "We represent other people's minds using simulations of our own minds." Such an approach, though reasonable at first glance, does not make room for the broad diversity in how people's minds work. There is a further risk that researchers, assuming that reading is a singular activity, draw on their own personal instincts and defaults as they create their research questions: "Often the tendency [is] to consult one's own experience and use one's own intuitions to design experiments—or simply to presume that all other humans experience thought the same way" (Otis 2015a, 47).

Maryanne Wolf (2016, 3–4) observes that we should probably expect readerly variation because the capacity to read is not hardwired: "*We were never born to read.* The brain that reads is not a given. Literacy is a cultural invention, which means that there is no genetic program that can dictate its design. . . . Because the acquisition of reading is not biologically determined (like language or taste), there exists no one, ideal, universal design" (emphasis in original). Reading is a highly complex mental activity. It is actually quite difficult to describe much of what occurs in our minds as we decode and interpret the marks on the page, converting them into some form of mental life. A whole research enterprise is dedicated to teasing out the fine details of our mental processes, but we still have much to learn. Brain science offers one kind of window, and Renate Brosch (2017) discusses a "default" mode of reading, which proceeds through the dorsal systems of the brain. The initial automatic processing of words "hovers on the threshold of consciousness and cannot be fully remembered once the reading is completed" (256). It is "continuous, fluid, transient, and indistinct" (257). And when readers do make the effort to articulate these responses, we find that how they vivify the written words in their heads not only incorporates personal memories and understandings, as most people would expect, but also activates variable and very personal mental habits and tendencies beyond that initial default autoprocessing, which seems to surprise people rather more.

We will never be able to specify every detail of the variety of possible reading behaviors. Nevertheless, the fact of its essentially plural nature is vital to a useful understanding of how reading works across a population of diverse mental traits and approaches. In addressing the fact of this multiplicity of activities known as reading, we may find Martin Heidegger's (2012, 117) observation helpful: "The human sciences . . . must necessarily remain inexact precisely in order to be rigorous. That is not a deficiency; it is their merit." Describing reading is inexact work; we will be truer to the complexity of its conditions if we keep this proviso in mind. The complex endeavor of reading is sometimes more productively understood through "fuzzy" frameworks. Readers often behave untidily, with important implications for how we frame, analyze, and apply research findings.

Much evidence about reading behaviors comes from laboratory constructs. But psychological metrics often compute the measurable in ways circumscribed by the focus of the research question. In this chapter, I address questions arising from readers' personal defaults and readerly idiosyncrasies as broadly categorized through Edwin Hutchins's (1995, xii) useful concept of *"naturally situated cognition"* (emphasis in original). Reading, of course, is not "natural," but readers do assemble personal structures of tacit and default behaviors and assumptions that they apply to their "free" reading; this assemblage provides a core understanding out of which more deliberate learned responses may develop. Self-aware readers, who acknowledge their default preferences, are in a better position to fine-tune behaviors to serve a particular end, such as studying. Hutchins entitled his book *Cognition in the Wild* (1995); the idea of "reading in the wild" may serve as a helpful counterweight to some excesses of the research lab and may provide useful grounding for the steps we take to develop more specialist forms of reading.

Evidence and Experience

Most of this chapter addresses ways in which readers differ from each other. But before I turn to that topic, I want to make a brief digression on the subject of reading and evidence. Politicians and officials making policy about the teaching of reading are committed to "evidence-based practice" (see, for example, how the selective use of particular kinds of evidence has informed the British government's ongoing insistence on phonics testing [Grundin 2018]). Yet, given that they are addressing processes that are "continuous, fluid, transient, and indistinct" (Brosch 2017, 257), many reading policies are unproductively wedded to a concept of evidence that is hamstrung by its overreliance on measurement and replicability. Much of what is vague but highly meaningful about reading and its pleasures is lost in translation when replicability takes priority over individuality.

SOTL is not immune to arguments about what constitutes standards of evidence (Chick 2013, 18). But I propose to step outside even the disciplinary arguments about what counts. For the moment, I propose to put the word *evidence* itself to one side and instead consider ways in which we may gain *knowledge* about the complex activity we call reading. Introspective consideration of our own behaviors, comparative conversations with other readers about their ways of responding, and qualitative and quantitative research to formalize some of these potential findings all have radical utility, whether in informal or formal venues. I suggest an additional route to increased knowledge: the activity of teaching. We all certainly hope that students learn something from their classes, but I am talking here about what their instructors learn.

Observant and sensitive teachers of early reading, for example, are an excellent resource for enhancing a nuanced understanding of the varied processes through which we interpret the written word. My own contribution in this chapter is based on a different kind of classroom. For nearly twenty years, I acted as the instructor for a graduate course *about* reading, aimed primarily at preservice librarians but also including teachers and literary scholars. Through thirteen iterations of this course, I taught more than 250 such students, with class sizes ranging between 10 and 30. These adults reported on their own reading behaviors both individually and collectively, with provision for some anonymous testimony; they conducted a self-assessment of their personal silent reading of a short story; they read over thirty articles by both scholars and practitioners (updated every year but with continuities as well), plus a complete book on the subject of reading (most recently, Mendelsund 2014); they responded to some of these readings with journal entries assessing their personal academic reading strategies; and they joined in group and class discussion on every article. They also interviewed a reader other than themselves and presented a case study to their classmates, an assignment that persevered through all iterations of the course, with the consequence that I have moderated more than 250 examples of these external readers. The chapter draws on this very deep well of teaching experience to augment the more structured accounts of reader variation developed through my research projects. Instructors in other kinds of classes will develop different insights; the library orientation of my own class permits my students and me to investigate an unusually broad range of reading situations.

It is now impossible to disentangle the perspectives I have brought to these classes from what the thoughtful contributions of the students have given back to me. My experience of these courses is not "evidence" in the technical sense of the term, and I do not quote any student directly or draw formal conclusions. Nevertheless, my understanding of readers has been both refined and expanded through more than five hundred hours of class time. The commentary on readerly variety that follows arises from that rich background, and I wish to acknowledge the active influence of all my students on the framework below.

It is also important to note what I have not been doing in my classroom. I am not teaching a literature course. We do sometimes talk about aspects of literary reading, but we align them alongside or in counterdistinction to the many other different ways that ordinary people read for pleasure. In my classroom, when we take account of the "systematic, analytical, distanced reflection" that Anezka Kuzmicova (2016, 218) says is primarily valued in the academy, it is only as one particular kind of reading behavior. As a consequence, we frequently explore interpretive behaviors that are "good enough" rather than maximally efficacious, behaviors that at best simply suffice the reader to keep moving forward (Mackey 1997) and that may be described as potentially sloppy at the careless extreme. In effect, our class discussions address many questions of reading in the wild as well as reading in the academy, although, needless to say, it is impossible to conceive of any graduate class as "wild" in its own right. In this particular classroom setting, insight comes from many quarters, not just through the refinement of literary attention or the development of strategies to "master" content, valuable though such processes undoubtedly are.

How Readers Differ

Both my formal research (intense qualitative work with more than one hundred individual readers) and my teaching experience in the reading course corroborate the idea that the cognitive and affective activities of reading are invisibly individual. To the outside eye, all readers behave in much the same way, focusing on the marks in front of them as they bring words to life in the mind. Eye movements are measurable; brain scanning offers information about blood flows and activity in brain cells. But the internal experience of reading is personal, available to an outsider only through the reader's own account of it, which is partial and usually limited to what can be expressed in words.

The model of reading variation that follows is based on reading for pleasure—"free voluntary reading" (Krashen 2011), or reading in the wild. An awareness of the functions of leisure reading is part of the content expertise of librarians, but investigating its nature is valuable for a much broader range of readers and students. Leisure reading may involve fiction or nonfiction, and many individuals classify reading to gain information as a form of reading for pleasure. Stephen Krashen says free reading is essential for the development of success. Much of our skilled reading activity necessarily occurs automatically; as long as we need to pay attention to every decoding detail, we are like the learning driver or emergent bicycle rider, impeded by our inability to "outsource" essential processes to automatic procedures that do not need monitoring. Until we get past needing to interpret every word separately, we cannot build fluidity and automaticity. Krashen suggests that it is necessary for learning readers to spend more time reading than school hours permit and that voluntary reading is the most effective route to achievement. Reading for pleasure is also an efficient way to recruit the brain's tacit processes. While a reader concentrates on salient content, the nonconscious part of the mind distributes the necessary background functions that smooth the way to automatic processing. These generalities apply to most readers. The variations in how people read for pleasure, however, are considerably greater than these relatively simple sentences indicate.

Variations on a Reading Theme: Habitual Responses

Some of the ways in which readers differ from each other are external and relatively obvious. Other points of difference are tacit and often unexamined even by the reader involved. The categories below are not necessarily comprehensive, but they certainly encompass a very wide range of individual variation.

Optimal Reading Conditions

Readers differ in the conditions they prefer for best reading success. Some need peace and quiet or a particular kind of background music; others are perfectly able to focus even in a setting of general uproar and potential distraction. Some have switched largely to audiobooks and podcasts. Sitting comfortably with a cup of tea or coffee, with or without the resident pet on hand, is the optimal setting for some; others do their best reading while commuting; and many require at least a small dose of reading in bed before they can fall asleep. In like manner, many students also need a specific setting for optimal studying; although they may not have thought about it very hard, they can describe it when asked. Articulating what works best for them can be surprisingly useful, as many of my students' reading journals have attested.

Conjuring Mental Images

Such differences, of course, are surface variations, but readers' internal behaviors are not identical either. To begin with, readers produce different forms of what is frequently called "mental imagery." The word *imagery* skews pictorial in its everyday meaning, but mental imagery is multisensory (De Koning and van der Schoot 2013). Many readers do indeed see visual images in their minds, sometimes like a movie playing before their internal eye, sometimes full of freeze-frame pictorial detail. Other readers have an acoustic bias, and their response to the words on the page is to hear them—all of them, in some cases—with a particular narrative voice included in the mix; or, for others, mainly the dialogue, with or without appropriate accents added in. Some readers produce a sketchier, more nebulous response, taking account of movement and feelings without much visual or aural detail at all. The scholarship surrounding this kind of variation is unusually divided. Some authors assume a visual default (MacKenzie 2017; Gormley and McDermott 2015); others are more dismissive about the value of visualizing while reading (Mendelsund 2014). Detailed and explicit consideration of the range of possible responses is less common (but see Otis 2015b; Mackey 2019). Ben Alderson-Day, Marco Bernini, and Charles Fernyhough (2017, 101) provide a rare empirical glimpse of distinctive forms of response in their survey of 1,566 adult readers. Of these participants, 48 percent say they have visual or other sensory experiences when reading all or most of the time, while 26 percent never or only very occasionally do so; and 51 percent hear characters' voices all or most of the time, while 21 percent never or only very occasionally hear voices.

Scientific studies designed to probe the reading mind frequently do not allow for such variety of internal behavior. To take a particularly narrow example, Gordon H. Bower and Daniel G. Morrow (1990) seem to assume the necessity of a visual bias, as they require participants in their study of mental models to memorize a floor plan and then interrogate them on their recall of visual details from this predetermined setting. Pedagogical advice also often skews visual in restrictive ways. A Google search for "reading and visualization" turned up dozens of sites insisting that children must learn to visualize to become successful readers. A greater respect for inherent reader preference might provide a broader yet subtler account of how mental models work divergently for different readers. Locking participants into an artificial model based on assumptions about a singular reading process diminishes the validity and the utility of both research findings and pedagogical recommendations.

Temporal Priorities

The variations described so far are part of what might be called the spatial framing of the text, the location of the reading act, and the opening up of a text world in a reader's mind. There are also temporal variations. Edward Chittenden and Terry Salinger (2001, 89) suggest that there is a spectrum of reading behaviors between those who read for momentum and those who read for accuracy: "The basis for the accuracy-momentum distinction hinges on the theoretical conception that anticipation and accountability are the dual requirements for constructing meaning from text. Anticipation sustains the momentum and flow of the action through time, while accountability ensures that the action stays on course." Momentum readers prioritize forward movement through a text. If they come across something they don't understand, they will likely keep reading in the hope that further information will be provided—they may even speed up. Momentum is not equivalent to speed per se, but their reluctance to stop and check may mean that momentum readers reach the end of a text more quickly and are more readily able to assess the gist of a text. Accountability readers, in contrast, *do* stop and check. They do not like to keep going when their understanding is vague, so they look up words, refer to an earlier segment of the text for clarification, return to the list of characters or the map at the beginning of the book, and so forth. This approach runs the risk of stalling, but it is arguably more thorough.

With momentum at one end of the spectrum and accountability at the other end, many readers fall somewhere in between; the text itself also plays a role in guiding reader reaction. Nevertheless, many people can identify whether their default tendencies veer toward one end or the other of this spectrum.

Tracy Linderholm's (2006) study of the role of the reader's purpose in framing reading seems to have located both readers with a bias toward momentum and others favoring accountability, as her description of their activities indicates. She does not use this terminology, nor does she attend to this distinction except to discount momentum readers as misguided. She refers to reading for pleasure but is dismissive of its inherent value: "When reading for entertainment purposes, readers' verbal protocols indicated that they generated more free associations, which are associations loosely based on text ideas that become transiently activated during reading, and generated more evaluative comments on the writing or interest value of the text. . . . In other words, these readers processed texts at a rather shallow level" (71). Her overriding priority is recall, so it is not surprising that she valorizes the strategies of the accountability readers. She points out that students who read and reread without pausing to paraphrase and make "coherence-building inferences" (72) recall less well. But even on those occasions when recall truly is the major reason for reading, a more useful strategy for helping readers improve their test scores might be for them to be alerted to their own default preferences to help them learn to change mental gears when required.

Reasons for Reading

So far, I have described variations in response behaviors, but readers also bring preferences to bear on why and what they choose to read. Again, we are talking about a continuum rather than a binary division, but for simplicity, I address the far ends of the spectrum.

Some readers relish risk-taking. Franz Kafka (1977) famously describes the scale of emotional risk that reading can offer: "I think we ought to read only the kind of books that wound and stab us.... We need the books that affect us like a disaster, that grieve us deeply, like the death of someone we loved more than ourselves, like being banished into forests far from everyone, like a suicide. A book must be the axe for the frozen sea inside us. That is my belief" (letter to Oskar Pollak, January 1904). Even without subscribing to Kafka's draconian ethos, readers know that there are true emotional risks in starting a new fiction or a particular biography or some kinds of history books. What will happen to our feelings by the time we end it? How brave must we be to keep reading it? What uncomfortable truths may we learn about ourselves or about the world? A novel engages our emotions, and that simple fact renders us vulnerable. Yet the risk is contained to something we hold in our hands; we can close it and put it down. A book sometimes serves as a testing ground for us to establish our own personal limits—of courage, of endurance, of self-awareness.

Many readers relish that risk; others choose to read for safety, turning to a book for comfort when the rest of life is too challenging. This particular form of variation is often situational; students writing exams will often revert to safer bedtime reading, for example, but make a much more adventurous choice during the summer holidays (Mackey 2003). Some kinds of reading offer safe havens in different ways. One of the appeals of series reading is that a certain amount of information is already available about the story world and, importantly, about the degree of emotional havoc an author is likely to wreak. A new book in a cherished series offers the prize of novelty and comfort in one package.

Rereading may also provide an emotional safety net; readers know to brace themselves for any upsetting content, though they may be devastated all over again (a slightly different issue). Series readers who gain access to their books out of order may reread to establish an orderly chronological sense of the doings of their fictional world. But, of course, rereading is not just a safe option; risk-loving readers may reread to address the dangerous issues raised by a text in more informed or reflective ways.

A different kind of risk/safety formula may apply in the classroom. Textbook reading is inherently risk-reduced in many ways, offering a kind of safety net for instructors and students alike. "Wilder" reading challenges students; for example, they may be sent out to make their own selections and defend them in a classroom setting, a riskier but more dynamic activity. One focus of contemporary pedagogy is on the need for a classroom to be a safe space; I submit that a classroom can be emotionally safe and intellectually risky at the same time, and I argue for a principled assessment of where the lines of risk and safety should reasonably be drawn. Once again, simply articulating priorities in this area can be useful.

Big-World Reading versus the Novel Novel

Many readers relish fictional worlds that burst the boundaries of a single title. Such a big-world approach may involve a series of books, a transmedia telling that distributes the complete story over a variety of vehicles, a concatenation of retellings in different media forms, or an online augmentation of the original world via authorized or fan additions. Some readers contribute to the enlargement of a particular world through fan fiction or complex world-building and mapping. Big worlds may also be informational, as readers build taxonomies or develop complex historical understanding. Acquiring expertise about a particular big world holds compelling appeal for some enthusiasts (Mackey 2009).

Other readers are not interested in returning over and over again to the same universe. They want the story to be over when they shut the book at the end. They prize novelty and look for a fresh start when they pick up a new story or topic. And, of course, some readers occupy an intermediate point on the spectrum, happy to read a series that captivates them but frequently seeking singular works.

In theory, academic reading encompasses a big-world approach, with content from one required text surviving in students' minds to inflect subsequent reading. In reality, however unfortunately and maladaptively, many students operate on a stand-alone basis, digesting individual readings or textbook chapters in atomistic and short-term ways. Exploring and perhaps expanding how readers set limits to particular study experiences can be productive. What do students think they are or should be doing "between" one course and the next, especially if the two courses are not explicitly linked through a hierarchy of required courses and prerequisites? Could they benefit from more conscious attention to the need to make connections? Does our system of end-of-term exams train them to consider that a course is finished and may be safely forgotten after that end date? A big-world education looks very different from one composed of separate building blocks that never quite link together.

The Constant and the Inconstant Reader

What factors lead readers to turn to reading in the first place is also variable. A helpful distinction separates "flow" readers from "event" readers, though once again these are not absolute terms, and many readers successfully alternate between both conditions. Flow readers always have reading on the go. They are the people with the stack of books at their bedside, whose suitcases or Kindles are stuffed with holiday reading. A flow reader dreads the moment when there is nothing available to read. Event readers, on the other hand, like reading well enough but do not need always to be doing it. They require a reason to read—for example, a book is such a best seller that everybody else is reading it and talking about it, the movie is about to come out, or their book group is going to discuss it. Once they finish their "event" read, they are perfectly happy to stop reading for a while until the next motivating factor arises. Some event readers operate on a binge-and-fast basis.

One reason this distinction is so useful is that, for many people, flow reading is part of their schema of what establishes a person as a reader. Many flow readers think of event readers as not really readers at all. Some event readers internalize the concept of flow as essential to the schema of being a reader and assess themselves in exactly the same negative way. Life events (e.g., having a baby, entering graduate school, accepting a new job or promotion, or acting as a caregiver) can reduce flow readers to the more limited palette of event reading. They sometimes regard this shift as a loss of the reading habit or even as the erosion of their overall ability to read. The idea that reading activities naturally peak and recede at various points in the trajectory of an individual life may console some readers who find themselves in a temporary trough and are concerned that they have forever lost the capacity for sustained reading.

Self-perception creeps into all kinds of reading. Students frequently lament their loss of time and autonomy to sustain an independent reading life. This is not a trivial irony. I have lost count of the students who say to me, "I used to be a reader, but then I came to university." There may not be a cure for the assault of academic learning on students' free time, but some discussion of the trajectory of a reading life can be helpful.

Even if flow reading is not possible for students with heavy course loads, this sense of being overwhelmed is not equivalent to a life sentence of being a nonreader. Perceiving oneself as an event reader, perhaps for the first time ever, is not a negative character assessment. Yet how people think of themselves as readers is often a strong feature of their sense of personal identity, and their instructors can do worse than give them a bit of time and space to reflect on these changes. Many of us, readers and nonreaders alike, operate on an implicit hierarchy: flow reading is better than event reading, which is better than not reading at all. Unpacking what "better" means in this context is a useful if sometimes sobering activity.

Students who are convinced that their voluntary reading lives are over may sour on the academic reading that seems to have undermined their sense of themselves as readers. Countering the depressing impact of this life turn is a valuable pedagogical exercise on many levels, and being honest about the opportunity costs of studying—the evisceration of wider reading time being one core example of loss—is salutary for everyone.

More Variations: Contingent Positions

So far, I have focused on large-scale reading preferences that frequently click into action as a default approach. Some distinctions are more situational, and I briefly explore how a particular context may affect how we read at any given moment.

Situated and Dedicated Reading

Two kinds of contemporary reading event are now commonplace. Situated reading is often fragmented, a momentary encounter with a text relevant to an ongoing social exchange. A prime example involves a conversation during which one participant whips out a mobile phone for a brief moment of Google research in order to augment the face-to-face exchange with further facts or examples. Much texting is also situated. Historical examples of situated reading undoubtedly included participants in a conversation consulting the newspaper carried by one of them, but there is no doubt that the advent of smartphones exponentially increased the social prevalence of situated reading.

Dedicated reading, in contrast, has been around for a long time. It is "appointment" reading, the kind that involves a deliberate decision to sit down with a text. Some dedicated reading may also be situated (the commuter focused on a book in the middle of a crowd comes to mind), but most dedicated readers can block out the situation of their reading if they are determined to do so. Probably very few contemporary readers will be found at either of the extreme ends of this continuum, but many readers will know that their preferred form of engagement veers one way or the other.

The distinction between situated and dedicated reading provides the raw material for an ongoing social argument about the state of contemporary reading. On one level, never have so many people read so much. At the same time, much of that reading comes in bite-sized fragments whose role is to contribute to the conversation rather than serve as a step away from the public world into a textual encounter of the kind that fosters an isolated silence (see Mackey 2020, for further discussion of this topic).

In my own classrooms, I have been surprised by the kinds of situational reading that have arisen as students turn to their computers for information to supplement our discussions. Often, I have noticed that a student seems to be prioritizing engagement with their screen, typing rather than listening, appearing to be distracted, only to discover, when I reach my office at breaktime, that this person has been engaged in sending me a relevant link. We tend to think of academic reading as usually dedicated, but I suggest that the current classroom is more complex. Nevertheless, dedicated academic reading time remains essential to success, and its significance should be articulated to and by students.

Stance

Louise Rosenblatt's ([1978] 1994) distinction between efferent and aesthetic reading remains useful after many decades. Efferent reading is reading for the purpose of taking something away. Aesthetic reading is done for the experience of dwelling in the world of the text; takeaway is not a feature. Readers may start reading with a particular stance in mind, but it is commonplace for their priorities to shift during the act. People who settle down for a careful read, with a view to creating a critical response later, may find themselves carried away by the story and reach the end without retaining all those details that were going to be noted so thoroughly. Alternatively, somebody planning a mindless reading romp through an escapist text may wind up learning a great deal of peripheral information about a particular topic that stays with them for life.

A different take on stance comes from J. Yellowlees Douglas and Andrew Hargadon (2001, 156), who distinguish between immersion and engagement in a text. Immersion is the state of being completely absorbed in the universe created by the writing; the only working schemas in the reader's mind are those of the text world. Engagement allows for a partial commitment to the text world, augmented by the devotion of mental energy to connected issues. For example, an engaged reading may include attention to the language of the telling as well as the events of the story, or it may involve awareness of how the story was told differently in the movie with a comparative perspective in constant play, or it may involve applying knowledge from a later book in the series as a kind of artificial foreshadowing device. The engaged reader remains committed to the overall zone of the text but is not entirely submerged in and captivated by the narrated universe.

It is certainly possible that immersed reading is less critical than engaged reading, but for many individuals, it is a necessary and highly valued first step. Rosenblatt is eloquent about the limitations of an instructional focus that insists only efferent reading has any utility, and her cautions are still worth reading many decades later: Linderholm's dismissal of the "shallow" work of what Rosenblatt would surely describe as an aesthetic reading is a reminder of the related perils of a singular approach to reading research.

Implications

Reading for recreational purposes is often taken completely for granted, but I have outlined many ways in which that activity is individualized:

Habitual responses (general preferences to which readers usually default)

- preferences in setting and conditions for reading
- instinct for visual, acoustic, or emotion-based imagery
- placement on a momentum/accuracy spectrum
- predilection for risky or safe reading
- enjoyment of big worlds or singular universes
- designation as a "flow" or an "event" reader

Contingent variations (specific conditions that may vary from one reading event to the next)

- situated or dedicated reading
- efferent or aesthetic stance
- immersed or engaged relationship with the text

Developing Personal Understanding

Placing oneself as a reader on such a rough-and-ready list is instructive, even when it is achieved "only" in the context of recreational reading. It is always useful to be aware that one's own behaviors are not inevitable, that there are other ways of achieving the same end of enjoying a reading experience. It is a radical step from a singular, sometimes vague presumption that there is no way other than one's own of performing the activity of reading to the idea of plural and distinctive options. Developing greater capacity for metacognition through a consideration of alternative approaches is often a precursor to more sophisticated learning.

Sometimes the simple act of naming an aspect of our reading processes is enough to empower readers to make adjustments. The momentum/accuracy spectrum offers a useful example. Labeling myself as a reader at the far momentum end of the scale allowed me to consider the value of reining in this default tendency for particular reading tasks. It remains a strenuous challenge for me to read more deliberately, but it has improved my reading tool kit to be aware of the occasional need for such efforts. I also benefit by simply recognizing that "accountability" advice may need to be adapted to be useful to me.

Awareness of reader variation is also useful for abating the sense of many nonvisualizing readers that they are somehow deficient. Evidence is scanty, but it seems likely that visualizers are in a majority; and some approaches to the teaching of reading suggest a deficit model for everyone else. Simply knowing you are not alone in your acoustic or affective mode of response can in itself be powerful. It is also useful for the visualizers to be less monolithic in their schema of reading, perhaps particularly useful for those visualizers who teach early readers.

Similarly, being alert to the difference between efferent and aesthetic reading can be a game changer. It is exceedingly commonplace to hear readers berating themselves for their poor recollection of what they have recently read. An awareness that recall is not always the priority of the reading mind can be liberating. Such self-knowledge can also offer strategic help. I know, for example, that my personal default behavior is nonvisualizing, momentum-driven, aesthetic by preference, and frequently immersed. This combination does not foster reliable memory work, and I have learned that rereading is very often my best strategy if I do want to develop a critical analysis. At a minimum, I now know that mine is not the only and inevitable way to read, and knowledge of such plurality helps me consider ways in which I might alter or refine or even resist my normal tendencies as needed. The challenge to change myself as a reader operates on a very different basis from the charge to change another reader.

Instructors who are self-aware readers themselves may bring a more nuanced understanding into the classroom. My own experience is that students benefit enormously when I let them into the secret that, although I am a teacher, I am very far from being an ideal reader and must acknowledge and sometimes resist my innate tendencies in order to develop a productive approach to my work. I always make this point right at the beginning of the course, and students immediately feel safer talking about their own reading in this classroom.

Refining Our Collective Awareness

It seems fairly obvious that readers, students and instructors alike, who can articulate their own personal reading proclivities in the awareness that not everybody behaves the same way have a valuable metacognitive tool for exploring ways to make their reading processes more effective in terms of their own personal purposes. Is there any collective value to a finer-grained understanding of readerly variation?

As citizens, we perceive ourselves to be stakeholders in public literacy concerns. Parents, employers, politicians and other policy makers, teachers, librarians, and journalists and other writers all participate more or less directly in the inculcation and application of literacy. But this list only scratches the surface. Literacy is a factor in most aspects of Western daily life in the twenty-first century. We draw on our literate skills as citizens, as patients, as workers, as consumers, and in many other roles. Understanding the necessary and inherent diversity of a society of readers enables us to open more subtle and sophisticated conversations about how we govern both our communications with each other and our own private reading capacities.

Inside the academy, the issue is no less important. Sometimes changing readers is crucial. Sometimes respecting their readerly autonomy takes priority. Sometimes respecting readerly autonomy is actually the best first step to developing change. However we look at it, the fact of reading heterogeneity matters to us all. For those who work to improve reading for learning, a more subtle sense of where readers are starting may help fine-tune the steps that will lead them to a desired destination.

Acknowledgments

The author owes a great debt to every University of Alberta student who took LIS 580, Contemporary Theories and Practices of Reading, between 1999 and 2017. She is also grateful for ongoing research support from the Social Sciences and Humanities Research Council of Canada.

References

Alderson-Day, Ben, Marco Bernini, and Charles Fernyhough. 2017. "Uncharted Features and Dynamics of Reading: Voices, Characters, and Crossing of Experiences." *Consciousness and Cognition* 49:98–109.

Barsalou, Lawrence W. 2008. "Grounded Cognition." *Annual Review of Psychology* 59:617–645.

Bloch-Schulman, Stephen, Susan Conkling, Sherry Lee Linkon, Karen Manarin, and Kathleen Perkins. 2016. "Asking Bigger Questions: An Invitation to Further Conversation." *Teaching and Learning Inquiry* 4 (1): 108–114. http://dx.doi.org/10.20343/teachlearninqu.4.1.12.

Bower, Gordon H., and Daniel G. Morrow. 1990. "Mental Models in Narrative Comprehension." *Science* 247:44–48.

Brosch, Renate. 2017. "Experiencing Narratives: Default and Vivid Modes of Visualization." *Poetics Today* 38 (2): 255–272.

Chick, Nancy L. 2013. "Difference, Privilege, and Power in the Scholarship of Teaching and Learning: The Value of Humanities SOTL." In *The Scholarship of Teaching and Learning in and across Disciplines*, edited by Kathleen McKinney, 15–33. Bloomington: Indiana University Press.

Chittenden, Edward, and Terry Salinger. 2001. *Inquiry into Meaning: An Investigation of Learning to Read*. With Anne M. Bussis. Rev. ed. New York: Teachers College Press.

De Koning, Bjorn B., and Menno van der Schoot. 2013. "Becoming Part of the Story! Refueling the Interest in Visualization Strategies for Reading Comprehension." *Educational Psychology Review* 25:261–287.

Douglas, J. Yellowlees, and Andrew Hargadon. 2001. "The Pleasures of Immersion and Engagement: Schemas, Scripts and the Fifth Business." *Digital Creativity* 12 (3): 153–166.

Gormley, Kathleen, and Peter McDermott. 2015. "Searching for Evidence—Teaching Students to Become Effective Readers by Visualizing Information in Texts." *Clearing House* 88 (6): 171–177.

Grundin, Hans U. 2018. "Policy and Evidence: A Critical Analysis of the Year 1 Phonics Screening Check in England." *Literacy* 52 (1): 39–46.

Heidegger, Martin. 2012. *Contributions to Philosophy (Of the Event)*. Bloomington: Indiana University Press.

Hutchings, Pat. 2005. "Building Pedagogical Intelligence." *Carnegie Perspectives*. https://files.eric.ed.gov/fulltext/ED498958.pdf.

Hutchins, Edwin. 1995. *Cognition in the Wild*. Cambridge, MA: MIT Press.

Kafka, Franz. 1977. *Letters to Friends, Family, and Editors*. Translated by Richard and Clara Winston. New York: Schocken Books.

Krashen, Stephen. 2011. *Free Voluntary Reading*. Santa Barbara, CA: Libraries Unlimited.

Kuzmicova, Anezka. 2016. "Audiobooks and Print Narrative: Similarities in Text Experience." In *Audionarratology: Interfaces of Sound and Narrative*, edited by Jarmila Mildorf and Till Kinzel, 217–238. Berlin: Walter de Gruyter.

Linderholm, Tracy. 2006. "Reading with Purpose." *Journal of College Reading and Learning* 36 (2): 70–80.

MacKenzie, Brooke. 2017. "The Power of the Picture." *Literacy Today* 35 (3): 32–33.

Mackey, Margaret. 1997. "Good-Enough Reading: Momentum and Accuracy in the Reading of Complex Fiction." *Research in the Teaching of English* 3 (4): 428–458.

———. 2003. "Risk, Safety, and Control in Young People's Reading Experiences." *School Libraries Worldwide* 9 (1): 50–63.

———. 2009. "Exciting yet Safe: The Appeal of Thick Play and Big Worlds." In *Play, Creativity and Digital Culture*, edited by Rebecca Willett, Muriel Robinson, and Jackie Marsh, 92–107. New York: Routledge.

———. 2019. "Visualization and the Vivid Reading Experience." *Jeunesse: Young People, Texts, Cultures* 11 (1): 38–58.

———. 2020. "Who Reads What, in Which Formats, and Why?" In *Handbook of Reading Research*, vol. 5, edited by Elizabeth B. Moje, Peter Afflerbach, Patricia Enciso, and Nonie K. Lesaux, 99–115. New York: Routledge.

Mendelsund, Peter. 2014. *What We See When We Read: A Phenomenology with Illustrations*. New York: Vintage Books.

Otis, Laura. 2015a. *Rethinking Thought: Inside the Minds of Creative Scientists and Artists*. Oxford: Oxford University Press.

———. 2015b. "The Value of Qualitative Research for Cognitive Literary Studies." In *The Oxford Handbook of Cognitive Literary Studies*, edited by Lisa Zunshine, 505–524. Oxford: Oxford University Press.

Rosenblatt, Louise. (1978) 1994. *The Reader, the Text, the Poem: The Transactional Theory of the Literary Work*. Carbondale: Southern Illinois University Press.
Sternberg, Robert J. 1997. *Thinking Styles*. Cambridge: Cambridge University Press.
Wolf, Maryanne. 2016. *Tales of Literacy for the 21st Century*. With Stephanie Gottwald. Oxford: Oxford University Press.

Margaret Mackey is Professor Emerita in the School of Library and Information Studies at the University of Alberta. Her research explores young people's literacies in print, media, and digital formats. Her most recent book is *One Child Reading: My Auto-Bibliography* (2016).

2

UNDERSTANDINGS OF READING

Insights from Faculty Development with Reading Apprenticeship

NELSON GRAFF
REBECCA KERSNAR
DAN SHAPIRO
RYNE LEUZINGER

This chapter seeks to consider the following questions: If faculty in various disciplines do not see themselves as reading teachers, in part because they believe they do not have the expertise to teach reading, what happens when those faculty are given an opportunity to develop expertise in teaching reading? Is an introduction to pedagogical strategies sufficient, or are there other elements of the practice of teaching reading that interfere with faculty engaging with students around disciplinary texts? What does it look like when faculty developers try to bring content area reading and disciplinary literacy together in work with faculty?

Faculty, staff, and administrators at California State University, Monterey Bay (CSUMB), have been enacting a "Vision of the Possible" (Hutchings 2000, 12) through the widespread adoption of a new methodology to advance students' reading skills across disciplines. This study investigates an intervention in which faculty participated in a community of practice to consider disciplinary reading for their students through apprenticeship in the reading and problem-solving practices of their disciplines using the Reading Apprenticeship (RA) framework. In *Leading for Literacy*, Ruth Schoenbach, Cynthia Greenleaf, and Lynn Murphy (2017) present a comprehensive justification and strategy for institutionalizing RA that engages educators in collaborative professional development. Their approach utilizes, and thus models and reinforces, RA philosophy and classroom practices, tools, and other strategies. Providing educators with contextualized professional development in RA has the potential to support them and their students in becoming the kind of "self-regulated learners" that Linda B. Nilson (2013) describes in *Creating Self-Regulated Learners: Strategies to Strengthen Students' Self-Awareness and Learning Skills*. The extent to which providing faculty with professional development in RA helps college educators and their students become stronger self-regulated learners who take responsibility for—and revel in—their own learning is central to the work and research presented in this chapter.

Since 2016, professional development opportunities related to RA have taken place at our institution in a variety of forms, ranging from one-hour workshops to half-day workshops to three-day retreats, all led by college educators with advanced certification in RA. The faculty response to these opportunities has been enthusiastic. However, recognizing that introductory workshops alone are not sufficient to support faculty adoption of RA routines, the director of Communication across the Disciplines (our institution's writing program) and the teaching and learning specialist for the Center for Teaching, Learning, and Assessment began facilitating ongoing communities of practice for faculty who had completed at least one of the introductory workshops. The first iteration of these semester-long groups involved early faculty adopters of RA from across a variety of disciplines as well as instructors who teach first-year seminar and foundational courses in communication, mathematics, and statistics. These communities of practice met regularly over a semester to discuss their adoption of RA routines and the challenges and opportunities they faced in using this new approach in their teaching. Such ongoing professional development addresses the fact that faculty typically don't see themselves as "reading teachers" and tend to believe that explicitly teaching reading skills in college is remedial work. Facilitators aim for faculty to experience a fundamental shift in how they think about reading and its role in student learning by coming to a newfound understanding of reading as a skill one is always advancing, which therefore requires support up to and even into graduate school.

As detailed in *Reading for Understanding: How Reading Apprenticeship Improves Disciplinary Learning in Secondary and College Classrooms*, RA is an organizing paradigm for subject area teaching rather than a program or curriculum. This paradigm for reading instruction resonated with this group for a variety of reasons, such as the way in which it treats all students as capable learners, creates a collaborative climate of inquiry, builds on students' interests and curiosity, taps into students' knowledge and experience, and harnesses their preference for social interaction to serve academic goals (Schoenbach, Greenleaf, and Murphy 2012, 4). RA focuses on the idea that "when teachers become more aware of the complexity of how they themselves make sense of text, they gain new appreciation for the reading difficulties students may face. Teachers can then begin to apprentice their students to the reading craft by making their invisible comprehension processes visible to their students. As apprentices, students, in turn, become empowered as readers, able to tap and expand their own knowledge. In the course of doing so, they begin to own and improve their reading processes" (12–13). RA is a versatile framework in that it comprises a variety of "routines" such as "Talking to the Text" and "Building a List of Reading Strategies" and tools such as metacognitive logs that can be flexibly employed at different points in instruction depending on the needs of a given course. In RA, learners engage multiple dimensions simultaneously: the social dimension, to strengthen community and build safety for risk-taking and maximizing participant strengths; the personal dimension, to develop reader identity, agency, and purpose; the cognitive dimension, to develop the mental processes required for successful disciplinary reading, including problem-solving strategies; and the knowledge-building dimension, to cultivate—while reading—the knowledges that readers bring to disciplinary texts.

To build RA dimensions, participants engage in extensive reading and metacognitive conversation, or interaction with others about reading to consider difficulty, discovery, and the strategies needed to problem-solve text. RA routines and strategies can help students and those facilitating their learning become more effective and confident learners and teachers within disciplinary communities. But as we discuss in this chapter, creating an "RA classroom" requires both students and faculty to make challenging—and often troublesome—transformations in the way they use, engage with, and talk about reading.

Although research into the efficacy of RA exists at the secondary and community-college levels, little research has been done on RA at the four-year college level, and less on the impact of RA professional development on faculty attitudes toward reading instruction. In our preliminary findings, faculty seemed to share common struggles as they tried to apply RA routines in their classes, struggles that suggested the need for conceptual shifts about the nature of reading and the teaching and learning of reading. The way that their talk about their classrooms both approached and retreated from those conceptual changes evoked for us the literature on threshold concepts. This led us to explore the relevance of Jan Meyer and Ray Land's (2003) threshold concepts and question whether conceptual thresholds exist for faculty that, when crossed, enable them to better apprentice more students into disciplinary reading, discourse, and problem-solving. After analyzing transcripts from two semester-long communities of practice, we found preliminary evidence for at least two distinct threshold concepts that may suggest strategies for helping faculty overcome—and maybe even embrace—common struggles with reading instruction: *reading difficulties catalyze learning* and *reading is active learning*.

Rather than being specific to RA, these threshold concepts may be common to many approaches to teaching reading, as evidenced by our own research and similar struggles experienced by faculty described in other chapters of this book. As such, the preliminary findings of the research presented here have significant implications for supporting student success and, in particular, for the design and implementation of professional development on teaching reading across the disciplines. In the following sections, we briefly review relevant literature on threshold concepts and faculty development, describe how we are engaging faculty with RA at our institution, present our research process and preliminary findings, and discuss implications of those findings for understanding connections among pedagogical practices and understandings of and attitudes about academic reading among faculty.

LITERATURE REVIEW: THRESHOLD CONCEPTS AND FACULTY DEVELOPMENT

According to Meyer and Land (2003, 1), a threshold concept is "akin to a portal, opening up a new and previously inaccessible way of thinking about something. It represents a transformed way of understanding or interpreting, or viewing something without which the learner cannot progress." Such concepts therefore allow learners changed understandings and self-perceptions as well as an insider's view and relationship to a discipline. Meyer and Land attribute five characteristics to threshold concepts: (1) they are transformative, as they create substantial perceptual shifts in learner perspective that can alter feelings, values, identity, and performance; (2) they are likely irreversible, that is, such concepts once comprehended are difficult to unlearn; (3) they are integrative, as learning them involves relating many elements together to create a bigger picture; (4) they are generally bounded, that is, they inhabit territory with other threshold concepts that can help define the boundaries between disciplines or academic territories; and (5) they are troublesome, or difficult for learners to understand due to their complexities, counterintuitive qualities, unique disciplinary meanings, and other challenges (Meyer and Land

2003; Perkins 1999). Based on the metaphor of crossing a threshold, Meyer and Land highlight the liminal states that may characterize engaging these concepts, when learners are between not understanding and understanding, sometimes oscillating and regressing before potentially being transformed by the new concept (Meyer and Land 2005).

Threshold concepts in various disciplines are defined and developed in a few different ways, usually either empirically through examination of student work, through surveys of or collaboration with disciplinary experts, and through conversations with students. Such work offers tentative ideas about troublesome concepts for college readers. As suggested by Brian Gogan (2013), because of the strong interrelationship between reading and writing (and in this case information literacy), troublesome concepts for one are likely to be troublesome for others. Gogan, for instance, analyzed the discussion questions that students asked while leading discussions of scholarly articles in their disciplines and established that rhetorical genre awareness is as much a threshold concept for readers as it is for writers. Brittney Johnson and I. Moriah McCracken (2016) make a similar case regarding connections between the framework for information literacy and the threshold concepts described in *Naming What We Know* (Adler-Kassner and Wardle 2015). The overarching concepts for writing studies listed in *Naming What We Know* are the following: writing is a social and rhetorical activity, writing speaks to situations through recognizable forms, writing enacts and creates identities and ideologies, all writers have more to learn, and writing is a cognitive activity.

Despite the significant work that has been done to develop and investigate threshold concepts for disciplines and, to some degree, the pedagogical approaches that will support students encountering and crossing those thresholds, less scholarly work has been done about the thresholds faculty themselves must cross to enact those pedagogies successfully. Studying preservice teachers, Peter Smagorinsky, Susan Cook, and Tara Johnson (2003) use a Vygotskian framework of concept attainment to describe the difficulties new faculty have with understanding and enacting constructivism. While these scholars do not write in terms of threshold concepts, their description of concept development as a "twisting path" mirrors the threshold concept framework's description of crossing thresholds as iterative and characterized by oscillations and setbacks. Brian Hand and Lori Norton-Meier (2018) similarly describe the difficulty that teachers have in seeing learning as negotiation, which turns out to be a threshold for both students and faculty (though the authors do not use that term). Explicitly engaging the threshold concept framework, Jessie L. Moore (2012) describes designing for transfer of learning as a threshold concept, demonstrating the ways in which it meets Meyer and Land's categorization and what strategies professional developers can use to help faculty encounter and cross those thresholds.

The Journal of Faculty Development dedicated an issue to threshold concepts in educational development that explores the threshold concepts framework for "understanding the mixed responses we often received when we work with faculty to support substantial changes in their teaching strategies, changes that have the potential to be both profoundly troubling and profoundly transformative" (King and Felten 2012, 6). Potential threshold concepts identified in this volume most relevant to our work with RA include variation in student learning (Meyer 2012), designing for transfer (Moore 2012), and students as coinquirers (Werder, Thibou, and Kaufer 2012). Each of these studies touches on faculty threshold concepts directly relevant to the effective implementation of RA routines and strategies (Schoenbach, Greenleaf, and Murphy 2012), but none explicitly identify disciplinary reading as the topic of student learning or thresholds that faculty themselves have to cross as teachers of disciplinary reading.

This chapter adds to the work of these previous scholars by bringing together understandings about successful learning practices for disciplinary reading with faculty development to describe the troublesome encounters that faculty had with perspectives on the nature of reading, the relationship of reading to learning disciplinary content, and the status of difficulty in disciplinary instruction involving texts.

Methodology

In the fall of 2017, CSUMB facilitators led eleven to fourteen faculty participants in RA professional development through an initial six-hour overview and five two-hour teaching cooperatives, each scheduled three weeks apart and repeated for two subgroups. The participants had responded to a general call to all CSUMB faculty. Those participants included faculty teaching first-year communication, first-year seminar, literature, and a variety of mathematics and science disciplines. RA teaching cooperatives proceeded in two phases: (1) faculty-posed inquiry and reflection on their classroom RA challenges, and (2) practice of RA routines using metacognitive tools and texts related to faculty disciplines, interests, and shared purposes. To investigate facilitator and faculty co-op participation, RA teaching cooperative sessions were recorded, and the first, third, and fifth (final) sessions were transcribed. These data were initially coded to trace the development of faculty ideas about academic reading, student learning, teaching strategies, and teacher self-efficacy. Through an iterative process of comparing codes, rereading the transcripts to create summarized episode narratives, and ongoing discussion, we identified two conceptions of reading around which faculty continued to struggle throughout the sessions: *reading difficulties catalyze learning* and *reading is active learning*.

Preliminary Findings

In the following sections, we define two potential faculty threshold concepts suggested by our research, *reading difficulties catalyze learning* and *reading is active learning*; illustrate how RA professional development engages faculty with these threshold concepts; and provide preliminary evidence that these concepts are troublesome, transformative, and integrative for faculty. Because we have studied just two communities of practice over a single semester, more research is needed to establish these as genuine threshold concepts, in particular regarding whether they have the features of being irreversible and bounded. However, based on the work related to RA that we have done with faculty over the past three years, we believe both are strong candidates.

Threshold Concept 1: Reading Difficulties Catalyze Learning

One area of struggle we encountered in the RA communities of practice focused on the relationship between reading difficulties and student learning, what faculty should do when reading difficulties are exposed through metacognitive conversation, and whether faculty should encourage—and even plan—student encounters with reading difficulty. We refer to this threshold concept as *reading difficulties catalyze learning*. Below, we describe the threshold concept, articulate its relevance to RA, and provide evidence suggesting that it was both troublesome and transformative for faculty. Comments by faculty across the community-of-practice meetings suggested ways in which the concept was also integrative, allowing faculty to connect different teaching and learning experiences including students' avoidance of (or refusal of) reading, their levels of engagement, their reticence in asking questions and preference for lecture versus discussion, and faculty's own anxieties about instructional strategies and assigning reading.

RA routines and strategies create learning experiences that help students detect, normalize, and work productively with difficulty and confusion. However, educators may believe it is their responsibility to reduce difficulty and confusion for students, or worse, avoid it (e.g., by not assigning texts deemed too difficult). Accepting that reading difficulty and confusion should be normalized and that the college educator's role should be to help students identify and employ strategies for engaging with challenging texts was a struggle for faculty but one that transformed how they facilitated learning. Schoenbach, Greenleaf, and Murphy (2012, 6) are aware of this tension, noting that "teachers may try to teach 'around' the text altogether with lectures and PowerPoint presentations, or they may try to 'protect' students from dry or difficult texts with alternatives that never challenge them or help them grow as readers and learners."

Avoiding difficulty can have the unintended consequences of (1) leaving students disengaged while their teachers do the thinking and problem-solving for them and (2) preempting students' ability to develop and apply their own reading and problem-solving strategies. This is something RA explicitly tries to avoid; as Schoenbach, Greenleaf, and Murphy (2012, 24) note, "more reading, more text-focused discussion, and more talk about reading and problem-solving processes—these distinguish Reading Apprenticeship classrooms from content area classes in which students are expected, but not taught, to handle complex reading tasks."

Redefining the role of the college educator from one who is expected to share disciplinary knowledge to one who invites students into challenging learning experiences normalizes difficulty and confusion. Faculty were comfortable asking students to summarize, interpret, and apply what they learned from assigned readings, often expressing frustration when students were not able to perform as expected. They were less comfortable asking students to identify reading difficulties and use metacognitive conversation to describe and share their strategies for working with difficulty and confusion. We believe this is in part because most faculty learned how to read college-level texts largely on their own and, consciously or unconsciously, assume their students should do the same. Consequently, most faculty have paid little attention to—and have little experience, modeling, or training—explicitly helping students learn how to make meaning from complex disciplinary texts. For example, when asked why he chose to participate in the community of practice after participating in an introductory RA workshop, one participant responded, "Oh, it was just something that I hadn't thought about before . . . , you know, how I read it in a nonlinear fashion . . . starting with the figures and going to the different places."

The RA framework asserts, backed by research, that faculty will reach more students more effectively if they use metacognitive conversation to help students engage with challenging texts (Schoenbach, Greenleaf, and Murphy 2012). As a starting point, engaging students in metacognitive conversation can help faculty understand what their students can and cannot yet do. For example, implementing RA helped one participant realize she didn't understand her students' thought processes as they interacted with exam questions: "That was kind of like a lightbulb moment for me, with this Reading Apprenticeship, was when... Rebecca said, 'Well, what are you thinking when you look at the problems—like, what is the thought process behind that?' and I was like, wait a minute, there's no way for me to see what a student is really thinking about on this problem."

It was not enough for faculty to realize that avoiding difficulty robbed students of opportunities to develop reading and problem-solving skills. They also needed explicit approaches to help students learn how to engage with difficulty, which is one of RA's overarching goals. Achieving this goal requires that faculty understand and model their own problem-solving processes, something that does not typically come naturally to faculty, who sometimes confuse showing students the answer with showing students how to solve the problem. For example, in the following exchange, one of the facilitators asks a participant whether or not he had modeled problem-solving for students before they had to solve problems on their own:

FACILITATOR: Did you start with a modeling process?

PARTICIPANT: Um, not for this. Because what I didn't do... now that you put it that way, what I didn't do was, like, let's put the existing ones up on the overhead or something, right?... I just added that little teeny clarification in the question, and I... *but*, but to your point, I still didn't model, right? I still didn't bring up the old ones and say, okay, this is what I had in mind.

The distinction between showing "what I had in mind" and showing students the thinking behind engaging successfully with the difficult task is lost in this moment with this faculty member.

To foster the idea and practice that difficulty is a place to begin, every community-of-practice session began by having participants share their responses to the following prompt: "Please choose a moment in your class that surfaced some confusion, uncertainty, or difficulty of any kind about any element of the RA four dimensions (social, personal, cognitive, or knowledge-building—including metacognitive conversation and extensive reading). Come prepared to describe it briefly (no more than two minutes) and with a question that will help us investigate it." This prompt reliably catalyzed excellent discussions that helped faculty increase their understanding of RA and its potential for improving student learning in their classrooms. As participants began to see difficulty as an exciting place to begin their own exploration of RA, rather than something to explain away or avoid altogether, they began implementing RA strategies in their classrooms, as illustrated by this participant's description of how her classroom practices have changed as a result of participating in the RA community of practice:

> I gotta tell you guys, I really love this thing. So, last year . . . they basically just summarized . . . but now they had to turn [in] the reading logs and list all of the places where they had issues [difficulty] . . . so the, the annotation that I got back was very different than the one that we did before. . . . I also had them turn [the reading log] in with their portfolio, sort of a review of the class and just telling me what was helpful. . . . A lot of them talked about how this was really helpful to them.

Faculty also began normalizing difficulty in the classroom and seeing positive results. One participant explained, "I've been pushing the reflection throughout. . . . They're expecting that I'm going to ask that question . . . What was difficult, and how did you try? What worked, and what didn't work? . . . So I think that they are thinking that's part of the class now, that I'm going to ask them that question no matter what . . . the kind of quality of reflection is slowly getting better."

It was not unusual for faculty to report students' experiences with RA routines and strategies as remedial or pointless. Upon further inquiry, this was often because the texts assigned were not sufficiently challenging for their students, which led to another common transformation for faculty: intentionally seeking out challenging texts. In referring to a new RA routine she had learned, one participant shared, "I want to do it with one of the really hard readings, like from semester two. There's the rhetorical situations and their constituents. It's, like, just ridiculously hard, and, like, maybe go through the first page or something."

As faculty learned RA strategies for helping students work through difficult text, they began challenging students more, but in more effective and supportive learning environments. The following two excerpts from the final meeting of the semester illustrate the ways in which the same instructor can move between a nuanced application of RA and a preliminary understanding of what it means for students to encounter difficulty in reading:

> PARTICIPANT: Yeah, so the first thing I thought about was some students who were ahead, and they already sort of intuitively got it. . . . Some of the other students were not as prepared. And so I keep going back to the reading logs. And so, what they, they would try to find ways around it. . . . And what I need to do next year perhaps is to perhaps have them do personalized reading strategies. So, you know, "Okay, you got this. Now what can you do? What's the next step that would work for you?" Instead of saying, "Okay, I already know how to do this." You know, what can you [do] instead? So I think that would help instead of just having it be a one-time process, have it be something that evolves.

In this excerpt, the participant is reflecting on ways that she can differentiate her use of reading logs to reflect on strategies so that all of the students in her classes continue to find them useful throughout the semester. A little later in the same session, that participant is thinking about applying RA in an upper-division, theory-heavy class:

> PARTICIPANT: I want to do this. I need to do this for the upper-division students. How do I do this in a way that doesn't make them uncomfortable, because some of them are seniors who are about to graduate? And they can't read. No, I shouldn't say that. Their comprehension skills need some work. How can I do this?
>
> [Talks about some of the challenges she has with this particular course.]
>
> PARTICIPANT: And then now, I have to say that you need to sort of remediate your reading in order to understand.

The move from seeing how all of her students can benefit from metacognitive reflection to seeing a focus on strategies as remedial for upper-division students is directly contradictory and reflects a liminal grasp of RA and learning to read.

As evidenced in these exchanges, apprenticing students in disciplinary reading and thinking—using written or visual texts—requires educators to create learning experiences that help students detect, normalize, and work productively with reading difficulties and confusion using metacognitive conversation. This was both troublesome and transformative for faculty. Although we are not sure whether any participants completely crossed the *reading difficulties catalyze learning* threshold, over the course of the semester, most participants came to see reading difficulties not as a barrier to learning that instructors need to explain away but as an opportunity to help students develop and apply learning strategies by employing a process of inquiry.

Those faculty who experienced the greatest success with RA began to transform their approaches to facilitating student learning. However, some faculty appeared to engage with this threshold concept more than others. Those faculty who struggled more with RA tended to revert to familiar pedagogical approaches in which they found themselves trying to explain away difficulty and confusion for their students. This variation in efficacy further suggests that *reading difficulties catalyze learning* is likely a genuine threshold concept that, when fully crossed, transforms how faculty use reading to apprentice students into disciplinary thinking and discourse.

Threshold Concept 2: Reading Is Active Learning

Another area of struggle we encountered in the RA communities of practice focused on the nature of reading itself and the relationship between reading and content learning, identified here as the threshold concept *reading is active learning*. While we do not have evidence that crossing this threshold is irreversible, we discuss the ways in which this concept was troublesome and transformative for faculty. The concept is also integrative in that it brings together many apparently disparate elements of the teaching-and-learning experience, including learning theory, linguistics, disciplinary epistemology and reasoning processes, and even the relationships among disciplines. While all co-op participants considered questions about the nature and role of reading in learning, the framing of reading as active learning caused struggle most significantly among faculty in the STEM (science, technology, engineering, and mathematics) fields. Importantly, for participants across the disciplines, engaging with this threshold concept also involved thinking carefully about how limited time constrains their teaching.

The RA framework conceptualizes reading as an active learning process and orientation, aiming to "bring students into an active relationship with texts they encounter" (Schoenbach, Greenleaf, and Murphy 2012, 11) as they associate knowledge, interpretation, and inquiry with words, sentences, and visual information on the page (19). Within an RA process, metacognitive conversation becomes a vehicle for making thinking visible and the solving of text problems collaborative, so learners build literacy stamina and disciplinary ways of being that support their growing independence over time.

Disciplinary experts can benefit from participating in text-based inquiry communities with other educators, particularly as a means of gaining insight into students' literacy challenges, the complexity of reading, and the value of shared inquiry about text, and of building confidence as disciplinary literacy leaders. Schoenbach, Greenleaf, and Murphy explain (2017, 54), "Similarly, by having challenging experiences in which they themselves learn from text, building knowledge intentionally about words, content, and genres with which they were previously inexperienced, teachers come to reassess the role texts may play in learning. And by contrasting their approaches to texts and tasks to those held by teachers of other disciplines, teachers begin to see the uniquely disciplinary aspects of their literacies and to value the contribution they are uniquely positioned to make to their own students' learning." In effect, participation in an RA learning community, including inquiry about challenging texts with other disciplinary experts, may help faculty identify as disciplinary literacy leaders and see the value of students' in-class active reading engagement (Nilson 2016).

Ongoing collaboration around the RA framework surfaced faculty struggles with *reading is active learning* in a variety of ways. The very notion that reading requires active, strategic engagement is challenging for both students and faculty. Many students see others making sense of text and fail to recognize the mostly invisible process that is happening for other readers (Beers 2002). Sense-making in reading takes many forms, from the interpretation of obscure literary texts and interrogation of complex concepts—which clearly call for problem-solving—to identifying and extracting key details from textbook chapters. This range in the need for sense-making and the invisibility of sense-making processes made it seem to faculty as though some texts or tasks should require no strategy instruction. As one faculty member put it, "Maybe it's the class I'm doing is just structurally a little bit different. Because right now they aren't solving problems. They're not interpreting texts. The text that we have at this point is very much just here's some background information. There's nothing really to interpret about it." While it may be true that many of the students found the background information in the texts without conscious effort, others may have required strategy instruction to find that background information (Braten and Samuelstuen 2004). The idea that texts are transparent and information is simply there for students to internalize is a common perception among both faculty and students.

This struggle over what it means to actively engage with texts in their classes particularly arose among STEM faculty. One member expressed that struggle in the following way: "I mean, we have some of the same commonalities with . . . there's, like, a procedural fluency that we need in our subject area, and then there's, like, this conceptual deep understanding that seems sometimes at odds with one another. And that there's certain things where it needs to be precise, and then there's other things that can have multiple interpretations. Does that make sense, or, like, . . . or multiple thought processes in it?" This commentary suggests that active engagement is required only for particular reading tasks—for instance, interpretation—rather than for all reading tasks. Procedures and precision, by this accounting, do not require any strategic thinking to recognize; only interpretation requires strategies. Yet that perception changed for some over time. One STEM faculty member said, "A recurring theme that we've had in this, where I guess you can say it's difficulty on my part buying into it entirely and trying to get away from just this is... this is right. This is how, how you do it and trying to get more into the thought process behind it. The more I've been thinking about this sort of thing, I'm seeing how I can implement it in aspects of not just this class but the, the other one that I do, particularly the problem-solving aspects of it." Regardless, the perspective that content and strategies are separate helps explain why faculty who see their classes as content-heavy wrestle with the time it takes to include strategy instruction in their classes. Indeed, faculty across the disciplines—composition, first-year seminar, science, mathematics—all commented that they had to negotiate the apparent time conflict between covering the material they had planned to teach and teaching students reading strategies. A first-year seminar instructor came to the realization that "this is very precious, very important for students' learning, because it, it kind of switches the content into the process." But time repeatedly arose as an area of conflict.

Part of what makes the challenge of this concept clear is the oscillation (Gogan 2013) around it. For instance, one instructor found that his students were finding it challenging to talk to the text (an RA routine sometimes described as "thinking aloud on paper"). In asking them to do so, he assumed that students just didn't feel comfortable, noting, "What I'm looking for is having a way to get folks to kind of feel more comfortable doing it... ways that you've seen people get buy-in a little faster." In this inquiry, he was treating literally the idea that reading is active. However, after facilitators and participants asked questions—"Do you give them... things specifically they are looking for... like something I understood or didn't understand? Why are they talking to the whole text? They should be talking to the text at places that are difficult"—he realized that the readings for which he was asking students to talk to the text were easy for students. So their difficulty was in consciously applying reading strategies when a text was transparent to them. The practice for this instructor at this time was likely more mimicry (Gogan 2013) than having crossed the threshold of understanding. In describing his change of perspective about his experience, the instructor commented, "Thanks for the insight. 'Cause I was like, gosh, this seems like it would make a lot of sense to do, and it should be kind of easy, so why are they kind of, like, struggling with it?"

Another faculty member's comments revealed a second manifestation of this notion that text is transparent, reporting that in his class, "they do three quizzes, so if they understand... what they've read, then they can answer the quizzes." Faculty across the disciplines often use reading quizzes as tools to assess students' compliance with assignments or comprehension of the reading. Depending on their structure, those quizzes may represent an expectation that texts are repositories of facts to be recalled (which may be true in some instances) or that the aspects of the text that matter are both clear and the same for every reader.

In contrast, another faculty member explicitly connected quiz-taking with the metacognitive routines with which students were engaged. She described noticing "a correlation there between people who did well on the quiz and the people who spent a lot of time actually doing the reading logs." Once she noticed the connection, she was able to use the reading logs to help her students: "Then I decided to use the reading log, which was great! It worked out really well. I saw a lot of people getting it. You know, if you don't understand the question, take out the reading log. And then I held up the [metacognitive] bookmarks, and I would walk around and say, 'Do you need a bookmark? Okay, just remember to use the [strategies] from the bookmark to understand the question before you start writing anything.'" She was helping students see that the processes they engaged in to read strategically would support them not only in using their class text but also in reading and comprehending quiz questions.

As faculty engaged with this aspect of the threshold concept, it transformed their ideas about who they are as teachers (i.e., that they *are* reading teachers) and how they valued reading. But this transformation also evoked another element of the threshold concept, the place of reading in the ongoing life of the classroom. In the field of writing studies, scholarship has moved from cognitive into socio-cognitive (e.g., Smith 2019), highlighting the notion that the activity of writing (and reading) occurs in a social context. The implication that reading is neither something mastered and moved beyond nor simply an individual activity separate from the life of the class proved troublesome. In larger professional development settings, faculty sometimes expressed doubts about the value of strategy instruction for upper-division students, and this clearly became an issue for some of the instructors in the co-ops as well. One instructor, for instance, worried that teaching reading strategies to her upper-division students would communicate, "You need to sort of remediate your reading in order to understand."

Although the concern that focusing on strategies with upper-division students would seem like remediation arose in the last meeting of the semester, this faculty member and others made comments throughout recognizing their roles in creating value around the text in the class. One noted, "Um . . . I have been doing in-class . . . I do in-class assignments every time, and this semester I have been specific in saying, 'Can you find this definition in your reading? Can you find the relationship for, say, speed in your reading and use it to solve this problem? Can you find this in your notes? So look it up.'" In this way, the faculty member was demonstrating for the students *how* to use their textbook and reminding them that it was a resource for their continuing work in the class.

In a different fashion, another instructor described using reading as active learning by relating it to a final assignment: "I have them do, they do a pretty large essay at the end of my class, but every reading we do focuses towards that essay, so if they're doing a metacognitive reading log for every reading, well, now they have a huge amount of information from which to write." This practice of expecting students to assemble their knowledge across a semester or major is not new with RA, but it was new to these faculty to make this explicit for students and show them how their ongoing work supports them in doing so. Additionally, the same faculty member who used reading logs to support students' writing noted, "It serves a dual purpose for me, then. It makes them a better reader, but now they're also building up a large amount of content knowledge which they can use."

The above comment arose amid a recurring conversation about reading logs, which made it clear that some faculty found troublesome the idea that reading and reading logs could have a classroom role beyond being an assignment. One instructor described assigning reading logs but then struggled to build interaction around them or explain their purpose to students. She noted that part of her difficulty was that she herself would not use such logs. However, the fact that many of the faculty had recommendations for building class interaction around text preparation—from using the logs for planning to asking students to share their logs in conversation in class to prompting students to find particular information in their logs—suggested that others did see the logs as tools to engage students with the readings rather than just to hold them accountable for reading. Yet even instructors who believed strongly in asking students to use reading logs did not always bring them into the classroom as a locus of metacognitive conversation.

The ways that faculty brought reading into the ongoing life of the classroom often depended on the role that faculty themselves saw for reading as an essential component of student learning. Many faculty in STEM fields doubted students' ability to learn their content by reading. Struggle over this aspect of the framework manifested as concern that the content itself was not amenable to learning through reading. While faculty in the humanities and first-year seminar saw reading instruction as closely aligned with their disciplinary instruction, faculty in mathematics and science felt more conflict about the prospect of students learning content from reading. One STEM instructor, in fact, expressed some of the stress that arose from the conflict between his hope and his experience: "I see that eureka moment, but it, it's . . . I just don't see it coming out of the reading. I hate to say that. I wish I could." Others repeatedly commented that focusing on reading meant reducing the amount of time they could lecture, highlighting the implicit (and often explicit) notion that content learning in these fields came through lecture.

Still, some inquiry challenged the assumption that content transmission should be prioritized over in-class metacognitive inquiry with text. For example, one faculty member (who had much earlier experience as a student in a lower-division STEM course now taught by another faculty member in the group) asserted, "I remember doing that experiment. But if you ask me [to] define turbidity . . . I remember the word but not necessarily [the] definition. But I do remember . . . which of those lakes you should be in, [which] I should not have been in, [that] the ocean was fine, and why that was fine. . . . I think that's more the purpose you're wanting students to walk away with—right? Like, ten years from now, what do you want them to remember from this class? What are they going to use?" In this way, some faculty, in thinking about content, started considering learning that would most readily transfer to other contexts and enhance disciplinary facility. Such considerations may open a window for faculty to consider using some class time for metacognitive conversation in relation to text.

As with *reading difficulties catalyze learning*, it would be difficult to claim that any faculty fully crossed the threshold of understanding *reading is active learning* in one semester, but the talk across the semester demonstrated faculty struggling with the concept and being transformed by their encounters with it. Two elements of the learning communities seemed to make the most difference for faculty encountering this threshold concept: the interdisciplinary makeup of the groups and the facilitators' emphasis on inquiry. The multidisciplinary community helped faculty members see outside their disciplinary perspectives. One STEM faculty member noted, "I thought it was really nice to have the humanities side . . . really pushed me to explain all the things I think about, really slow down and then . . . 'cause it kind of more made me think about . . . well, what am I expecting [of] my students?" Because she was working with other faculty who did not have the same background or make the same assumptions, the experience activated her own metacognition. And another commented about the facilitators, "You were definitely prompting me to think about things in a different way I hadn't really thought about." Because the facilitators and other group members frequently asked participants to explain their perspectives, the conversations surfaced many assumptions about the relationships between reading and learning.

CONCLUSION

If *reading difficulties catalyze learning* and *reading is active learning* are genuine threshold concepts for college educators, as our experience and this preliminary research imply, this has significant implications for professional development. As the literature on threshold concepts makes clear, threshold concepts are not mastered over a semester, much less during a single class or workshop (Land, Meyer, and Flanagan 2016; Land, Meyer, and Smith 2008; Meyer and Land 2006). Rather, mastery requires ongoing exploration and support from experts and peers as learners take different paths through liminal zones. This means that professional development needs to be designed to (1) create encounters with threshold concepts that can feel unsettling for college educators, who are often more comfortable sharing content knowledge than facilitating learning, and (2) provide the support college educators need to cross thresholds.

The potential benefits to students from providing college educators with professional development on teaching reading are great, particularly for those students least well served by pedagogical approaches that assume students no longer need reading support once they enter college. Educating an increasingly ethnically, racially, economically, and cognitively diverse student body will require that more college educators transform how they facilitate learning by mastering threshold concepts such as *reading difficulties catalyze learning* and *reading is active learning*, that those facilitating professional development learn how to help college educators encounter and master those threshold concepts, and that institutions of higher education value, incentivize, and support the necessary professional development.

Asking faculty who see themselves as content area experts to additionally identify as disciplinary literacy leaders can require a substantial transformation in the way they envision educator and student roles, classroom purposes, and the function of disciplinary text in the learning process. RA, a metacognitive framework for disciplinary reading and problem-solving, provides powerful tools and scaffolding to inspire faculty to make this leap, but some conceptual hurdles may be more challenging for faculty to recognize and embody. If faculty developers have a clearer understanding of the threshold concepts associated with such a transition, they may be better able to encourage faculty growth and a more central role for disciplinary reading in higher-education classrooms.

References

Adler-Kassner, Linda, and Elizabeth Wardle, eds. 2015. *Naming What We Know: Threshold Concepts of Writing Studies*. Logan: Utah State University Press.

Beers, Kylene. 2002. *When Kids Can't Read: What Teachers Can Do*. Portsmouth, NH: Heinemann.

Braten, Ivar, and Marit S. Samuelstuen. 2004. "Does the Influence of Reading Purpose on Reports of Strategic Text Processing Depend on Students' Topic Knowledge?" *Journal of Educational Psychology* 96 (2): 324–336.

Gogan, Brian. 2013. "Reading at the Threshold." *Across the Disciplines* 10 (4). http://wac.colostate.edu/atd/reading.

Hand, Brian, and Lori Norton-Meier. 2018. "I Will Just SWH It: The Learning Lens of Teachers as They Engage in the Exploration of Argument-Based Inquiry." *Journal of Adolescent and Adult Literacy* 62 (2): 223–226.

Hutchings, Pat. 2000. *Opening Lines: Approaches to the Scholarship of Teaching and Learning*. Menlo Park, CA: Carnegie.

Johnson, Brittney, and I. Moria McCracken. 2016. "Reading for Integration, Identifying Complementary Threshold Concepts: The ACRL Framework in Conversation with Naming What We Know—Threshold Concepts of Writing Studies." *Communications in Information Literacy* 10 (2): 178–198. https://doi.org/10.15760/comminfolit.2016.10.2.23.

King, Catherine, and Peter Felten. 2012. "Threshold Concepts in Educational Development: An Introduction." *Journal of Faculty Development* 26 (3): 5–7.

Land, Ray, Jan H. F. Meyer, and Michael T. Flanagan, eds. 2016. *Threshold Concepts in Practice*. Rotterdam, The Netherlands: Sense.

Land, Ray, Jan H. F. Meyer, and Jan Smith, eds. 2008. *Threshold Concepts within the Disciplines*. Leiden, The Netherlands: Brill.

Meyer, Jan H. F. 2012. "'Variation in Student Learning' as a Threshold Concept." *Journal of Faculty Development* 26 (3): 8–13.

Meyer, Jan, and Ray Land. 2003. "Threshold Concepts and Troublesome Knowledge: Linkages to Ways of Thinking and Practicing within the Disciplines." In *Improving Student Learning—Ten Years On*, edited by Chris Rust, 53-64. Oxford: OCSLD.

———. 2005. "Threshold Concepts and Troublesome Knowledge (2): Epistemological Considerations and a Conceptual Framework for Teaching and Learning." *Higher Education* 49 (3): 373–388.

———. 2006. *Overcoming Barriers to Student Understanding: Threshold Concepts and Troublesome Knowledge*. New York: Routledge.

Moore, Jessie L. 2012. "Designing for Transfer: A Threshold Concept." *Journal of Faculty Development* 26 (3): 19–24.

Nilson, Linda B. 2013. *Creating Self-Regulated Learners: Strategies to Strengthen Students' Self-Awareness and Learning Skills*. Sterling, VA: Stylus.

———. 2016. *Teaching at Its Best: A Research-Based Resource for College Instructors*. San Francisco: Wiley.

Perkins, David. 1999. "The Many Faces of Constructivism." *Educational Leadership* 57 (3): 6–11.

Schoenbach, Ruth, Cynthia Greenleaf, and Lynn Murphy. 2012. *Reading for Understanding: How Reading Apprenticeship Improves Disciplinary Learning in Secondary and College Classrooms*. San Francisco: Wiley.

———. 2017. *Leading for Literacy*. San Francisco: Wiley.

Smagorinsky, Peter, Susan Cook, and Tara Star Johnson. 2003. "The Twisting Path of Concept Development in Learning to Teach." *Teachers College Record* 105 (8): 1399–1436.

Smith, Anna. 2019. "Waves of Theory Building in Writing and Its Development, and Their Implications for Instruction, Assessment, and Curriculum." In *Theoretical Models and Processes of Literacy*,

7th ed., edited by Donna E. Alvermann, Normal J. Unrau, Misty Sailors, and Robert B. Ruddell, 65–83. New York: Routledge.

Werder, Carmen, Shevell Thibou, and Blair Kaufer. 2012. "Students as Co-inquirers: A Requisite Threshold Concept in Educational Development?" *Journal of Faculty Development* 26 (3): 34–38.

Nelson Graff is faculty in and director of the Communication across the Disciplines program at California State University, Monterey Bay. He coedited the collection *Literacy, Economy, and Power: Research and Writing after "Literacy in American Lives."*

Rebecca Kersnar is a faculty member and the teaching and learning specialist for the Center for Teaching, Learning, and Assessment at California State University, Monterey Bay. She is one of the primary leads of the Reading Apprenticeship initiative on campus.

Dan Shapiro is director of the Center for Teaching, Learning, and Assessment at California State University, Monterey Bay.

Ryne Leuzinger is a faculty member in the library at California State University, Monterey Bay, where he serves as Coordinator for Information Literacy Instruction. His research interests include the intersection of written communication and information literacy and the role of assignment design in information literacy instruction.

3

"MIND THE GAP"

Investigating Faculty Reading Practices

HEATHER C. EASTERLING
JOHN ELIASON

> When I read, I'm looking at someone's possible answer to a puzzle. . . . [I'm] trying to answer a political problem.
> —Political science faculty member
>
> As I read, I'm always holding in the back of my mind what I'm reading for: how does this fit what I'm thinking about?
> —History faculty member
>
> My reading practices vary depending on where I am in the writing process with a project. . . . I don't have one way of reading, but with many purposes and projects, different practices.
> —English faculty member
>
> As scholars we read to answer questions.
> —Biology faculty member

When college and university faculty offer critiques of student reading, how often do they reflect on their own development as readers and on their reading practices as experts within disciplines and professions? As faculty particularly interested in the challenges of college-level reading for students, we have developed a distinct curiosity about how we as English studies professors and selected colleagues in other disciplines ground our perspectives on reading. As Alice Horning emphasizes, disciplinary experts "understand and produce meaning in texts by working before, after, around and within them in specific ways" (2012, 1). But do such disciplinary experts routinely externalize practices that they by now have internalized? And might they underestimate their own practices' utility as narratives for teaching reading? We set out to learn more about faculty reading practices as a possible and potentially valuable entry point for addressing students as college-level readers.

With this project, we were mindful of the large-scale importance of reading not only in disciplines but in everyday life. Wringing from faculty the ways in which they think about the teaching of reading seems paramount in an era when many connect reading skills to the very function of the US democratic republic. Furthermore, we recognize excellent work in this vein by scholars such as Horning, Robert Scholes, and Ellen Carillo. We enthusiastically support such efforts to improve and intensify reading pedagogy; at the same time, we are provoked by Nancy Chick's assertion that any pedagogy of college-level or expert reading must "reflect... what scholars do" (Chick et al. 2009, 50). Therefore, we sought to investigate faculty members' often-unarticulated assumptions and practices of reading. Our inquiry was grounded in an attendant hypothesis that the unpacking of faculty approaches might suggest productive strategies both for articulating faculty perceptions about their students as readers and for teaching reading.

This chapter thus describes an institutionally grounded study of faculty reading that we conducted and offers some of the ideas that emerged from the study's small-group conversations, facilitated by us with colleagues on our own campus. As faculty teaching at an undergraduate-focused Jesuit university of just over five thousand undergraduate students, we know firsthand that Gonzaga University and its faculty take teaching and learning seriously. A high percentage of our students arrive on campus having prepared well academically and are in possession of a genuine earnestness about succeeding in college and afterward. Transitioning to college-level reading is nonetheless a challenge for many of them and can be as routinely underexamined by faculty here as elsewhere. Knowing this, we sought to query our colleagues' ideas and experiences of disciplinary reading for themselves and their students, in the process observing that simply being asked to unpack their reading practices was meaningful not only to us as facilitators and researchers but also to our faculty participants, who vividly cared about reading and its instruction, even as they admitted giving it less attention than they know most students need.

As we worked through the series of small-group discussions, what emerged from our analysis were what we call reading stories, as well as related suggestive themes regarding faculty reading practices and meta-awareness. We also came to recognize the possible significance of these themes for considering and supporting students as college-level readers.

And while we acknowledge the relatively limited scale of our study as well as a methodology tending toward the anecdotal, in our project we sought precisely to listen to our faculty colleagues' stories and their stated understandings and dispositions. In the pages that follow, we present our study as a distinctive approach to addressing student reading challenges. Moreover, as this chapter's final section discusses, plans for this study include using it as a pilot from which to implement faculty development opportunities and Scholarship of Teaching and Learning (SOTL) projects on reading.

Literature Review

Faculty concerns about students as college-level readers across the curriculum have been rightfully central to what could be called the story of the gap between faculty expectations and student abilities. In *Reconnecting Reading and Writing*, Alice Horning and Elizabeth Kraemer (2013) highlight work that scrutinizes student reading as an area of scholarly inquiry. As coeditors, they and the other contributing authors argue for increased faculty attention to students' abilities, assumptions, and deficits; to the cognitive as well as affective dimensions of the act of reading; to reading as an element of disciplines' discursive practices; and to pedagogy. Scholes (2002) observes in "The Transition to College Reading" that such granularity in approaching reading is particularly warranted because faculty often do not "see" reading (166). Scholes means not only that faculty do not have ready access to students' reading practices and assumptions because of the inherently private nature of reading but also that faculty have not worked deliberately enough to respond critically to student reading practices. Though one of the discursive practices that most defines the academic communities that students encounter in higher education, reading is easily overlooked and too often underinstructed. As Chick and her colleagues caution, "Students asked to read in complex ways may not successfully negotiate this task simply because we ask them to" (Chick et al. 2009, 410).

Relatedly, faculty may not easily and automatically access what they do as expert readers. As Carillo notes, "discussions of reading [with faculty] can quickly morph from questions of how [to read] to questions of what [to read]" (2015, 148). Thus, while a gap often exists between student practices and faculty expectations for college-level reading, we argue that minding the gap of student reading and faculty expectations must entail minding a second gap. This second gap pertains to what can be an occupational hazard for many faculty: the more they immerse themselves in their professional communities, the more they are challenged to see—to really contemplate—what they do as readers. Mary Lou Odom identifies a phenomenon of faculty requiring but not explicitly teaching more expert, often disciplinary, reading. She posits that if faculty neither realize nor make explicit such specialized reading, a problematic cycle emerges wherein students' abilities and approaches as more novice readers collide with their instructors' tacit expectations: "Such a cycle is all the more problematic," Odom notes, "when it is not apparent to faculty . . . themselves. Reading has in many ways become an invisible component of academic literacy" (Odom 2013, 4). Carillo (2018, 70) offers a similar point: "Students need models of what it looks like to read, to do this work." This important scholarship on student reading and reading pedagogy has led us to theorize that faculty must reflect on and richly see their own reading practices, dispositions, and contexts before teaching their students to be the metacognitive readers that Horning (2012, 1) characterizes as "understand[ing] and produc[ing] meaning in texts by working before, after, around and within them in specific ways."

Our theorized gap, developed through our inquiry into "seeing" faculty reading, builds on recent attention to reading practices and expertise from within writing studies circles as well as from psychology. This conceptualization of a gap—which impacts students as college readers but involves faculty reading—particularly approaches reading as a key practice of disciplinary expertise, a conceptualization that has gained greater exposure through the work of James Paul Gee (2015) and others within the "new literacy studies." This idea of reading also has developed from the discourse-community movement's notion that "discourse community membership implicates people in interpretive activities," including "how a text is read" (Bizzell, quoted in Harl 2013, 46).

This link between reading, discursive practices, and disciplinary identity also is explored by Ira James Allen (2011), who takes up David Bartholomae's striking description from "Inventing the University" (1986) of college education as a kind of advanced literacy project, making explicit, where Bartholomae does not, that reading must be seen as part of this essential discursive literacy. And scholars including Carolyn Miller, Charles Bazerman, David Russell, and Paul Prior have shown through their attention to genre, genre theory, and activity systems why faculty should remember that people read texts to create what Bazerman summarizes as "new realities of meaning, relation, and knowledge," where each text "is embedded within structured social activities and depends on previous texts that influence the social activity and organization" (2003, 309, 311). In our view, the layers of complexity to reading and the practices of engagement will remain largely inaccessible to students unless faculty commit to making their own practices visible.

As part of developing methods and bringing together concepts for investigating the reading practices of faculty, we have benefited in particular from applying the behavioral science approach of educational psychologist Patricia Alexander. She provides an interpretive lens for better understanding expert practitioners in a field of knowledge, as well as a helpful framework for outlining the differences between novices and experts. Alexander's research has long focused on the psychology of "domain learning" within the academy. When we consider domain learning in light of professed textual practices of readers, we embrace Alexander's point that levels of expertise are differentiated not simply in terms of varying knowledge levels. The differentiation also exists via different interpretive strategies with texts and information and different levels of "interest" as a function of affect and motivation. The differences in reading practices, in other words, depend on more than knowing or not knowing. Alexander (2003, 3) unfolds what she sees as the important implications of this model of domain learning that her research has revealed: that knowledge, strategic processing, and interest—and their interplay—are at the heart of domain learning and disciplinary expertise and that this interplay also changes over the journey from novice ("Acclimation") through "Competence" to expert ("Proficiency").

These implications are significant to us as we focus on a college-reading gap that concerns not just student readers but also faculty as readers and as instructors assigning reading to students. Alexander helps us recognize that the students are, by definition, likely to be not yet at competence or proficiency. More novice readers, Alexander writes, "have characteristically limited and fragmented knowledge ... [a] piecemeal knowledge [that] comes with little personal investment in the domain and strong reliance on surface-level strategies" (4). By contrast, "not only is the knowledge base of experts both broad and deep, but the experts are also contributing new knowledge to the domain. . . . These experts are posing questions and instituting investigations that push the boundaries of the domain. For this reason, the level of strategy use among experts remains high, although those strategies are almost exclusively of a deep-processing kind" (4). In our view, these robust characterizations of learning provide a valuable lens for contemplating expertise, meta-reading, and the reading practices of students or novices and faculty. We therefore seized on an opportunity to build from the existing literature on reading and domain learning and opened up a multidisciplinary discussion of reading right on our campus.

Methods

We developed our study as exploratory research grounded in existing literature on reading and in our hypothesis that our faculty colleagues' reading stories were crucial to better understanding and approaching the often-perceived gap between student abilities and faculty expectations for college-level reading. We pursued this goal of learning about faculty experiences with reading via a focus-group-based study that we designed using principles of qualitative analysis; we made this decision because of this method's "exploratory and more hypothesis generating" strengths (Corbin and Strauss 2008, 25). With focus groups centered on faculty reflection and extended responses, our approach also was grounded in Carillo's concept of "Mindful Reading" (2015), with its emphasis on reading as a process of reflection, along with Mary Huber and Sherwyn P. Morreale's definition of SOTL as including scholarly work that helps create a "common language for trading ideas" (2002, 20). We thus sought to create a circumstance for colleagues from diverse disciplines in our institution's College of Liberal Arts and Sciences to "[make] explicit [their] disciplinary assumptions about what reading *is*" (Manarin, introduction to this volume; emphasis added). Allen's description and discussion of his survey-based investigation of faculty reading practices influenced our thinking about research process and methods. In "Reprivileging Reading: The Negotiation of Uncertainty," Allen (2011) characterizes his study as "impressionistic," adding that his survey "might better be seen as a pilot project, using a small sample of case studies" that is valuable precisely because it is "suggestive" exploratory research (118). We have situated our project along similar lines.

To do so, we designed and received Institutional Review Board (IRB) approval for a set of questions (see table 3.1) with which to investigate the reading practices and any existing reading pedagogies of fourteen faculty colleagues from across the liberal arts and sciences disciplines of our institution. Our participants—representing the disciplines of biology, communication studies, English, history, journalism, mathematics, modern languages, philosophy, physics, and political science—met in one of four different focus groups. Each group consisted of between two and five people. We convened every time under similar circumstances, meeting for seventy-five minutes in our university's Writing Center around a large conference table. We circulated our questions to the group just before we began. We were intentional about not asking faculty to prepare for the meetings. We desired instead to pose the questions as scaffolding for a conversation that could become somewhat organic with each group.

Table 3.1 Reading group discussion questions.

> 1. What is your name, your field, your specialty? What types of courses do you regularly teach to undergraduates here?
>
> FACULTY AS READERS:
>
> 2. What do you (disciplinary expert/professional) read in your field?
> 3. How did you develop professional/expert reading practices?
>
> STUDENTS AS READERS:
>
> 4. What do students read in your field?
> 5. What are the biggest difficulties students experience with readings in your field or in your classes? What makes reading challenging for them in your experience?
>
> THE TEACHING OF READING:
>
> 6. What specific reading practices, if any, do you teach your lower-division students? Your upper-division?
> 7. What is your discipline's/field's level of interest in the (related) subjects of reading, student-reading, and teaching-reading?

Moreover, the relatively small number of colleagues allowed for participants to have the time and space to elaborate on their answers to questions. Even more, it was important to our interest in their reading stories that faculty offer more spontaneous and unfolding responses—that is, while we sought the answers they provided as scholars and expert readers in their fields, we also wanted to encounter their thinking, their reflecting, about being asked such questions. If possible, we wanted to observe their own encounters, if any, with the second gap we had hypothesized between faculty and their awareness of how they had become and function as expert readers versus their assumptions and observations concerning their students' reading practices.

We collected our participants' responses for coding and analysis via our own note-taking and via audio-recording each meeting. After each session, we shared and discussed our written notes with each other to do some preliminary coding of major themes in our participants' characterizations of their own reading. This was followed by at least two further listening sessions of the audio from each meeting, using each successive listening to again take notes and recode for observed themes as well as any that were more emergent on a second or a third listening. Our work with these data initially took an in vivo approach, based on our desire to identify themes from our participants' own words about themselves as readers and their perceptions of their students as readers (Hedlund-DeWitt 2013; Corbin and Strauss 2008; Patel 2014). Our interest in a potential gap in faculty awareness of their own reading practices also led us to some values coding, wherein we assigned terms (not necessarily participants' words) to capture the surfaced values and attitudes of our participants concerning reading practices.

Findings and Discussion

Faculty as Meta-readers

What were the faculty reading stories and the emergent themes we found in our study? First, our colleagues told stories that indeed signaled them as what Horning calls "meta-readers": "expert readers are meta-readers" (2011, 2). Horning's work on expert reading as meta-reading references the medieval use of "manicules" as a notation of a reader's attention to a text that literally marked their process of making a text meaningful. Expert readers, Horning argues, apply a similar if usually less literal set of manicules derived from their own questions as well as their disciplinary grounding. The question of where to put the manicules resonated in what we heard from all our participants. Two of them, one from history and one from political science, described a metacognitive attention to published scholarship in their fields—specifically to texts' methodology and sources—and a process of reading directed toward "looking for a possible answer to a puzzle" and "fitting pieces into a larger framework." Similarly, a physicist colleague described reading published papers as one means of staying current in his field, but almost never completely. As he put it, his goal is not to understand the entire paper but to see what draws his attention. His reading seeks to make connections with questions or problems he already has in mind.

Across disciplines, we found further characteristics of faculty as meta-readers. In their language describing reading, faculty suggested a dynamic and interactive process reflective of Horning's description of literacy experts: those who "understand and produce meaning in texts by working before, after, around and within them in specific ways" (2012, 1). We also found faculty sharing an awareness that their reading practices vary depending on the occasion of reading and a related awareness that there are indeed ways of reading, not just one, a set of perceptions that affirm Norbert Elliot, Alice Horning, and Cynthia Haller's articulation of expert reading as "the ability to reflect on one's reading processes and make observations about those processes and cognitive strategies as mental processes of reasoning and memory accompanied by reading behaviors" (2018, "Literature Review," para. 1).

Faculty as Strategic Readers

Our participants' own reading stories thus foregrounded meta-reading and the various ways faculty read to understand and produce meaning. However, these faculty accounts also revealed a strikingly instrumentalist or strategic approach to much of their own academic reading. A history colleague, for example, described her common reading practice in terms of herself as a "filter": "I probably 'read' two hundred books last week," she related, but spent only "about four seconds per page," with her own critical questions and project at hand serving as a sifting device. The same colleague began by describing one of her frequent dispositions as a reader: "I read, holding in the back of my mind what I'm reading for: how does this fit with what I'm thinking about?" We were struck by these stories of incomplete reading as a common aspect of our colleagues' expert reading—indeed, of a quality we can term *strategic*. In his 2011 study of faculty reading practices, Allen confronts the challenge of these same findings that suggest no easy binary existing between faculty readers as the "deep" readers and student readers as the incomplete and strategic readers. For Allen, such incomplete reading by faculty points most importantly to the politics of academic labor and the pressure to publish, a timely and thoughtful argument. For us, however, this instrumentalism by faculty readers also provocatively reflects discursive and disciplinary expertise.

Our faculty participants described their reading almost entirely as strategic—a purposeful, partial reading that proceeded via ongoing negotiation between disciplinary texts and these readers' existing questions and frameworks. A math colleague corroborates this, explaining, "I read articles as well as textbooks for classes ... the kind of material I read matters less than the goal. When I read, I always have a goal, and reading always involves a pencil and paper [for] ... understanding details." Our colleagues described always reading *for* something, an approach that contrasts intriguingly with Keith Hjortshoj's observation regarding student readers in *The Transition to College Writing*: "The impression that college students do not know *how* to read usually results from the fact that they do not know *why* they are reading assigned text" (2009, 125). A more nuanced understanding of the place and value of this *"why"*—of strategic reading as part of growing disciplinary expertise—could contribute importantly to the story of college-level reading and of the gap we seek to investigate and ultimately bridge on behalf of better supporting students as college-level readers.

Certainly, distinct differences exist between expert and more novice or intermediate learners and readers, but as briefly explored above, our argument is that greater faculty awareness of and attention to their own highly purposeful reading can foster discussions with students about the disciplinary origins that inform purpose-driven practices. In turn, we consider this emphasis on unpacking point- or agenda-driven reading as a meaningful step toward addressing Carillo's notion of spotlighting process as well as purpose. Returning to Scholes's idea that faculty do not have ready access to students' reading practices, we suggest that though faculty do have access to their own practices and though they are indeed expert meta-readers as Horning claims, faculty may nevertheless need assistance—in the form of small-group discussions such as ours or via SOTL initiatives—in bridging the gap between what they expect and practice as meta-readers and what they expect and wish for their students as evolving readers. Faculty, in other words, may need intervention points before they can satisfy their own efforts to see or "read" their own students' needs and then respond pedagogically.

Reading to Produce versus Reading to Acquire

Alexander's characterization of domain experts as "contributing new knowledge," often specifically through "posing questions and instituting investigations that push the boundaries of the domain" (2003, 4), resonates broadly with our participants' descriptions both of how they read and of what reading is for in their work. This active and distinctly interactive work also points up a third and one of the most significant themes concerning faculty reading practices that emerged from our focus groups: faculty (expert disciplinary readers) read to produce, while student readers (novice and intermediate readers) more typically read to acquire. We find this suggestive distinction between readers in the higher-education setting crucial for confronting the transition to college-level reading for students and for our question concerning the significance of faculty to this transition for students. One participant's characterization of his reading adds nuance to this notion of reading to produce as a marker of expert reading: "Reading for [me] is a translation matter." Faculty read texts in order to translate them, he argues—into actions, into new textual forms, or into some kind of further application. This participant, a biologist, added that such translation work also meant a distinctly active movement of something read both inward and outward—toward oneself, toward existing questions, and toward existing context. Allen's study of faculty reading finds it to be fundamentally conversational, indeed to be a transactional process—suggestive of our biologist's sense of "translation"—not only between text and reader but between both of these and what Allen calls "a third, semi-impersonal party, a living context" (2011, 106). Such disciplinary context impels expert readers, according to Allen, enlivening texts and peopling the act of reading them with an imaginative or scholarly community. Our participants reflected in their own words Allen's contention that "much academic reading is motivated by the thinker-identity—by the desire to converse with the others one is reading" (107).

Reading to produce is thus a dialectical practice grounded in disciplinary identity, and many of our other participants described similarly dialectical and recursive practices as readers. Reading to produce versus reading to acquire offers a new formulation, we argue, of the gap between faculty and student readers that we find valuable for the way it adds particularities of disposition to existing formulations of novice and expert reading. None of this is a judgment of student readers, who are, by definition, entering higher education in order to develop higher-order and ultimately disciplinary knowledge and skills. As the work of Horning, Carillo, Alexander, and others clarifies, college students are not automatically purposeful meta-readers; neither are most students coming to reading with the disciplinary context and dialectical practice their faculty possess. Comments from our participants reflected this understanding of students as learners and of reading as a particular challenge. On the whole, they responded to questions about their experiences with students' reading not with disparagements but with thoughtful considerations of students' reluctance or difficulties. Several participants told us that their experiences suggested students often have minimal expectations of what reading a text or texts requires of them. One history colleague described her regular practice of asking her students (confidentially) to report how much time they spent on assigned reading for class and observed how little time many reported. To her, this pointed not to laziness or time-management problems but more significantly to students' overall conceptualization of reading as an activity.

Students, then, need support to develop further competence and disciplinary expertise as readers—to develop as meta-readers, purposeful readers, and active, productive readers. As David Bartholomae and Anthony Petrosky (2005) argue, students can become strong readers with the help of innovative critical reading and writing pedagogies. We argue that our study's granular unfolding of faculty reading can contribute in significant ways to such greater support and enhanced pedagogies. For example, its qualitative detailing of the practices and dispositions of expert disciplinary readers can illuminate and encourage dialectical practices and dispositions. In addition, the study's accompanying metacognition by faculty regarding themselves as readers can signal and model the importance of faculty making their practices visible to students and of drawing out students' own metacognition about their practices and then refining them.

Implications and Recommendations

Describing different types of SOTL research, Pat Hutchings (2000) has discussed the value of investigating "What Is": identifying and delineating existing teaching and learning problems. Making a different approach to broader concerns about college students' common difficulties with the expectations, practices, and demands of college-level reading, our study focused on one significant "What Is" of college-level reading: faculty reading and their knowledge of their own reading practices. We see this is as an importantly emergent "What Is" concerning college-level reading, compelling us to hypothesize that in order to provide richer support to student readers, faculty must have more and richer opportunities to think about their work and disciplines discursively. They must be offered (and create) chances to see, describe, and query themselves, according to our study's findings, as meta-readers, as strategic readers, and as productive readers in their fields.

Faculty development focused on such metacognition of reading could lend collaborative support and inquiry to faculty already invested in reading pedagogy. And this work could serve as a precursor to SOTL projects involving student reading as well as provide a rhetorical space for faculty to interrogate and describe how they came to be expert meta-readers. Conversations in faculty development sessions could surface to what degree faculty see their meta-reading as productive and goal-oriented and to what extent they see, or could come to see, their own reading strategies and ways of knowing as relevant to promoting student meta-reading practices.

This recommendation for a specific kind of faculty development emerges directly from how voluble our faculty participants were in our group discussions and from their spirited engagement with the topic of reading. Most faculty with whom we spoke reported finding real value in simply having the chance to speak with other faculty about these topics of expert, disciplinary reading and their respective processes and practices. Our participants also found helpful the opportunity to share perceptions of their students' reading difficulties and needs. While faculty readily made comments signaling meta-awareness of their fields and of their own uses of reading as a tool, they also often admitted that they had not previously thought much about or articulated the differences between themselves and their students as readers. Moreover, because our participants responded to each other with observations from their experiences rather than just to us, each small group discussion became a provocative, multivocal unfolding of new understandings and ideas.

This vigorous dialogue inspired us to envision how an enhanced focus on reading within faculty development efforts could reframe attention to student readers in novice-versus-expert terms and could harness faculty members' unique histories with reading and their discipline-specific reading practices as valuable pedagogical resources. We see faculty benefiting from concentrating on reading as a kind of "bottleneck" to student learning, borrowing that term from the language of Decoding the Disciplines, an ongoing pedagogical project that emerged in the 1990s from Indiana University's Freshman Learning Project. Seeing reading as such a bottleneck reframes it in perhaps subtle but meaningful ways, as difficulty with reading—and conceiving of reading as a productive, meta-aware activity—becomes a distinct impediment to students' ability to understand, engage with, and produce work in their disciplines. Moreover, the process of decoding a discipline involves, in part, the distinctly metacognitive modeling of effective practices by successful practitioners. With the decoding process "seek[ing] to make explicit the tacit knowledge of experts and to help students master the mental actions they need for success in particular courses" (Decoding the Disciplines, n.d.; see also Middendorf and Shopkow 2017; Pace 2017), students would benefit immensely from their faculty having such a structured setting in which to engage with other faculty, unveiling reading as well as negotiating how to model it.

What could this structure look like? Fundamentally, we propose offering opportunities for faculty simply to talk to each other about reading, seeding discussion with a set of questions such as those we used in our study. This talk would ask faculty to reflect and to bring to the surface important practices, moves, and habits of mind (see table 3.1). Discussion would delve into matters of unconscious competence, perhaps also asking participants to apply a "decoding" approach to their practices as well as more tacit assumptions and expectations. As part of this structure for faculty participants, we would suggest the provision and discussion of short readings drawn from the growing scholarship on reading and expertise, with the goal of giving faculty a new or more precise vocabulary for talking and thinking about reading as a practice of disciplinary knowledge and expertise.

Regardless of how such programming might go about exposing the gaps pertaining to college-level reading, to us it is essential that participants be supported in generating pedagogical innovations. While we want faculty to engage meaningfully with the insight of reading to produce versus reading to acquire as a significant divide between students and faculty, those faculty must then be afforded opportunities to develop classroom and assignment ideas for addressing this divide with students. As noted earlier, SOTL projects could be developed from this faculty activity, sponsored in part by departments and programs but also by institutional centers for teaching and learning. We see rich opportunities for student participation in such SOTL projects as well, including interviewing faculty about their reading practices, critiquing reading-centered assignments, and coauthoring undergraduate research projects on reading and reading pedagogy.

Conclusion

Central to our study as a whole is the recognition that even if faculty recognize themselves as meta-readers, they may not realize how they came to be such readers. Talking through their reading stories and their development as expert readers in small focus groups such as we convened—and in the programming and projects we've envisioned here—can provide faculty an opportunity to better see their own practices. This newly acquired vision, in turn, can give faculty insights into why it could be useful to invest teaching time in having students make explicit their own reading practices. Fostering metacognitive awareness would invite faculty and students to work together to set learning goals that foreground reading strategies, helping students meet the demands of college-level reading across the disciplines as well as setting students on a positive course for the experience of reading and beyond, throughout their lives. As Horning (2012, 1–2) reminds us, "all students can and must become more effective meta-readers and writers if they are to succeed in personal, educational, and professional venues and also as members of a democratic society."

Such new attention by faculty to these reading gaps does not of course remove or diminish the factors distinguishing novice or competent readers from more expert ones. As Alexander, Allen, Horning, and others have shown, expertise is both complexly and gradually acquired. Faculty engagement with reading as a key disciplinary and discursive practice, and with the gap between many students' reading and college-level demands, will not erase the inevitable distance between students as more novice learners and readers and their instructors' practices. And we are not advocating a simplistic approach of just asking faculty to tell students what they, the faculty, do as readers. Quite the contrary, the needed instructional design to scaffold a reading pedagogy must begin with faculty dedicating time and space to seeing their own expert reading practices in order to then explicitly and methodically develop a practice that embodies and applies specific ways of reading, including dispositions and habits of mind. Our primary concern, then, is advocating for developing awareness and metacognition, and perhaps ultimately a fundamental reconceptualization of what "reading" is, means, and does as students (learners) move from novice domains toward expertise.

What if reading were explicitly redefined by faculty, both to themselves and to students entering college, as meta-reading? What if a revision of prior expectations and practices from reading to acquire to reading to produce was foregrounded to students by faculty prepared to talk openly about themselves as readers and how reading functions as a key practice of not just acquiring but creating knowledge in their fields? What if the first year of college-level classes, across disciplines, centered on the reconceptualizing of reading that is central to growing disciplinary identity and expertise? How can we help faculty transform their self-knowledge as expert readers into effective reading pedagogy for their students? How might the scholarship of teaching and learning explore meta-reading? All such developments, both more modest and more startlingly comprehensive in aspiration, begin with minding the gaps explored here.

Acknowledgments

We deeply appreciate our faculty colleagues at Gonzaga University who dedicated time, thought, and optimism to this endeavor. Our discussions with them left us inspired to continue the quest for a better understanding of how faculty read and how they teach their own students.

References

Alexander, Patricia. 2003. "The Development of Expertise: The Journey from Acclimation to Proficiency." *Educational Researcher* 32 (8): 10–14. http://www.jstor.org/stable/3700080.

Allen, Ira James. 2011. "Reprivileging Reading: The Negotiation of Uncertainty." *Pedagogy* 12 (1): 97–120. https://doi.org/10.1215/15314200-1416540.

Bartholomae, David. 1986. "Inventing the University." *Journal of Basic Writing* 5 (1): 4–23.

Bartholomae, David, and Anthony Petrosky. 2005. *Ways of Reading*. Boston: Bedford/St. Martin's.

Bazerman, Charles. 2003. "Speech Acts, Genres, and Activity Systems: How Texts Organize Activity and People." In *What Writing Does and How It Does It: An Introduction to Analyzing Texts and Textual Practices*, edited by Charles Bazerman and Paul Prior, 309–339. New York: Routledge.

Carillo, Ellen C. 2015. *Securing a Place for Reading in Composition: The Importance of Teaching for Transfer*. Logan: Utah State University Press.

———. 2018. *Teaching Readers in Post-truth America*. Logan: Utah State University Press.
Chick, Nancy L., Holly Hassel, and Aeron Haynie. 2009. "Pressing an Ear against the Hive: Reading Literature for Complexity." *Pedagogy* 9 (3): 399–422.
Corbin, Juliet, and Anselm Strauss. 2008. *Basics of Qualitative Research: Techniques to Developing Grounded Theory*. 3rd ed. Los Angeles: Sage.
Decoding the Disciplines. n.d. Home page. Accessed April 14, 2021. http://decodingthedisciplines.org/.
Elliot, Norbert, Alice S. Horning, and Cynthia Haller. 2018. "Message in a Bottle: Expert Readers, English Language Arts, and New Directions for Writing Studies." *Composition Forum* 40. http://www.compositionforum.com/issue/40/message-bottle.php.
Gee, James Paul. 2015. "The New Literacy Studies." In *The Routledge Handbook of Literacy Studies*, edited by Jennifer Rowsell and Kate Pahl, chap. 2. London: Routledge. https://www.routledgehandbooks.com/doi/10.4324/9781315717647.ch2.
Harl, Allison L. 2013. "A Historical and Theoretical Review of the Literature: Reading and Writing Connections." In *Reconnecting Reading and Writing*, edited by Alice S. Horning and Elizabeth W. Kraemer, 26–54. Anderson, SC: Parlor.
Hedlund-DeWitt, Nicolas. 2013. "Coding: An Overview and Guide to Qualitative Data Analysis for Integral Researchers, Version 1.0." IRC (Integral Research Center) Resource Paper No. 1. https://www.academia.edu/9864164/Coding_An_Overview_and_Guide_to_Qualitative_Data_Analysis_for_Integral_Researchers.
Hjortshoj, Keith. 2009. *The Transition to College Writing*. 2nd ed. New York: Bedford/St. Martin's.
Horning, Alice S. 2011. "Where to Put the Manicules: A Theory of Expert Reading." *Across the Disciplines* 8 (2). https://clearinghouse.colostate.edu/atd/articles/horning2011/index.cfm.
———. 2012. *Reading, Writing, and Digitizing: Understanding Literacy in the Electronic Age*. Newcastle upon Tyne: Cambridge Scholars.
Horning, Alice S., and Elizabeth W. Kraemer, eds. 2013. *Reconnecting Reading and Writing*. Anderson, SC: Parlor. https://wac.colostate.edu/books/reconnecting/reading.pdf.
Huber, Mary, and Sherwyn P. Morreale, eds. 2002. *Disciplinary Styles in the Scholarship of Teaching and Learning: Exploring Common Ground*. Washington, DC: American Association for Higher Education.
Hutchings, Pat, ed. 2000. *Opening Lines: Approaches to the Scholarship of Teaching and Learning*. Menlo Park, CA: Carnegie Foundation for the Advancement of Teaching.
Middendorf, Joan, and Leah Shopkow. 2017. *Overcoming the Student Learning Bottlenecks: Decode the Critical Thinking of Your Discipline*. Sterling, VA: Stylus.
Odom, Mary Lou. 2013. "Not Just for Writing Anymore: What WAC Can Teach Us about Reading to Learn." *Across the Disciplines* 10 (4). http://wac.colostate.edu/atd/reading/odom.cfm.
Pace, David. 2017. *The Decoding the Disciplines Paradigm*. Bloomington: Indiana University Press.
Patel, Salma. 2014. "A Guide to Coding Qualitative Data." SalmaPatel.co.uk, September 18, 2014. http://salmapatel.co.uk/academia/coding-qualitative-research/.
Scholes, Robert J. 2002. "The Transition to College Reading." *Pedagogy* 2 (2): 165–172.

Heather C. Easterling is Professor of English at Gonzaga University, where she teaches lower-division literature and first-year seminar courses as well as upper-division courses in Renaissance drama and poetry. She has served as a Faculty Fellow and a Steering Committee member for the university's Center for Teaching and Advising and has extensive experience related to SOTL.

John Eliason is Professor of English and Director of the Composition Program and the Writing Center at Gonzaga University. He teaches lower- and upper-division writing courses, serves on the Steering Committee for the university's Center for Teaching and Advising, and has advised faculty engaged in SOTL work across the curriculum. John serves on the review boards for *Across the Disciplines* and the *WAC Journal*.

4

UNDERSTANDING HOW STUDENTS ACROSS THE DISCIPLINES READ IMAGES

DANA STATTON THOMPSON

> I follow it [the image] like a book... trying to take in as much information as possible.
> —Participant

Students in higher education encounter images on the internet, and especially social media platforms, on a daily basis. Because images are encountered so frequently on websites and phone apps such as Facebook, Instagram, Snapchat, Twitter, and YouTube, it is difficult to remember that images can be complicated, demanding, and problematic (Wardle and Derakhshan 2017). These characteristics provide ample reason to teach students to read images critically. Indeed, the literature on visual literacy from the past fifty years emphasizes a need to teach visual literacy skills to students across the disciplines (Fransecky and Debes 1972; Robinson 1990; Moore and Dwyer 1994; Elkins 2007; Mayer 2014; Baylen and D'Alba 2015; Little, Felten, and Berry 2015; Schellenberg 2015; Kędra and Žakevičiūtė 2019). As Rhonda Robinson writes, "We have agreed on the importance of these skills, and we now strive to develop and promote the inclusion of visual literacy in school curricula and activities" (1990, 433). Over twenty years later, Denise Hattwig et al. (2013, 61) continue this line of thinking, stating, "Across disciplines, students are being asked to produce projects and intellectual work using visual media, and they must develop the skills needed to find, interpret, evaluate, use, and produce visual materials in a scholarly context. Visual literacy competencies are essential for 21st century learners and must be supported across the higher education curriculum." Yet, as Jennifer Mayer (2014, 279) observes, "On university campuses, it is increasingly common for faculty members to incorporate visuals into required work for their classes in disciplines other than the visual arts; however, in many cases, visual literacy is not a formal outcome for university students." Furthermore, Susan Sweeney and David Hughes (2017, 64) note that "the integration of visual literacy training within the curricula, whilst commendable, remains in its infancy and tends to be ad hoc and informal (non-accredited) by nature." Acknowledging the future challenges of visual literacy education, Joanna Kędra and Rasa Žakevičiūtė (2019, 5) write, "The new (visual) literacy education is ephemeral, momentary, multitasking, simultaneous, random, non-structured; it happens digitally, switching between devices and (learning) platforms, but it also happens in physical contexts, such as classrooms. We are returning to the holistic view on knowledge and knowing, and thus, on teaching and learning." Indeed, as we move further into the twenty-first century, instructors must improve their understanding of the visual in addition to the more familiar textual environment of higher education.

Within this context, this exploratory study seeks to explain whether and how higher-education students critically read digital images independent of formal instruction on how to do so. It responds to Eva Brumberger's statement that "this is an area that merits further research, particularly since the ability to read images seems to be more and more important, regardless of academic or professional discipline" (2011, 44). By understanding whether and how students across the disciplines critically read images, it is possible to create instruction that supports this type of reading in the classroom.

LITERATURE REVIEW

Identifying Visually Literate Students in the Context of Critical Reading

The terms *critical reading* and *visual literacy* best explain the practice of critically reading images. Critical reading, according to Karen Manarin et al. (2015), can be understood as reading with two different goals: reading for academic purposes or reading for social or civic engagement. Reading for academic purposes includes "identifying patterns of textual elements, distinguishing between main and subordinate ideas, evaluating credibility, making judgements about how a text is argued, and making relevant inferences about the text" (4). Reading for social or civic engagement involves "sifting through various forms of rhetoric, recognizing power relations, questioning assumptions, engaging with the world, and constructing new possibilities" (6). Across these two types of reading, Manarin et al. (2015)

determine that four categories are consistent: comprehension, analysis, interpretation, and evaluation. The ability to critically read images, as opposed to critically reading text à la Manarin et al., is a skill found within the competencies of a visually literate individual.

Acknowledging the rise of visual culture in the past twenty years, the Association of College and Research Libraries' "Visual Literacy Competency Standards for Higher Education" contains a timely, comprehensive definition of visual literacy: "Visual literacy is a set of abilities that enables an individual to effectively find, interpret, evaluate, use, and create images and visual media. Visual literacy skills equip a learner to understand and analyze the contextual, cultural, ethical, aesthetic, intellectual, and technical components involved in the production and use of visual materials. A visually literate individual is both a critical consumer of visual media and a competent contributor to a body of shared knowledge and culture" (ACRL 2011). The "ACRL Visual Literacy Competency Standards for Higher Education" includes seven standards, defining the visually literate student as someone who

> (1) defines and articulates the need for an image,
> (2) finds and accesses needed images and visual media effectively and efficiently,
> (3) interprets and analyzes the meanings of images and visual media,
> (4) evaluates images and their sources,
> (5) uses images effectively for different purposes,
> (6) designs and creates meaningful images and visual media,
> (7) and understands many of the ethical, legal, social, and economic issues surrounding the creation and use of images and visual media, and accesses and uses visual materials ethically. (ACRL 2011)

Each standard is accompanied by a set of performance indicators and learning outcomes.

The four consistent categories of critical reading identified by Manarin et al. (2015)—comprehension, analysis, interpretation, and evaluation—are thoroughly explored in standards 3 and 4 of the "ACRL Visual Literacy Competency Standards for Higher Education." The first three performance indicators of standard 3 directly relate to critical reading:

> (3.1) the visually literate student identifies information relevant to an image's meaning,
> (3.2) the visually literate student situates an image in its cultural, social, and historical contexts, and
> (3.3) the visually literate student identifies the physical, technical, and design components of an image.

The four performance indicators of standard 4 also directly relate to critical reading:

> (4.1) the visually literate student evaluates the effectiveness and reliability of images as visual communications,
> (4.2) the visually literate student evaluates the aesthetic and technical characteristics of images,
> (4.3) the visually literate student evaluates textual information accompanying images, and
> (4.4) the visually literate student makes judgments about the reliability and accuracy of image sources. (ACRL 2011)

Parallels between these categories of critical reading can be drawn to the above performance indicators. Although each of these categories is an important element in critical reading, for the purposes of this study, I focus on evaluation as the skill that most directly corresponds to the process of critically reading images.

Examining Students' Evaluation of Images

The following studies give conflicting evidence about what criteria students use to evaluate images, how often students evaluate images, and whether students evaluate images at all. Investigating the image-seeking preferences of college freshmen, Laurie Bridges and Tiah Edmunson-Morton (2011) report that students do not mention evaluating images at all. They write, "In addition, because the respondents in our survey did not mention evaluating the images they might find or concern for copyright, we suggest librarians begin to consider integrating visual literacy instruction into standard information literacy instruction for undergraduates" (32). The fact that no student mentions evaluating images in the search process indicates it is possible that students are unaware of the connection between searching for images and evaluating images for use.

Brumberger (2011) examines the assumptions around the myth of the "digital native," an idea originally published by Marc Prensky in 2001. In her survey, she includes several questions about evaluating images and video. Two traits that she investigates include an "awareness of how easily visual material may be altered, and a concomitant mistrust of such information" (Brumberger 2011, 32). She finds that "the data do not offer clear cut evidence that respondents are consistently informed or critical viewers. That is, although respondents are inclined to assume that images have been altered, this tendency is not as strong as one might expect from students who are purportedly visually savvy media critics" (32). Her findings illustrate that while students report some assumption that images have been altered or manipulated, they do not do so consistently or constantly.

Alison J. Head and Michael B. Eisenberg (2010) investigate how students evaluate web content and library materials based on their disciplinary area of study. The different criteria for evaluating library sources and web sources in their survey include currency (i.e., the content's timeliness), charts (if charts exist, their value), whether different viewpoints are represented, whether the author gives credit to sources used, whether a bibliography is included, the author's credentials, familiarity of the source from previous usage, whether the student has heard about the source before, the publisher of the source, and whether the student got a librarian referral about the source (Head and Eisenberg 2010, 52–54). Students report evaluating charts found on the web more frequently than charts found in library sources, with students in the sciences reporting that they do so more often than students in other disciplines. Head and Eisenberg (2010, 17) also find that, in relation to evaluating information sources in general,

> One third of the students we interviewed used a minimalist "checklist" approach when conducting evaluation. These students said they relied on one or two criteria for assessing the quality of information they had found. If a source met their standards, they continued with fulfilling the rest of the research assignment. The checklist approach adhered to some of the rigors of applying accepted evaluation standards, in part, but students did not treat evaluation as a process—but rather as a procedural step or routine. The comments suggest evaluation was a hurdle they needed to clear, rather than an essential aspect of selecting and synthesizing information, and then formulating their own argument for an assignment.

Head and Eisenberg do not detail which criteria students include in their "checklist approach," nor do they mention what specific type of information sources the students are referring to. However, their findings illustrate that students are evaluating images (in this case, charts), and they are using some criteria when they evaluate information sources in general.

In her research examining college students' image-searching processes on the web, Youngok Choi (2010, 2023) finds stronger evidence of student evaluation, noting, "In order to extract the appropriate sources or resources, users consistently evaluate search results for decision making to meet their information needs. In this process, topic knowledge, a working stage, and task goal seem to have an impact on interpreting the meanings of an image and relevance judgement. . . . Furthermore, in assessing relevance of the found image, the participants seemed to rely on text within context of a page where an image presents its meaning." Although "topic knowledge," "working stage," and "task goal" are specific research domains to Choi's work, her research proves students are interpreting images to determine their relevance and are also using criteria, such as text, to do so. Choi further notes that participants also considered the credibility, reliability, and quality of web resources before making a final judgment in their search process. These criteria, again, are not specific to images necessarily; however, the images here were found on the web, so extrapolations can be made that these criteria apply, at least tangentially, to images as well.

Tammy Ravas and Megan Stark's case study (2012) discusses a librarian-led instruction session on visual literacy. They note that, at their university, all first-year students are encouraged "to engage and analyze information sources according to a set of guidelines, which include: bias, authorship, credibility, coverage/scope, purpose, timeliness, and reliability/verifiability" (41). They then report, "The students expressed frustration with these guidelines and suggested they were inadequate to provide a thorough analysis of the images" (42). Ravas and Stark continue:

> While their ability to evaluate the photographs seemed strengthened by the exercise, the discussion returned repeatedly to the difficulty of applying the same evaluation criteria to photographs that they would to more traditional sources. The typical criteria for evaluating sources were inadequate.... The students seemed reluctant to identify photography as a medium that can be fairly critiqued according to traditional scholarly standards. They seemed to believe that photographs evaded this kind of analytical reading simply by their nature. There was general agreement that, if the examination of visual material is part of scholarly work, it should be governed by different standards. There was not, however, agreement on what this different standard would include since there was such a strong feeling that there is some visual content that should not be judged. (43–44)

This interesting finding indicates that the criteria used for evaluating text and images, such as photographs in particular, should be differentiated.

The categories used by Ravas and Stark echo the categories included in a commonly used source evaluation tool currently used by librarians, the CRAAP Test, which includes the following criteria: currency, relevance, authority, accuracy, and purpose (Blakeslee 2004; California State University, Chico, 2010). These criteria are meant to apply to evaluating textual information. Christopher Toth and Hazel McClure (2017) and Dana Statton Thompson, Melony Shemberger, and Elizabeth Wright (2018) use and modify the CRAAP Test for evaluating infographics specifically.

However, based on my research in 2018, no widely recognized or used criteria exist for evaluating digital images.

Study Aims

To remedy this, I examined how college students evaluate digital images in the following exploratory, discovery-focused study. I investigated the following research questions using a mixed-methods approach:

RQ1: Do students evaluate digital images (such as charts, graphs, illustrations, or photographs)?
RQ2: If students do evaluate digital images, what criteria do they use?

Methodology

The Murray State University Institutional Review Board approved the study "Reading Digital Images: Evaluating Students' Visual Literacy Skills" in the spring of 2018, IRB #18-103.

Institutional Information

Murray State University is a four-year public university in Murray, Kentucky, located in the southeastern United States. This midsized regional university averages 9,500 enrolled students with approximately 8,100 undergraduate (60% female and 40% male) and 1,400 graduate students (66% female and 33% male) per academic year and a 15:1 student-to-faculty ratio. Undergraduate students are 82 percent white, non-Hispanic; 6.3 percent nonresident aliens; 6.0 percent black or African American, non-Hispanic; 2.2 percent identifying with two or more races, non-Hispanic; 2.3 percent with race and/or ethnicity unknown; 1.8 percent Hispanic/Latino; and 1 percent Asian (Murray State University 2019).

Study Design

I used a mixed-methods approach that included quantitative analysis of a survey consisting of ten multiple-choice questions and qualitative analysis for the associated open-ended questions (see appendix 1). The questions followed a forced-choice format, but answers were not required to continue to the next question. Question 1 asks students if they "read" digital images by interpreting, analyzing, evaluating, and comprehending, using the same categories from Manarin et al. (2015). Questions 2–7 ask students how often (on a scale from very often to never) they notice particular elements of digital images, including the formal elements, the affective elements, the text, the source, the context, and the purpose of the digital image. Question 8 asks, on the same scale, how often the students look up the digital image to verify that the information has not been misrepresented or manipulated. Question 9 asks students if they have been given criteria or been taught to evaluate images. Question 10 asks students to identify their major (see table 4.1 for this information).

I created and administered the survey using SurveyMonkey. To recruit students for the survey, I used a nonprobability, convenience sampling technique. I contacted twenty-three professors whom I know through library liaison support or information literacy instruction efforts and invited them to forward the survey to their students; nine responded that they did so. The survey was open for a period of two weeks and had a 100 percent completion rating. Seventy-three completed surveys were collected; sixty-three were completed online, and ten were completed in person during a multimedia writing course in the Journalism and Mass Communication Department. I collected informed consent from the participants when they started the survey.

Study Population

The students who responded to the survey indicated their academic discipline: forty-two business students (55%), twenty-one humanities and fine arts students (27%), five science and technology students (7%), four nursing and health professions students (5%), three education and human services students (4%), one agriculture student (1%), and one continuing education student (1%). Six students double-majored and so were counted in their respective majors' colleges. Two students did not provide information on their major. Although the sample is not representative of the larger student population or higher education in general, the data do provide a current snapshot of whether and how college students evaluate images on a midsized regional university's campus in the southeastern United States.

ANALYSIS

I first analyzed the quantitative data from questions 2 through 8 using descriptive statistics to summarize and describe the data. Each of these questions follows the same Likert scale according to frequency ("very often," "often," "not often," or "never"). Because of the small number of responses collected, the categories "very often" and "often" were combined, as were "not often" and "never," to provide a better representation of the data.

Each multiple-choice question included an open-ended response space where the students could include additional information about how the

Table 4.1 College and center representation by department.

Department	Number of participants	Percentage of participants
Arthur J. Bauernfeind College of Business		
Journalism and Mass Communication	22	
Organizational Communication	10	
Management, Marketing, and Business Administration	9	
Accounting	1	
	42	**55%**
College of Humanities and Fine Arts		
Art and Design	10	
English and Philosophy	2	
History	2	
Music	2	
Political Science and Sociology	2	
Liberal Arts	1	
Psychology	1	
Global Languages and Theater Arts	1	
	21	**27%**
Jesse D. Jones College of Science, Engineering, and Technology		
Institute of Engineering	2	
Occupational Safety and Health	2	
Earth and Environmental Sciences	1	
	5	**7%**
School of Nursing and Health Professions		
Applied Health Sciences	4	5%
College of Education and Human Service		
Community Leadership and Human Services	2	
Early Childhood and Elementary Education	1	
	3	**4%**
Hutson School of Agriculture		
Pre-veterinary Medicine	1	1%
Center for Adult and Regional Education		
Integrated Studies	1	1%
	77*	**100%**

Italics denote departments in which students are double-majoring.
*Six students double-majored, and two skipped the question.

elements mentioned above informed their understanding of a digital image. I analyzed this qualitative data using an inductive, open coding process. I then established codes by identifying emerging themes and subthemes. Combining quantitative and qualitative data worked well for this study since participants could elaborate on their selected answer, which only indicated the frequency of the behavior and identified the "what." Including a space for short answers made it possible to also analyze the "how" and "why" of their responses.

Findings and Discussion

Understanding the Concept of Critically Reading Images

A majority of students reported that they do read images (89%). Only 8 percent of students reported that they do not, with 3 percent of students reporting in the short answer space that "it depends" (question 1). Because all of the students continued the survey and indicated in their other answers that they do, in fact, use certain criteria (such as formal elements, affective elements, source, and purpose) to evaluate images, it is possible that students do not equate "reading images" with evaluating specific criteria since they have not received formal instruction on critically reading images. This finding concurs with Sweeney and Hughes's (2017) assessment that the integration of visual literacy training in the curricula tends to be informal (64), which, as seen here, can lead to an uninformed population. Additionally, although the majority of students in this study reported that they do evaluate digital images, they did not use all criteria with the same frequency and relied unevenly on the criteria outlined by the "ACRL Visual Literacy Competency Standards for Higher Education" for evaluating images, especially in regard to standards 3 and 4. This could be directly tied to students' interest level, which seemed indicative of whether they would spend the time to read an image. Students commented, "It depends on what it is over. If it is needed for an assignment or something that interests me, I'll analyze what the graph is saying and if it's accurate or not," "If it's a compelling picture, I will study it," "It depends on what the image is and if it's appealing or not. It must grab my attention and stand out," and "I'm curious to see what it's telling me." These statements could indicate that students use the same type of "checklist approach" mentioned by Head and Eisenberg (2010) and that they investigate an image further only depending on their interest level in the image.

Understanding Images

Related to students' understanding of the concept of critically reading images as a whole, analysis showed that different criteria either led to in-depth understanding, helped with understanding, led to only superficial understanding, or had no impact on understanding.

The Relationship between Text and Image

Most students reported that textual elements helped with understanding: "I usually use [the text] to form a basis of understanding about the image," "It helps to understand what the graph's goal is—what was measured by the graph," and "[The text] gives more comprehensive understanding." This echoes the quantitative results, in which students reported that they most frequently (82% very often/often) noticed the text surrounding a digital image such as the caption, data, and headline (question 4), which directly corresponds to the first performance indicator of standard 3 and the third performance indicator of standard 4. This aligns with Choi's (2010) finding that students use criteria such as text to determine relevance and interpret images.

In addition, students frequently commented on the relationship between text and image in their responses to the open-ended questions: "I often look to see how the image relates to a story or gives more detail or an illustration of what the writing is trying to say," "The text helps me to sometimes understand what is not readable in the image," and "The caption is vital to understanding the image." Students also frequently commented that the purpose of the surrounding text was to explain the image: "Text is one of my main focuses when viewing an image. The text gives the most obvious information," "It gives you a description of what the image is," and "This supports the image just in case I may not understand what the digital image is there for, but it also helps explain the author's reasoning for the image." These statements correspond to the fact that higher-education students participate in a heavily text-based environment in the United States that privileges textual information over visual information.

Context

Most students also reported that context led to an in-depth understanding of an image: "The context explains to me a deeper meaning of the image," "An image can change its impact and meaning after understanding the context of it," and "I want to know who or what the source of the image is it is important to know and understand the background of the source in order to understand the image." This qualitative finding parallels the quantitative finding in which students reported that they frequently (70% very often/often) noticed the context of the digital image (question 6), which directly corresponds to the second performance indicator of standard 3.

Purpose

Some students reported that examining the purpose of an image was helpful for their understanding: "It helps you understand why the image was produced altogether," "It lets me know how to interpret the image," "The purpose is the main concept to review when attempting to understand an image, in my opinion," and "The purpose is a small part of my understanding." This finding is reflected in the quantitative data, in which students reported that they sometimes (66% very often/often) noticed the purpose of the image (question 7), which directly corresponds to the first performance indicator of standard 4.

Formal Elements

For a few students, criteria such as formal elements led to a more in-depth understanding of an image or helped their understanding: "I like [how] the formal elements inform you about the small details and the character of the digital image. Helps you to look into the inner message of the digital image," "They make the image more interesting which makes me want to pay attention longer. The longer I pay attention, the higher understanding I have," and "They often help interpret the meaning." For others, the same criteria had no effect on their understanding: "They don't really, I don't know the formal aspects," "They don't inform me of anything I can think of," and "My understanding is not changed very much based on the formal elements." This dovetails with the quantitative finding in which students reported that they only sometimes (63% very often/often) noticed the formal elements of an image (question 2), which directly corresponds to the third performance indicator of standard 3 and the second performance indicator of standard 4.

Affective Elements and Feelings

A few students reported that affective elements helped them with understanding: "I feel like my initial emotions help me create an idea about how I should understand a digital image," "I hope that it helps me understand what [the] photographer was trying to convey," and "If you're emotional, you likely understand the image's meaning." Other students reported that the affective elements did not add to their understanding of the image: "I can't say that they do," "This is not something I often think about, but probably should," and "Walking past something I don't think to do that." This dovetails with the quantitative finding in which students reported that they sometimes (63% very often/often) noticed the affective elements of an image (question 3), which are not addressed in the "ACRL Visual Literacy Competency Standards for Higher Education."

Students also commented on their emotional response to digital images in the open-ended responses: "I think that often an image like a political cartoon makes me happy or I find it funny. On the other hand, with photos, especially in breaking news stories I'm often sad or sometimes upset by the images because they show tragic situations and sometimes graphic images that make me feel for the subjects of the story who went through the ordeal," "My emotions toward a photo ARE [sic] my understanding of a digital image. If an image makes me sad, then I think it's a sad picture," and "An instant emotional response acts as a guide for my cognitive interpretation." Interestingly, students also commented on how having to read an image made them feel: "When characters represent positive emotions or when images contain material that interests me, my mood is changed. When images portray beliefs that I do not agree with, I am angered easily," "In some instances, I get annoyed with the graph, but other times if it's easy to comprehend it breaks up monotony," and "It depends a lot on the source of the image. If it's a complex graph I'm expected to decipher for a class, then I'm not happy." This frustration is likely borne from a lack of instruction on how to read images such as charts, graphs, and photographs. These statements also align with Ravas and Stark's finding (2012) that students expressed frustration with the prescribed criteria for evaluating images (in their case, photographs).

Sources and Credibility

Some students reported that the source did not help their understanding of the image or led to only a superficial understanding: "I don't usually pay attention to the source, so I wouldn't know," "Unless I am citing the image, I do not pay attention to this info," "Most of the time I might see or skim over the attribution of the image, but I often don't see it or remember it," and "The source does not influence my understanding, but I should view it more." This reflects the quantitative finding in which students reported that they much less frequently (33% very often/often) noticed the source (creator, publisher, and/or website) of the digital image (question 5), which directly corresponds to the fourth performance indicator of standard 4.

This self-reportage directly contrasts with the fact that students cite credibility as a main concern when considering the source of an image or whether or not to look up an image: "The source tells me the level of credibility of the digital image," "Credibility and biases can be evaluated and help understand the meaning of the image," "Sometimes if an image looks wrong I look at the source to check for credibility," "When I do look up the digital image, I first Google it then go to the most official/reliable website to verify it," and "I didn't always do that but after the past two years of fake news, I catch myself doing this quite often." This corresponds with Choi's (2010) finding in which participants also considered the credibility, reliability, and quality of images found on web resources before making a final judgment in their search process. This finding does contradict the fact that students reported that the source did not help their understanding of the image or led to only a superficial understanding, in addition to the fact that students reported that they rarely examine the source of an image. This discrepancy could mean that students understand that they should be exhibiting these behaviors but have not put these behaviors into practice. Because of the prevalence of "fake news" in the media in the past several years, students have likely encountered more emphasis, both online and in the classroom, on fact-checking.

Discipline-Specific Knowledge and Genre-Specific Images

Students were also asked if they had been given criteria or been taught to evaluate images (question 9). Fifty-eight percent reported that they had not received this type of instruction, and 42 percent reported that they had. Those subjects were journalism, art and design, English, statistics, science, organizational communication, and information studies. Students mentioned journalism and art and design the most.

Students also frequently referenced one genre of an image to the exclusion of others when providing short answers. This indicated that students use different criteria depending on the type of digital image they are evaluating (charts, graphs, illustrations, or photographs). Photographs were by far the most frequently mentioned genre. This finding could be because students are more likely to encounter a photograph in an online environment than a chart, graph, or illustration. This also follows Ravas and Stark's (2012) finding that students believed visual materials should be governed by different standards than the criteria developed to evaluate text.

Limitations

Because of the sampling method and number of participants, the data are not representative of the entire population of college students, so the results of this study cannot be generalizable. Additionally, the response rate was indeterminable because professors did not state the number of classes or number of students per class they had distributed the survey to. Lastly, question 1 asked an "and/or" statement, meaning that a "yes" response might indicate that students did any or all four actions (interpret, analyze, evaluate, and comprehend) in order to read images. It is possible that respondents were not able to distinguish between these four actions.

Moving Forward

Future Areas of Study

This exploratory study provides several different avenues for future exploration in the scholarship of teaching and learning (SOTL) community. In particular, developing specific evaluative criteria for different types of images seems a worthy endeavor, especially as it realizes that how students evaluate images might depend on what type of image is being evaluated. A second future area of study would explore how different students in particular majors explain how they evaluate images and whether those students use genre-specific terms. For example, are art students more likely to specifically and exclusively mention art, are business students more likely to specifically and exclusively mention graphs, and are journalism students more likely to specifically and exclusively mention photographs?

From Results to Practice in the Classroom

As Pat Hutchings (2000, 8) notes, "the scholarship of teaching and learning is characterized by a transformational agenda." With this study, I originally wanted to both transform current curricula and "understand or improve student learning in higher education and the teaching approaches and practices that affect student learning" (Chick 2019). Specifically, I wanted to discover which criteria students use to evaluate images independently of instruction. As this study shows, in order for students to evaluate images outside of the classroom, they must be taught how to do so in the classroom.

After the conclusion of this study, I developed the Digital Image Guide (DIG) Method, addressing the need to establish specific criteria to evaluate digital images (see table 4.2). Instructors can use the DIG Method to teach their students to critically read images (Thompson 2019). To develop this evaluation tool, I first adapted a series of questions found in an online research guide about how to evaluate digital images (University of

Table 4.2 The Digital Image Guide (DIG) Method.

The DIG Method
Analyzing:
Review and describe the image. Who, what, when, and where do you see **represented** in the image?
Review the text. What **textual information** is provided (caption, date, and/or headline)?
React to the image. How does the image make you **feel**?
Interpreting:
Determine the **source** (creator, publisher, and/or website) of the image. Who created the image? Who owns and/or published the image?
Determine the **message** of the image. What is the message? Who is the intended audience?
Search for other online sources that further contextualize the image. How does context (social, cultural, historical, and/or political) inform the image?
Evaluating:
Think back to your first reaction to the image. How might your reaction **impact** how you view the image?
Refer back to the other websites that have published the image. Has the image been **misrepresented** or **manipulated**?
Assess the **reliability** and **accuracy** of the image. Is the image reliable and accurate? Why or why not?
Comprehending:
What **judgments** can you make about the image based on your evaluations above and the available information?
Do any of your **biases** or points of view impact how you view the image? If so, how?
What is the **purpose** of this image (to inform, to instruct, to sell, to entertain, to enjoy, and/or to persuade)? Why do you think so?

California, Irvine 2020). I also referenced questions found in *The Visual Literacy White Paper* (Bamford 2003, 6–7) and *Visual Literacy for Libraries: A Practical, Standards-Based Guide* (Brown et al. 2016, 20). The questions I created were then organized according to the steps of critical reading as found in Manarin et al. (2015). After several additional rounds of revisions, I codified the resulting schema as the DIG Method.

The questions in the "Analyzing" section of the DIG Method ask the student to review and describe the image, review the textual information included in the image (if any), and describe their initial reaction to the image. In the next section, "Interpreting," the questions ask the student to determine the source and the message, as well as search the internet for the image to provide context. The third section, "Evaluating," asks the student to evaluate how their feelings might impact how they view the image, as well as evaluate whether the image has been manipulated or misrepresented. The next question in the "Evaluating" section asks the student whether the image is reliable and accurate and asks them to provide reasoning for their response. The final section of questions addresses comprehension. This set of questions asks the student to provide their own judgment of the image based on the information they have accumulated thus far, to assess that judgment in regard to their biases, and finally to determine the purpose of the image (Thompson 2019).

Teaching students how to read images critically should happen in introductory courses, starting with the basic criteria of affective elements, context, formal elements, purpose, source, and text, as found in the DIG Method. Then, as students move through the curriculum, the process of critical reading can become more discipline-specific and privilege certain criteria over others, depending on the discipline. By learning how to read digital images critically, a student will become able to evaluate complicated, demanding, and problematic images as a "critical consumer of visual media and a competent contributor to a body of shared knowledge and culture" (ACRL 2011).

This exploratory study shows that students *are* evaluating images. This evaluation happens in degrees and frequently depends on the students' discipline and interest level in the individual image. Some aspects, such as text, context, and purpose, can be very helpful for overall understanding, while other criteria, such as the formal and affective elements, may depend more on the education or inclination of the individual. There seems to be a strong disconnect in students' understanding of the relationship between sources and credibility. This disconnect is very concerning in this age of disinformation, prevalent social media use, and ever-increasing available information. At its core, critically reading images comes down to evaluating images; instructors should impress on their students the importance of critically reading images wherever they encounter them, even (and especially) outside of the classroom.

Appendix: Survey Questions for Evaluating Students' Visual Literacy Skills

Q1 When you encounter a digital image (such as a photograph, chart, graph, or illustration), do you "read" (interpret, analyze, evaluate, and/or comprehend) it? (Fixed-response)

Yes

No

Please explain your answer. (Open-ended)

Q2 On the following scale, how often do you notice the formal elements (color, line, balance, saturation, etc.) of a digital image? (Fixed-response)

Very often

Often

Not often

Never

How do the formal elements inform your understanding of the digital image? (Open-ended)

Q3 On the following scale, how often do you notice how digital images make you feel (happy, sad, amused, angry, joyous, uneasy, etc.)? (Fixed-response)

Very often

Often

Not often

Never

How do your emotions inform your understanding of the digital image? (Open-ended)

Q4 On the following scale, how often do you notice the text surrounding the digital image (caption, date, headline, etc.) (Fixed-response)

Very often

Often

Not often

Never

How does the accompanying text inform your understanding of the digital image? (Open-ended)

Q5 On the following scale, how often do you notice the source (creator, publisher, and/or website) of the digital image? (Fixed-response)
Very often
Often
Not often
Never
How does the source inform your understanding of the digital image? (Open-ended)

Q6 On the following scale, how often do you think about the context (social, cultural, historical, political, etc.) of the digital image? (Fixed-response)
Very often
Often
Not often
Never
How does context inform your understanding of the digital image? (Open-ended)

Q7 On the following scale, how often do you think about the purpose (to inform, to sell, to entertain, or to persuade) of the digital image? (Fixed-response)
Very often
Often
Not often
Never
How does the purpose inform your understanding of the digital image? (Open-ended)

Q8 On the following scale, how often do you look up the digital image to verify the information has not been misrepresented or manipulated? (Fixed-response)
Very often
Often
Not often
Never
If you look up the digital image to verify the information is correct, how do you do so? (Open-ended)

Q9 Have you ever been given criteria or been taught to evaluate images? (Fixed-response)
Yes
No
If "yes," what were those criteria and in what class? (Open-ended)

Q10 What is your major? (Open-ended)

References

ACRL. 2011. "ACRL Visual Literacy Competency Standards for Higher Education." http://www.ala.org/acrl/standards/visualliteracy.

Bamford, Anne. 2003. *The Visual Literacy White Paper*. Adobe Systems. https://www.aperture.org/wp-content/uploads/2013/05/visual-literacy-wp.pdf.

Baylen, Danilo M., and Adriana D'Alba, eds. 2015. *Essentials of Teaching and Integrating Visual and Media Literacy*. Cham, Switzerland: Springer International.

Blakeslee, Sarah. 2004. "The CRAAP Test." *LOEX Quarterly* 31 (3): 6–7.

Bridges, Laurie, and Tiah Edmunson-Morton. 2011. "Image-Seeking Preferences among Undergraduate Novice Researchers." *Evidence Based Library and Information Practice* 6 (1): 24–40.

Brown, Nicole E., Kaila Bussert, Denise Hattwig, and Ann Medaille. 2016. *Visual Literacy for Libraries: A Practical, Standards-Based Guide*. Chicago: ALA Editions.

Brumberger, Eva. 2011. "Visual Literacy and the Digital Native: An Examination of the Millennial Learner." *Journal of Visual Literacy* 30 (1): 19–46.

California State University, Chico. 2010. "Evaluating Information—Applying the CRAAP Test." https://library.csuchico.edu/sites/default/files/craap-test.pdf.

Chick, Nancy. 2019. "A Scholarly Approach to Teaching." The SoTL Guide. http://sotl.ucalgaryblogs.ca/understanding-sotl/a-scholarly-approach-to-teaching/.

Choi, Youngok. 2010. "Effects of Contextual Factors on Image Searching on the Web." *Journal of the American Society for Information Science and Technology* 61 (10): 2011–2028.

Elkins, James. 2007. *Visual Practices across the University*. München: Wilhelm Fink.

Fransecky, Roger B., and John L. Debes. 1972. *Visual Literacy: A Way to Learn—a Way to Teach*. Washington, DC: Association for Educational Communications and Technology.

Hattwig, Denise, Kaila Bussert, Ann Medaille, and Joanna Burgess. 2013. "Visual Literacy Standards in Higher Education: New Opportunities for Libraries and Student Learning." *portal: Libraries and the Academy* 13 (1): 61–89.

Head, Alison J., and Michael B. Eisenberg. 2010. *Truth Be Told: How College Students Evaluate and Use Information in the Digital Age*. Seattle: Project Information Literacy Progress Report. https://projectinfolit.org/pubs/evaluating-information-study/pil_evaluating-information_2010-11-01.pdf

Hutchings, Pat. 2000. *Opening Lines: Approaches to the Scholarship of Teaching and Learning*. Princeton, NJ: Carnegie Foundation for the Advancement of Teaching.

Kędra, Joanna, and Rasa Žakevičiūtė. 2019. "Visual Literacy Practices in Higher Education: What, Why, and How?" *Journal of Visual Literacy* 38 (1–2): 1–7. https://doi.org/10.1080/1051144X.2019.1580438.

Little, Deandra, Peter Felten, and Chad Berry. 2015. *Looking and Learning: Visual Literacy across the Disciplines*. San Francisco: Jossey-Bass.

Manarin, Karen, Miriam Carey, Melanie Rathburn, and Glenn Ryland. 2015. *Critical Reading in Higher Education: Academic Goals and Social Engagement*. Bloomington: Indiana University Press.

Mayer, Jennifer. 2014. "Visual Literacy across the Disciplines." In *Research with the Disciplines*, 2nd ed., edited by Peggy Keeran and Michael Levine-Clark, 277–299. Lanham, MD: Rowman and Littlefield.

Moore, David M., and Francis M. Dwyer, eds. 1994. *Visual Literacy: A Spectrum of Visual Learning*. Englewood Cliffs, NJ: Educational Technology.

Murray State University. 2019. "Common Data Set." https://www.murraystate.edu/headermenu/administration/PresidentsOffice/institutional-effectiveness/OfficeOfInstitutionalResearch/CommonDataSet.aspx.

Prensky, Marc. 2001. "Digital Natives, Digital Immigrants." *On the Horizon* 9 (5): 1–6.

Ravas, Tammy, and Megan Stark. 2012. "Pulitzer-Prize-Winning Photographs and Visual Literacy at the University of Montana: A Case Study." *Art Documentation: Journal of the Art Libraries Society of North America* 31 (1): 34–44.

Robinson, Rhonda. 1990. "Investigating Visual Literacy: Developing Skills across the Curriculum." In *Investigating Visual Literacy*, edited by Darrell G. Beauchamp, Judy Clark Baca, and Roberts A. Braden, 433–436. Bloomington, IN: International Visual Literacy Association.

Schellenberg, Julia. 2015. "Visual Literacy Practices in Higher Education." Master's thesis, Tallinn University.

Sweeney, Susan, and David Hughes. 2017. "Integrating Visual Literacy Training into the Business Curriculum: A Case Study at Dublin Business School." *DBS Business Review* 1:61–97.

Thompson, Dana Statton. 2019. "Teaching Students to Critically Read Digital Images: A Visual Literacy Approach Using the DIG Method." *Journal of Visual Literacy* 38 (1–2): 110–119. https://doi.org/10.1080/1051144X.2018.1564604.

Thompson, Dana Statton, Melony Shemberger, and Elizabeth Wright. 2018. "Evaluating Visuals: Increasing Visual Literacy Skills with Infographics." In *Senses and Experiences: The Book of Selected Readings*, edited by Danilo M. Baylen, 98–110. International Visual Literacy Association. https://ivla.org/wp-content/uploads/2020/09/Thompson_2018.pdf.

Toth, Christopher, and Hazel McClure. 2017. "Ethics, Distribution, and Credibility: Using an Emerging Genre to Teach Information Literacy Concepts." In *Information Literacy: Research and Collaboration across Disciplines*, edited by Barbara J. D'Angelo, Sandra Jamieson, Barry Maid, and Janice R. Walker, 257–270. Fort Collins, CO: WAC Clearinghouse.

University of California, Irvine. 2020. "Visual Literacy: Evaluate Images." Last modified September 14, 2020. https://guides.lib.uci.edu/visual_literacy/visual_literacy_evaluateimagesquestionnaire.

Wardle, Claire, and Hossein Derakhshan. 2017. *Information Disorder: Toward an Interdisciplinary Framework for Research and Policy Making*. Council of Europe Report. https://rm.coe.int/information-disorder-toward-an-interdisciplinary-framework-for-researc/168076277c.

Dana Statton Thompson is a research and instruction librarian and assistant professor at Murray State University, where she teaches courses on information literacy and serves as a liaison to the College of Business. She is also a member of the board of directors for the International Visual Literacy Association. Her research and teaching interests focus on the intersection of visual literacy and news literacy, the integration of visual literacy instruction into higher education, and SOTL.

5

STUDENT READING OF DOCUMENTARY AND FICTION FILM

ELIZABETH MARQUIS

Film occupies a significant place within an increasingly mediated world. Like written texts, films require viewers to engage with, respond to, navigate, and interpret them—to *read* them in a number of ways. Nevertheless, scholars of teaching and learning have not yet considered extensively what student reading of film entails and how effective film reading might be supported. And, of course, while film reading may share some features with the reading of written texts, film's unique characteristics (e.g., the combination of sounds and images that proceed largely at a fixed and predetermined pace) suggest that it might require similarly distinct reading strategies and raise novel considerations for readers and educators. This chapter thus seeks to add to the growing body of scholarship exploring questions about the teaching and learning of reading by extending such questions to the case of reading film in an academic setting.

Investigating student reading of film is increasingly important, given that instructors across disciplines draw on both fiction and documentary films to support learning in their courses and programs (Marquis et al. 2020; Sealey 2008). For example, audiovisual texts are called on to help elucidate complex and abstract concepts (Andrist et al. 2014; Calcagno 2015; Pelton 2013), to elicit student empathy (Blasco and Moreto 2012; Happel-Parkins and Esposito 2015; Marcus and Stoddard 2007), and to encourage critical thinking and deep approaches to learning (Bright 2015; Olson, Autry, and Moe 2016). Scholars have likewise described using films as part of teaching professional skills (Ber and Alroy 2002; Lumlertgul et al. 2009), disciplinary ways of thinking (Calder 2006), and media literacies (Holland 2014; Sigler and Albandoz 2014). Given growing student interest in learning with and through popular culture (Peacock et al. 2018), film can also serve to enhance student engagement and motivation (Algeo

2007; Kabooha 2016; Swimelar 2013); it offers entry points for rich discussion (Madsen 2014; Travis 2016) and often appeals to a wide variety of learners (Brown et al. 2017; Luccasen and Thomas 2010). Lendol Calder (2006, 1364), for example, positions film as a powerful tool that "awakens [students'] capacity for wonder."

While the existing scholarship begins to indicate the multiple, significant roles film might play in classrooms, many questions about the pedagogical functioning of media texts remain unanswered. For example, much scholarship in this area has attended more to instructors' pedagogical choices and goals than to direct evidence of student learning with and through film (e.g., Calcagno 2015; Luccasen and Thomas 2010; Marquis et al. 2020; Travis 2016). This instructor focus even characterizes much work focusing on film studies teaching specifically (e.g., Achberger 2014; Lameborshi 2014; McEntee 2007), mirroring a trend that Randy Bass and Sherry Lee Linkon (2008) note within scholarship examining the teaching and learning of literature. At the same time, while some research has begun to fill this gap by exploring the efficacy of particular deployments of film, our understanding is marred by a more fundamental lack of attention to how students approach the *process* of reading films. Whereas the nascent body of existing empirical scholarship has focused largely on what Pat Hutchings (2000) might call "what works?" questions, in this chapter I instead investigate a "what is?" question, asking what happens when students attempt to read and analyze film texts in academic contexts.

Just as studies of expert thinking and practice can inform educational efforts (Forsberg et al. 2014; Middendorf and Pace 2004), attending to how students approach and respond to texts can reveal important insights about their thinking, which can in turn help refine pedagogical approaches (Bloch-Schulman 2016; Calder 2006). As Jeffrey L. Bernstein (2010, 50) points out, for example, educators are often limited in our ability to support student skill development by the fact that we see only the end result of student learning in tests and assignments: "If all we see is the final product, we have limited ability to judge what students do right and what they do wrong *as they are working through the steps involved in performing the task*. Thus, our ability to help *build* [a] skill (rather than merely *assessing* its presence or absence) is limited" (emphasis in original). Greater attention to the steps students take—to the ways in which they approach and work through tasks such as reading and interpreting texts—is therefore pedagogically important.

Against this backdrop, the present chapter describes a pilot study conducted to investigate student reading of films at a research-intensive university in Ontario, Canada. In particular, it explores the following research questions: How do students approach and experience the process of viewing films in the classroom? To what elements of films do they attend? How do they make sense of and respond to film texts? Do they approach documentaries and fiction films differently?

Participants and Methodology

To focus my exploration of how students approach reading film texts in academic settings, I framed the present study around a first-year Global Challenges course, which is mandatory for all students in one program at McMaster University. McMaster is a midsized, medical-doctoral institution in Hamilton (Canada), with a reputation for being highly research-intensive while also valuing effective and innovative teaching and learning. The program in question is a small, interdisciplinary program (about sixty-five students per year) that aims to provide students with a broad-based, liberal arts education and to help them develop skills that support scholarly inquiry into issues of social concern. The Global Challenges Inquiry course is an early entry into this process, asking students to develop their capacities to engage critically with scholarly and popular perspectives on contemporary challenges and injustices and to develop, investigate, and respond to their own researchable questions relevant to the course focus. I have cotaught the class since 2014, making frequent use of documentary and fiction film clips as examples meant to stimulate discussion and analysis of global challenges and means of responding to injustice. The course thus provided a concrete context through which to examine how students read films in relation to particular pedagogical goals (the discussion and analysis just mentioned) with which I am deeply familiar.

After receiving clearance from the university Research Ethics Board, I invited all current students in the program to participate in a "think-aloud" exercise, wherein they were asked to verbalize their thought processes as they encountered sections of two film texts. Think-alouds have been used extensively in educational research and practice and are understood to offer meaningful insights into student thinking (Banning 2008; Miller-Young 2013) and the ways in which students work with texts specifically (Bernstein 2010; Calder 2006; Bloch-Schulman 2016). They often involve asking participants to read a written text, intermittently speaking their thoughts and observations as they go. In the present case, I adapted the think-aloud process for use with audiovisual (rather than written) texts, selecting brief segments (five to six minutes each) from the beginnings of two feature-length films and asking participants to pause the clips and voice what they were thinking, noticing, or wondering as they watched.

One of these texts was a documentary, *Human Flow*, while the other was a fiction film, *Children of Men*. The selected *Human Flow* clip shows refugees arriving on the shores of Greece and features images of life in a refugee camp, including a section that cuts among lengthy shots of individual refugees standing in front of a tent wall. The selection from *Children of Men* establishes the film's dystopian universe: a world marked by violence, human infertility, xenophobia, and rampant nationalism. Without providing a great deal of explanation, it introduces the film's protagonist and illustrates his reactions to a series of events, including the death of the world's youngest person, a bomb exploding in a coffee shop, and the ongoing detention of refugees in England. As these descriptions suggest, these films were selected because they both take up issues related to refugees and human migration and thus were relevant to (but had not been used directly in) the Global Challenges course that all participants had taken.

Acknowledging the broad range of ways in which film might be utilized in class contexts, participants were asked explicitly to approach these clips as they would if the clips were presented in that mandatory course—as examples meant to prime discussion and analysis of global challenges. Given the unfamiliarity of the think-aloud process, participants were first given a chance to practice by thinking aloud with a brief trailer. They then had an opportunity to ask questions before proceeding to complete the think-aloud process with the two focal clips. To account for possible ordering effects, I alternated the sequence of the primary clips for different participants so that half completed the think-aloud with the clip from *Children of Men* first, while the other half began with *Human Flow*. After the think-alouds, participants answered a series of open-ended interview questions about the think-aloud process, the clips they had just viewed, and their typical experiences of interacting with film texts in academic contexts. This kind of exit interview is recommended in scholarship discussing think-alouds (e.g., Charters 2003), as it allows for a kind of triangulation that helps address the fact that think-alouds are necessarily incomplete and partial, and it contributes additional information about participant thinking. After the session, participants were sent a ten-dollar gift card in recognition of the time they spent taking part in the study.

Twenty-two students (of approximately 275 in the program) elected to participate—a fairly large sample size for think-aloud research, which typically involves only small numbers of participants (Charters 2003; Bernstein 2010). These students were drawn from all levels of the program, and few noted having any formal training in film analysis. All participants had taken the required Global Challenges course in their first year of university, though the design of that course had shifted over the years in which they were enrolled, and it was obviously a more recent experience for some than for others. Nevertheless, no participants expressed substantial uncertainty about the course context or the way in which they were being asked to approach the film clips for the purpose of the study.

After the data collection, the think-aloud and interview recordings were transcribed and analyzed using a qualitative approach (as recommended by Charters 2003) in order to explore the depth and complexity of participant reading strategies. In particular, I drew on constant comparative analysis (Merriam 2009) to interpret the transcripts, looking inductively to the data for patterns in how students responded when presented with documentaries and fiction films in the context of this study. This inductive approach allowed findings to emerge through the interpretation of the data themselves, as opposed to testing preexisting hypotheses—a process that is both appropriate and necessary given the exploratory nature of the project and the lack of existing research in the area. Guided by my research questions, I paid particular attention to what students notice, the questions they do and do not ask as they watch, and the strategies they use to interpret films. After an open coding phase, I reread all items coded at central branches of the code tree to check for consistency of application and to group ideas into broader conceptual categories where appropriate. These steps were intended to enhance the trustworthiness of my analytical process and to allow for the identification of key themes. I also considered the extent to which participants' approaches differed for the documentary and fiction film examples, supplementing my own analysis of this issue with participants' responses to interview questions taking it up directly. Key ideas arising from this process are presented below.

Findings

Overall, the data made clear that students take a broad range of approaches to reading and interacting with films in this particular context. While there were several instances in which participants engaged actively in questioning and interpreting the filmic examples, some participants also described taking a more passive and uncritical approach to film reading. These varying approaches (and the substrategies connected to them) were not mutually exclusive but instead overlapped and were often deployed simultaneously or iteratively by participants. While they are described separately below for clarity, these processes should be seen as potential constituent parts of a more complex reading process.

Questioning and Assessing the Text

Across the data, participants frequently took an active, inquisitive stance to interacting with and interpreting film texts. In particular, three broad strategies stood out in this regard: questioning content, questioning focus and intent, and critiquing social and political implications.

Questioning Content

When watching both the documentary and fiction film clips, participants spent ample time asking questions about the content represented. These were often concrete queries about setting, location, and plot, as students attempted to orient themselves to what was happening in the films. Viewing a sequence in *Children of Men* that included images of people detained in cages, for instance, one asked, "I'm guessing those people are immigrants, so why are they arrested? And were they originally British people that were taken out, or are they trying to get into the country?" Similarly, considering an interview with a refugee arriving on a beach in *Human Flow*, another participant noted, "I'm just wondering if they came all the way from Iraq. I'm just wondering where is it they are right now. Just wondering how far they had traveled."

Participants also posed questions about what might have led to the real or fictional situations represented or about how various elements of a film's plot interconnected. After viewing the *Children of Men* clip, for example, one participant said, "I want to know what happens, I guess, but then, also, how did things get this way? . . . Or, how specifically is infertility linked to this thing with immigration? I can kind of see where that would come from, but what's the direct linkage that they're going to draw here?" Some participants also raised broader queries about the people or issues that the films take up or the nature of the world represented. Viewing an image from *Human Flow*, for example, one student noted, "I guess I'm kind of thinking about what her life would be like, that little girl. What she would do every day in these camps." In spite of minor variations in focus, the process of asking content-based questions remained fundamental to most participants' interactions with both clips, suggesting that actively attempting to parse out what is happening and understand the nature of the world presented is a key component of what students are doing when presented with film content in course contexts.

Questioning Focus and Intent

Participants also engaged actively in questioning the focus of the film or the intent of the filmmakers, though this strategy was less common than asking questions about content. Some puzzled about why a particular shot might have been selected or what it was intended to convey, for example, or about what the larger purpose of the film might be. Noting a definition of *refugee* overlaid on one of the images in *Human Flow*, for example, one participant explained, "With the ending quote, I think it was interesting especially right after all of those nondialogued scenes with different people. I just kind of asked myself, like, what exactly are you trying to say here, and what exactly are you trying to show here?" Similarly, watching another sequence in *Human Flow*, in which individual refugees are filmed silently standing in front of a tent wall, another asked, "Is he trying to make us feel like they're actually human beings, instead of just a number? What's the purpose of making them stand in front of this thing?"

Interestingly, while students asked questions about intent and focus in relation to both clips, some argued in interviews that they are more attuned to intentionality when watching fiction films. One pointed out that fictional texts, as opposed to documentaries, have an element of deliberateness that "really changes the way I think of it. Like, I know that [things] were put there, this is a set, and everything in this frame is meant to be there." Such comments imply that some students may be less likely to consciously attend to the constructed nature of documentaries. However, another participant suggested that they consider questions of intent and purpose for both documentary and fiction films, but in slightly different ways: "[With *Children of Men*,] I was paying attention to all the writing that you could see in the background and all the advertisements that you saw in that city street ... because I was kind of looking to everything for meaning. But I guess in the second film [*Human Flow*], I was kind of just looking at how the filmmaker was trying to frame it. And I was kind of looking for maybe biases but also just things that seemed intentional." Such comments, along with examples of questioning intent across both clips used in the think-alouds, highlight that this strategy may be a relatively common one for students interacting with both fiction and nonfiction examples.

Critiquing Social and Political Implications

Building on the process of actively questioning the text, participants also engaged widely in assessing the social and political implications of the films they watched for the study. Indeed, this kind of ideologically focused interpretation was nearly as common as questions about content, perhaps because the Global Challenges course focuses heavily on social and political issues, and the films themselves relate clearly to that course focus.[1] Given this framing context, students proposed and explored many preliminary arguments about how the films represent issues such as immigration and how these representational choices might function to reproduce or destabilize prevailing views and practices.

Several participants suggested that *Human Flow* served to confront Western audiences with a different, perhaps more humanizing view of refugees than they might typically encounter—for example, often pointing to the way filmic choices enabled this shift in perspective. As one put it, "The length of time that they're holding on these people makes me able to see them for long enough that I can start to, like, see different people I might know, as opposed to just another face, a mass, a bunch of different people." Similarly, *Children of Men* was repeatedly described as offering a warning or a commentary about contemporary issues such as xenophobia, inequality, and authoritarianism. One participant ventured the following preliminary interpretation: "I think it's almost trying to make a commentary on our disregard for groups of people ... and how we all do that in our day-to-day lives and kind of push some things to the side as less important and are so able to avoid feeling uncomfortable because of the sufferings of others."

In addition to highlighting the social and political messages the films convey, some participants offered commentary that engaged with the ethics and politics of the texts themselves. Some noted the problematic racial politics of *Children of Men*, for instance; one participant observed that the film has "a lot of white characters. Not many people of color so far," while another asked, "Why does it have to be a white guy who saves the world? He's not the one who is the most impacted, I'm assuming, so why does it have to be him?" Others questioned the ethics of particular choices made in *Human Flow*, noting, for example, that "the camera being so close seems kind of invasive for these people who are just getting [off] a boat," or wondering "how [an individual in the documentary] feels about being filmed and if he knows why." In a similar vein, one student offered the following observation about the scene from *Human Flow* in which refugees are filmed in front of a tent wall: "I always just kind of hate when there's, like, 'Oh, here's some poor, oppressed people who had some troubles; we're gonna make them stand in front of this camera, so you can eyeball them, look them down.' ... It's weirdly dehumanizing, and it's supposed to be humanizing, but it's not." As these comments suggest, participants attempted to unpack the politics of both the documentary and the fiction film in several ways. Importantly, in the context taken up by the present study, this focus suggests a process of reading textual details through the lens of course goals, as participants attended to the interplay of filmic choices and issues of social justice and ethics, a lens I surely also applied in my selection of the texts and analysis of participant responses.

Reading Strategies Supporting Questioning and Assessment

To help themselves address and explore the three broad kinds of questions described above, participants also called on a range of substrategies that are worthy of mention. Generally speaking, these fell into two broad groups: working with textual details and making connections beyond the text.

Working with Textual Details

Participants paid considerable attention to observing particular formal features of the texts and considering the implications of those features. Perhaps not surprisingly, given that few had film studies training, students were particularly likely to note elements of dialogue, plotting, or mise-en-scène (i.e., entities that appear before the camera, such as sets, costumes, performers, and lighting). Nevertheless, several also observed salient choices connected to cinematography, editing, narration, and sound, though they did not always have the vocabulary to describe these in concrete terms. More than simply highlighting the presence of these formal features, participants often worked with these choices to help them understand the issues of content, intent, and politics described above. This process can be seen, for example, in the previously provided quotations about cinematography and staging in *Human Flow*.

In addition to describing and analyzing the work of particular formal choices, participants paid some attention to connecting the dots among textual features, considering how individual choices worked in concert with one another, and, at times, looking to how particular textual elements confirmed or disconfirmed their earlier interpretations. After hearing a line from *Children of Men* that explicitly acknowledged the infertility crisis in the world of the film, for example, one student exclaimed, "Oh, okay. This is all making sense now. I was so confused. I was like, 'Why is he the youngest person in the world?' I thought he was, like, a baby who was born really prematurely, but now I understand, infertility." Similarly, some called on previous sequences to help them situate moments that followed, as with one participant who responded to a shot of a destroyed landscape in *Human Flow* by noting, "I'm assuming this is back home, where [two women] were talking about" in the previous scene. Some participants also attempted to connect textual features in order to articulate the social implications of the clips. Considering *Children of Men*, for instance, one puzzled, "It feels like it will be a warning . . . for something. It seems to me like it's something environmental, because there's clearly something health-wise going on with fertility, and there also seems to be clearly issues with politics . . . and authoritarianism, because of the sign that said it's illegal to avoid fertility tests. It seems like people's bodies to some extent are being controlled or monitored, especially if they know who the youngest person in the world is." While this individual struggled to fully piece together a critique that they thought the film was making, this quotation demonstrates how an attempt to synthesize various elements of the film was a foundational element of their process.

Finally, participants engaged in a fair amount of hypothesizing or filling in the blanks based on features of the texts they observed. Observing a shot of burning livestock in *Children of Men*, for example, one suggested, "That looks like a lot of burnt animals, so I'm guessing, like, mad cow disease or something like that." Likewise, following a sequence displaying a nationalistic advertisement on a train in the same film, another observed, "It's like that quote that they always say, that the sun never sets on Britain . . . the characters will probably have colonialist perspectives on things." This process of hypothesizing could also be seen in relation to the *Human Flow* clip, as indicated in the following think-aloud extract: "They're literally cooking over fire, or is this . . . ? Yeah. They maybe don't have electricity. I'm guessing they don't, given what those camps looked like, which is just showing how horrible the living conditions are in these camps." Again, a process of extrapolating from observed details works to shape the student's understanding of what is represented and, in turn, their sense of the implications of that film. This process was quite common[2] and sometimes led students to unique and idiosyncratic interpretations.

Making Connections beyond the Text

While participants were clearly engaged in working with the features of the clips, they also called on a number of strategies that involved drawing connections to entities outside of the films themselves. Not surprisingly, given the focus of the course and the films involved in the study, the most common approach in this regard was to consider ways in which the films called on or related to historical or contemporary events. Several participants pointed out that the imagery of immigrants being detained and transported in *Children of Men* was strongly reminiscent of Holocaust imagery, for example, and worked from this connection to consider how the historical reference strengthened the film's critique of othering and anti-immigration discourse. Students also referred to more contemporary issues, from Brexit to Canada's refugee policies and practices, to help themselves understand the clips and think through their relevance. Watching the beginning of the *Human Flow* example, for instance, one participant noted, "This immediately reminds me of Syrian refugees coming onto the Greece shores, from based on what I've seen in the news." Likewise, another suggested that *Children of Men* might be speaking to "concerns that we might have today with overpopulation. So maybe in this case, they tried to reduce overpopulation . . . by not allowing reproduction."

In addition to considering connections to contemporary or historical events and contexts, participants contemplated ways in which the films resonated with their own personal lives and experiences, using these connections to help them navigate and understand the texts themselves. Multiple participants talked about particular issues or concepts they had learned in courses they were taking, for example, sometimes explaining how those ideas shaped their attention to and interpretation of the clips. Similarly, a few participants mentioned their own or family members' experiences of immigration, or time they had spent volunteering in refugee camps or traveling to places relevant to the films. After watching the *Human Flow* clip, for example, one student explained, "This a very personal film to me, because my parents fled [country] for this particular reason. Sometimes I wish I could go back and stuff, and I wonder what it would be like." Others mentioned having particular interests and passions and suggested that these shape the features they attend to in films: "I care a lot about gender politics, or I care a lot about how race is portrayed," one student noted. "I think I pay attention to those things." Such connections to personal experiences and interests were made in relation to both documentaries and fictional examples.

Many participants also engaged in a process of considering the filmic examples in relation to broader genre conventions or other related cultural texts. While some considered how the *Human Flow* clip related to other documentary or news representations, this process was particularly commonly deployed in relation to the clip from *Children of Men*. Many participants observed that the film had resonances with other examples of dystopian science fiction, working from this connection to suggest what might happen in the film and what its social implications might be. Others broadened this process, focusing not only on a particular genre but also (or rather) on patterns they saw as common to Hollywood narratives more generally: "It's Hollywood," one participant observed, "so he's probably gonna fall in love with an immigrant." Similarly, another noted, "I feel like, maybe he'll be that kind of typical reluctant hero character that you see in a lot of stories, where something will happen and he'll, I don't know, start a revolution and save the world or something." As these examples suggest, this process of relating the focal clips to other texts and examples often informed and overlapped with the strategy of hypothesizing described above.

Finally, in the post-think-aloud interviews, participants also described actively attempting to connect filmic examples to the content and context of the course in which they are shown. Several students commented that, when viewing films in class, they try to consider how the text resonates with the goals and focus of the course and, as one put it, to "relat[e] it to other works we've been reading or talking about." Some also noted attempting to determine why, specifically, the instructor might have selected the film and what they hoped students might take from it. Just as students attend actively to the intent of filmmakers, then, so too do they often consider the pedagogical intent of their instructors when they watch films in academic contexts. Arguably, this process of reading the clips in relation to course content and goals is also reflected in many of the approaches discussed above. Because students in this case had been told to approach the films as they would in a course on global challenges, central strategies included considering the social and political implications of the texts and connecting the films to real-world issues. As one participant put it, "I think because you told me to think about it in terms of, like, first-year inquiry, which is about global challenges, I was definitely looking for themes on what is going on in the world today." By the same token, I would have also been looking for these connections between reading strategies and course goals in my analysis of the data.

Absorbing Information from the Text

As the above discussion makes clear, students in the present study engaged in a large number of processes to understand, work with, and assess the texts presented to them. But in spite of all this activity, some participants also noted that, in some cases at least, they experience viewing films as a comparatively easy or passive process of receiving information. With audiovisual texts, one student claimed, "it's easy to just kind of fall into a lull of things. And often it's fine because the narration carries you along, but I find especially when I'm forced to sit down and look critically at something, there are a lot of things . . . that sometimes just go over your head when you're just sitting there and passively absorbing." Similarly, another commented that information in films is "spoon-fed," adding, "It's really nice sometimes when you have to really be engaged in reading in a lot [of] your other courses and you just get to sort of be told the information by osmosis [with film]. Just get it without thinking too much." While these comments are somewhat at odds with all of the examples of active interpretation in the data (and with scholarship demonstrating that film reception is an active process—e.g., Hall [1973] 1996), they are nonetheless worth taking seriously as indications of how some students may position themselves in relation to films in their day-to-day practice. Students may typically be less engaged in active and critical reading than they were in this study, in which they were required to voice moment-to-moment analytical observations.

At the same time, some participants noted additional perceptions that might further influence how students engage with films in class settings. Several suggested that films are powerful or that they found them especially accessible, engaging, or interesting. Nevertheless, a few participants also indicated that films sometimes seem less important, academic, or relevant than lecture material or that they can be perceived as a break from the actual content. As one suggested, "the fact that it's a video or something makes it feel less serious, in a way." Given such perceptions, some students may attend less actively to films in class settings, even if they find films engaging and enjoyable.

Whereas the quotations above indicate that this more passive, less attentive approach to interacting with films may apply to both documentary and fiction film viewing, other elements of the data suggest that text type may figure importantly in shaping students' viewing practices in this regard. For instance, a number of participants suggested that they approach documentaries expecting to learn something from them. To some extent, evidence of this approach could be found in moments of the *Human Flow* think-alouds in which students remarked that they were not previously aware of an issue represented in the clip. While some participants suggested that this expectation to learn from documentaries made them more likely to pay attention and take the process of viewing nonfiction films seriously, others noted that it, along with the fact that documentaries represent real-world situations, also made them *less* likely to engage critically with the material presented. One suggested, "I always feel like in documentaries I'm a little more, like, attentive and I'm a little more likely to . . . look at the ideas and almost, like, take them as proof." Similarly, another student noted, "I feel like I'm less critical of the content that I'm being presented in a documentary, because for some reason, I automatically assume in a lot of contexts that this is the truth.... So I'm like, 'Okay. This is real information, and I'm taking in this knowledge just automatically.'" For some, the issue of intentionality noted earlier also figured here: because they were aware that all elements of fiction films are constructed or selected, they were more likely to engage critically with fictional examples.

In contrast, some participants argued that they tended to be much *more* critical of documentary films, precisely because such texts make truth claims and the representational stakes are thus higher. As one put it, "I would like to think I'm more critical of documentaries because they can be so easily twisted to convey whatever message they want to. So I would hope I'm more critical in asking, okay, well, are they presenting this in a fair way, is it biased, how are they asking these questions of the people, who are they, whose stories are they getting, what's their motivation and intent?" Still others noted that they engaged critically with both documentary and fiction, though in different ways, or they acknowledged that they knew they *should* engage more critically with nonfiction films than they typically do. Thus, the potential for encouraging increased critical engagement seems apparent, and students' capacities in this regard are borne out by their extensive, active engagement with both documentaries and fiction films in this study.

Discussion

Like all research, the present study has limitations that should be acknowledged. Most notably, the think-aloud process is an imperfect proxy for students' typical reading behavior. As many participants noted, the process of pausing the films and voicing their thoughts was somewhat unusual and unfamiliar, not least because a former instructor was there observing them. Nevertheless, this approach does offer a useful window into the kinds of thinking processes in which students can engage and has been widely understood to offer meaningful, if partial, insights (Charters 2003; Bernstein 2010; Calder 2006). It is also worth noting that students self-selected to participate and that, since I was the sole researcher, I was not able to have others corroborate my analysis. The comparatively large number of participants for a think-aloud study, the inclusion of interviews that allowed participants to flesh out the data they contributed, and the multiple stages of analysis conducted mitigate these concerns to some extent, though they should still be borne in mind when considering the study's implications.

Foremost among these implications is the finding that students engage in a complex and overlapping array of strategies to read films when they are asked to view such texts as examples meant to prime analysis and discussion of global challenges in a related course. Clearly, this is a particular context and set of pedagogical goals, which influenced both the data generated and my analysis of those data. As such, I do not claim that the findings presented here are necessarily generalizable. Nevertheless, they do offer insight into the underexplored issue of how students read film in one academic setting, documenting a preliminary set of strategies that others might consider and test in their own contexts.

Perhaps most notably in this respect, participants expended considerable energy asking questions about the content of the clips—trying to determine what was happening, where, to whom, and why. While such comprehension is a fundamental piece of understanding and analyzing filmic texts—and, indeed, strategies for helping students ask content-based questions have been developed by educators working at the pretertiary level (Golden 2001)—it is nevertheless the case that many university instructors presenting films might hope students will do more than simply comprehend the texts themselves. For individuals with such goals, the present data suggest the potential benefits of providing students with more information about the content of film clips in advance or, perhaps, of screening examples multiple times so that students can first read for content before moving on to other levels of analysis.

Moreover, given the diverse array of reading strategies students employed in this pilot, ranging from making connections to their own lives to looking for points of resonance with historical examples and genre conventions, it might also be productive for instructors to provide framing prompts or explicit instruction that encourages students to embrace reading tactics that seem particularly important or desirable. For example, the attention some students paid to questions of filmmaker intent in the present study gave me pause, given that texts can have meanings and social implications that outstrip what their creators might have intended (Lewis 2007) and that this focus on intentionality also contributed, in some cases, to reduced critical attention to documentary films.[3] With this concern in mind, I plan to make more explicit going forward the value of focusing filmic analyses in my classes on questions of function and effect rather than simply intention. I can also emphasize the value of, and perhaps provide further direction concerning, reading strategies that seem especially relevant to my pedagogical goals, such as considering connections to contemporary and historical examples or to other relevant texts in the service of thinking through the social implications of filmic examples.

Such potential revisions offer examples of the kind of refinement to pedagogical practice that authors such as Bernstein (2010) and Stephen Bloch-Schulman (2016) suggest think-aloud data can support.

At the same time, by drawing on interview data as well, this study also documents a tension between evidence of students actively reading film clips and a perception (held by some, at least) that engaging with film is a passive and potentially frivolous activity. The notion that film is unserious and unscholarly has been acknowledged in other research (Swimelar 2013; Travis 2016), further emphasizing the need for instructional interventions that make clear to students the significant educative work that film can perform, although it might appear to be just entertainment (García 2015; Johnstone, Marquis, and Puri 2018; Marquis, Johnstone, and Puri 2020). Equally importantly, the data also underscore the need to find ways to support meaningful, critical reading of films even when such texts are approached as sites of learning. This need is particularly pronounced in relation to documentary films.

While some participants in this study suggested that documentary is seen as more serious than fiction, echoing popular understandings of documentaries as "discourses of sobriety" (Nichols 2001), many students also indicated that they were more likely to approach documentaries uncritically because such texts represent reality. Indeed, a few suggested that they do not typically engage critically with documentaries even while they acknowledged or implied that they knew they probably should. While uncritical viewing is possible in any context and may be more likely outside of the classroom, it is also worth considering in academic settings specifically. As one participant noted, documentaries shown in classes might be seen as trustworthy since they have been selected by an instructor—particularly if they are not framed explicitly as starting points for discussion and critique. Exploring how to support active, critical reading of documentary films in and outside the classroom thus remains a compelling challenge for scholars and educators.

Likewise, future studies might also explore potential variations among different viewers' approaches to reading films in a variety of academic settings. Given other research that indicates distinctions between expert and novice approaches to tasks (Bernstein 2010; Bloch-Schulman 2016), for instance, we might consider how film reading strategies develop over time and with training. Similarly, studies could explore how viewer social location and identity interrelate with approaches to film reading in course contexts, drawing on related scholarship about film spectatorship more generally (e.g., hooks [1992] 2000). Considering the range of preliminary insights generated by this pilot study, such research is likely to prove useful in advancing our understanding of the process of reading film.

Conclusion

Complementing both the growing body of teaching and learning scholarship focused on reading written texts and research that explores the potential utility of using films in university classrooms, this study explored how students engage in and experience the process of reading films in one academic context. It documented several approaches that students take to reading documentary and fiction films when asked to approach these as they might in a Global Challenges course, generating useful considerations that provide a starting point for pedagogical refinement and further research. While these considerations are primarily relevant to teaching and research focused on film reading, some also seem likely to apply to the teaching and learning of reading more broadly. Most notably in this respect, although the present study emphasizes the importance of exploring how to support critical reading of documentary films, fostering meaningful critical reading practices remains an important challenge for all scholars and teachers of reading, regardless of the types of text on which they focus.

Notes

1. A follow-up interview question asking students whether they thought the clips were significant in any way provided additional opportunities for participants to speak to social and political implications if and when they saw these, which might also partially account for the prevalence of this practice.

2. As the previous quotations suggest, hypothesizing frequently happened unprompted during the think-alouds and interviews. Nevertheless, I sometimes asked participants during follow-up interviews what they thought might happen in the films, effectively inviting them to hypothesize and contributing to the commonality of this strategy.

3. The point about unintended implications should be taken not to suggest that films have effects on their own, without human intervention, but rather to underscore that the choices made in constructing films can have functions that were not consciously meant. For example, the creators of *Children of Men* may not have intended to reproduce a white savior narrative by casting Clive Owen as the film's protagonist, but this outcome can reasonably be read from the film nevertheless.

References

Achberger, Karen R. 2014. "Flipping German Cinema." *Cinema Journal Teaching Dossier* 2 (2). http://www.teachingmedia.org/flipping-german-cinema/.

Algeo, Katie. 2007. "Teaching Cultural Geography with *Bend It Like Beckham*." *Journal of Geography* 106 (3): 133–143.

Andrist, Lester, Valerie Chepp, Paul Dean, and Michael V. Miller. 2014. "Toward a Video Pedagogy: A Teaching Typology with Learning Goals." *Teaching Sociology* 42 (3): 196–206.

Banning, Maggi. 2008. "The Think-Aloud Approach as an Educational Tool to Develop and Assess Clinical Reasoning in Undergraduate Students." *Nurse Education Today* 28 (1): 8–14.

Bass, Randy, and Sherry Lee Linkon. 2008. "On the Evidence of Theory: Close Reading as a Disciplinary Model for Writing about Teaching and Learning." *Arts and Humanities in Higher Education* 7 (3): 245–261.

Ber, Rosalie, and Gideon Alroy. 2002. "Teaching Professionalism with the Aid of Trigger Films." *Medical Teacher* 24 (5): 528–531.

Bernstein, Jeffrey L. 2010. "Using 'Think-Alouds' to Understand Variations in Political Thinking." *Journal of Political Science Education* 6 (1): 49–69.

Blasco, Pablo González, and Graciela Moreto. 2012. "Teaching Empathy through Movies: Reaching Learners' Affective Domain in Medical Education." *Journal of Education and Learning* 1 (1): 22–34.

Bloch-Schulman, Stephen. 2016. "A Critique of Methods in the Scholarship of Teaching and Learning in Philosophy." *Teaching and Learning Inquiry* 4 (1): 80–94. https://doi.org/10.20343/teachlearninqu.4.1.10.

Bright, Anita. 2015. "Why Are We Watching Funny Videos in Our Pedagogy Course? Deconstructing Humorous Videos to Foster Social Activism in Educators." *European Journal of Humour Research* 3 (4): 36–53. https://pdxscholar.library.pdx.edu/edu_fac/95/.

Brown, Stanley P., JohnEric W. Smith, Matthew McAllister, and LeeAnn Joe. 2017. "Superhero Physiology: The Case for Captain America." *Advances in Physiology Education* 41 (1): 16–24.

Calcagno, Justine. 2015. "A Current Media Approach to Learning and Teaching in Psychology of Women Courses." *Psychology of Women Quarterly* 39 (2): 268–271.

Calder, Lendol. 2006. "Uncoverage: Toward a Signature Pedagogy for the History Survey." *Journal of American History* 92 (4): 1358–1370. https://doi.org/10.2307/4485896.

Charters, Elizabeth. 2003. "The Use of Think-Aloud Methods in Qualitative Research: An Introduction to Think-Aloud Methods." *Brock Education* 12 (2): 68–82.

Forsberg, Elenita, Kristina Ziegert, Håkan Hult, and Uno Fors. 2014. "Clinical Reasoning in Nursing, a Think-Aloud Study Using Virtual Patients—a Base for an Innovative Assessment." *Nurse Education Today* 34 (4): 538–542.

García, José. 2015. "Learning from Bad Teachers: The Neoliberal Agenda for Education in Popular Media." *Critical Education* 6 (13). http://ices.library.ubc.ca/index.php/criticaled/article/view/184935.

Golden, John. 2001. *Reading in the Dark: Using Film as a Tool in the English Classroom*. Urbana, IL: National Council of Teachers of English.

Hall, Stuart. (1973) 1996. "Encoding/Decoding." In *Media Studies—a Reader*, edited by P. Marris and S. Thornham, 41–49. Edinburgh: Edinburgh University Press.

Happel-Parkins, Alison, and Jennifer Esposito. 2015. "Using Popular Culture Texts in the Classroom to Interrogate Issues of Gender Transgression Related Bullying." *Educational Studies* 51 (1): 3–16.

Holland, Jack. 2014. "Video Use and the Student Learning Experience in Politics and International Relations." *Politics* 34 (3): 263–274.

hooks, bell. (1992) 2000. "The Oppositional Gaze: Black Female Spectators." In *Film and Theory: An Anthology*, edited by R. Stam and T. Miller, 510–523. Malden, MA: Blackwell.

Hutchings, Pat. 2000. "Introduction: Approaching the Scholarship of Teaching and Learning." In *Opening Lines: Approaches to the Scholarship of Teaching and Learning*, edited by Pat Hutchings, 1–10. Menlo Park, CA: Carnegie Foundation for the Advancement of Teaching.

Johnstone, Katelyn, Elizabeth Marquis, and Varun Puri. 2018. "Public Pedagogy and Representations of Higher Education in Popular Film: New Ground for the Scholarship of Teaching and Learning." *Teaching and Learning Inquiry* 6 (1): 25–37. https://doi.org/10.20343/teachlearninqu.6.1.4.

Kabooha, Raniah Hassen. 2016. "Using Movies in EFL Classrooms: A Study Conducted at the English Language Institute (ELI), King Abdul-Aziz University." *English Language Teaching* 9 (3): 248–257.

Lameborshi, Eralda L. 2014. "Contrapuntal Reading in World Cinema." *Cinema Journal Teaching Dossier* 2 (1). http://www.teachingmedia.org/contrapuntal-reading-world-cinema/.

Lewis, Randolph. 2007. "Questionable Intent: Documentary Cinema and the Authorial Fallacy." *Studies in Documentary Film* 1 (3): 265–278.

Luccasen, R. Andrew, and M. Kathleen Thomas. 2010. "Simpsonomics: Teaching Economics Using Episodes of *The Simpsons*." *Journal of Economic Education* 41 (2): 136–149.

Lumlertgul, Nuttha, Naruchorn Kijpaisalratana, Nuttorn Pityaratstian, and Danai Wangsaturaka. 2009. "Cinemeducation: A Pilot Student Project Using Movies to Help Students Learn Medical Professionalism." *Medical Teacher* 31 (7): e327–e332.

Madsen, Kenneth D. 2014. "Blue Indians: Teaching the Political Geography of Imperialism with Fictional Film." *Journal of Geography* 113 (2): 47–57.

Marcus, Alan S., and Jeremy D. Stoddard. 2007. "Tinsel Town as Teacher: Hollywood Film in the High School Classroom." *History Teacher* 40 (3): 303–330.

Marquis, Elizabeth, Katelyn Johnstone, and Varun Puri. 2020. "Just Entertainment? Student and Faculty Responses to the Pedagogy of Media Representations of Higher Education." *Pedagogy, Culture, and Society* 28 (1): 59–76.

Marquis, Elizabeth, Cassia Wojcik, Effie Lin, and Victoria McKinnon. 2020. "Meaningful Teaching Tool and/or 'Cool Factor'? Instructors' Perceptions of Using Film and Video within Teaching and Learning." *Journal of the Scholarship of Teaching and Learning* 20 (1): 130–150.

McEntee, Joy. 2007. "Inducing Double Vision, or Does the 'Threshold Concept' Account for How Students Learn about the Hollywood Film?" *Australasian Journal of American Studies* 26 (2): 131–151.

Merriam, Sharan B. 2009. *Qualitative Research: A Guide to Design and Implementation*. 3rd ed. San Francisco: Jossey-Bass.

Middendorf, Joan, and David Pace. 2004. "Decoding the Disciplines: A Model for Helping Students Learn Disciplinary Ways of Thinking." *New Directions for Teaching and Learning* 98:1–12.

Miller-Young, Janice E. 2013. "Calculations and Expectations: How Engineering Students Describe Three-Dimensional Forces." *Canadian Journal for the Scholarship of Teaching and Learning* 4 (1). http://dx.doi.org/10.5206/cjsotl-rcacea.2013.1.4.

Nichols, Bill. 2001. *Introduction to Documentary*. Bloomington: Indiana University Press.

Olson, Joann S., Linda Autry, and Jeffry Moe. 2016. "Moving beyond 'Bookish Knowledge': Using Film-Based Assignments to Promote Deep Learning." *Adult Learning* 27 (2): 60–67.

Peacock, Jessica, Ralph Covino, Jessica Auchter, Jennifer Boyd, Hope Klug, Craig Laing, and Lindsay Irvin. 2018. "University Faculty Perceptions and Utilization of Popular Culture in the Classroom." *Studies in Higher Education* 43 (4): 601–613.

Pelton, Julie A. 2013. "Seeing the Theory Is Believing: Writing about Film to Reduce Theory Anxiety." *Teaching Sociology* 41 (1): 106–120.

Sealey, Kelvin Shawn. 2008. *Film, Politics, and Education: Cinematic Pedagogy across the Disciplines*. New York: Peter Lang.

Sigler, Thomas, and Roberto I. Albandoz. 2014. "Beyond Representation: Film as a Pedagogical Tool in Urban Geography." *Journal of Geography* 113 (2): 58–67.

Swimelar, Safia. 2013. "Visualizing International Relations: Assessing Student Learning through Film." *International Studies Perspectives* 14 (1): 14–38.

Travis, Mitchell. 2016. "Teaching Professional Ethics through Popular Culture." *Law Teacher* 50 (2): 147–159.

Elizabeth Marquis is Associate Professor in the Arts and Science Program and the School of the Arts at McMaster University. Her teaching and learning scholarship focuses on film and media texts as public pedagogy, intersections between teaching and learning and questions of equity and justice, and student-faculty pedagogical partnership in postsecondary education.

II. READING IN SPECIFIC CONTEXTS

6

READING-TO-WRITE

Rehearsing the Doctoral Literature Review

ROSEMARY GREEN

Prelude

Doctoral students of any discipline are assumed to be proficient at reading, understanding, and writing academic discourse. Studies of doctoral education indicate otherwise; indeed, doctoral students can become overwhelmed by the quantity, complexity, and intensity of academic reading expectations (Green 2009; Kwan 2008). Nevertheless, "reading in graduate school is of utmost importance" because it is central to doctoral students' abilities to grasp foundational disciplinary knowledge and learn methods for gathering and synthesizing information during and beyond the doctorate (McMinn et al. 2009, 233).

Despite its role as a fundamental point of entry into the disciplines, effective academic reading is not easily defined, learned, or taught: "Learning to read *properly* becomes one of the most salient hurdles faced by students in postgraduate education" (Wohl and Fine 2017, 216). Tacitly prescribed by each discipline (Pace 2004), proper reading is identified, for example, by knowing how and when to deploy alternating strategies such as skimming and reading deeply (Wohl and Fine 2017). Doctoral students must read and appropriate rhetorically dense works while developing disciplinary-specific discursive practices, yet most are left to negotiate secondary discourses on their own (McAlpine 2012; Wohl and Fine 2017). The literature of doctoral pedagogies is clear: seldom are graduate students provided direct instruction in reading and writing literacies because, presumably, they have acquired such literacies elsewhere (Green 2009; Luke and Freebody 1997).

In this chapter, I detail the instructional approaches and activities used in a reading, writing, and research course in a doctor of musical arts (DMA) program at Shenandoah Conservatory, a conservatory of music in a private university in Virginia. The pedagogical focus of the course is the doctoral literature review that students drafted to support their particular research topics. I share student narratives to represent the reading practices and experiences of doctoral students of music, who, as their discipline required, routinely contended with multiple forms of academic rhetoric. The narratives I gathered from DMA student interviews and responses to writing prompts personalize what otherwise might be just a recounting of instructional exercises. The theme of reader agency emerged as I interpreted student narratives, and I drew on studies such as Lynn McAlpine's (2012), who centers the role of reading in the development of doctoral students' academic identity. Gary Alan Fine and Hannah Wohl (2018) consider academic reading in a similar vein, proposing that reading competence is a powerful influence on one's standing in an academic field. These works are among the few to associate doctoral students' reading practices with negotiating "actions in discursive situations" (Walker 2015, 4).

The Performers: DMA Students as Academic Readers

I hope to "shine a light" (McAlpine 2012, 351) on the perspectives and experiences of doctoral students as researchers-in-training learning to read (and write) as music scholars. McAlpine (2012) endorses direct pedagogy to support graduate reading processes, such as recognizing reading as an essential component of doctoral training, thereby ensuring that students are introduced to readings in a range of genres and scaffolding learners' engagements with "the reading practices essential to the doctorate" (359). In this context, genre "describes a form of discourse recognizable as a common set of structural or thematic qualities" (Hart-Davidson 2015, 39). Students of music encounter disciplinary-specific textual genres that vary considerably, and they must learn to move among these texts. DMA students read across literary genres that encompass histories, biographies, theses and dissertations, essays, analyses of musical works, critiques and reviews, and empirical research. For example, DMA students read articles from journals such as *Nineteenth-Century Piano Music* and *Jazz Research Journal*; annotated historical editions of musical scores; compendia of analytical, theoretical, and musicological texts; and treatises on historical performance practices. No single formula for reading these literary forms is available or even feasible; readers must adjust their strategies to accommodate the purpose, audience, and stylistic conventions of each genre.

All graduate students arrive at text with their own schema; "one right [graduate reading] practice" does not exist (Roldan and Turns 2018, n.p.). They must decide for themselves which texts to read, which to set aside, and "'what counts' as reading" (Baker et al. 2019, 143). Literature reviewing requires reading extensively and deploying multiple reading-to-write strategies. When students of any discipline are encouraged to uncover their own methods of textual engagement, as were students in the Advanced Research and Writing course, they begin to comprehend increasingly "complex negotiations" with disciplinary-specific discourse and the communities that privilege those discursive practices (Baker et al. 2019, 150). This chapter aims to make visible the practices and experiences of doctoral students immersed in music scholarship and details reading-to-write activities that otherwise might have remained "unspecified" (Pace 2004, 13). While the reading-to-write experiences and practices of doctoral students of music frame this chapter, students in all disciplines face similar challenges with text. Indeed, the studies cited here originate from several fields, demonstrating interest in academic reading across multiple disciplines.

The research, teaching, and learning project outlined in this chapter is informed by frameworks of critical literacy (Gee 1996; Lea and Street 1998; Luke and Freebody 1997). All doctoral learners must confront and then train themselves in secondary discourses that function to socialize newcomers to the scholarship of their research fields (Gee 1996; Green 2009). They must learn to read themselves into disciplinary-specific ways of thinking and doing; they must unpack and decode value-laden language of their fields of study. Critical readers, such as the DMA students in this project, recognize the significance of interrogating the privileged text of published scholarship (Green 2009; Luke and Freebody 1997). Referencing the process of decoding the disciplines (Middendorf and Pace 2004; Pace 2004), J. Peter Burkholder (2011, 94) grants that, while music history students must learn facts, they also learn "how to think like music historians" by reading from and writing about music scholarship. Implicit in the model of decoding the disciplines is a critical perspective, one that requires examining power relationships ever present in academic fields.

By and large, academic reading is subordinate to academic writing, in part because the act of reading for any purpose is undertaken privately and usually silently (Kwan 2008; McAlpine 2012; van Pletzen 2006). The dominance of writing over reading is challenged by work from Sarah J. Mann (2000), from Ermien van Pletzen (2006), by essayists in the recent collection *Reconnecting Reading and Writing* (Horning and Kraemer 2013), and by contributors in this collection.

DOCTORAL READERS AND THE LITERATURE REVIEW

I frame DMA students' encounters with reading-to-write as a trajectory through which students strengthen their literacy skills and gain confidence as academic readers and incoming members of scholarly communities. Attempting to move beyond individual courses and instructional practices to reach broader teaching and learning settings, I describe instructional activities that may be transferable to other disciplinary settings. I contend that the scholarly literature review acts as a vehicle through which students learn academic literacies, particularly academic reading, and it was a principal requirement of the course. The first of the following sections addresses the centrality of the literature review in the disciplines. In the next sections, the design of the Advanced Research and Writing course is described, and examples of instructional activities are outlined. Student narratives illustrate their reflections on their experiences with reading-to-write literature reviews, and the chapter closes with a brief discussion.

MAIN THEME: CENTERING THE LITERATURE REVIEW

Chris M. Golde (2007, 2) identifies the literature review as a "signature pedagogy" of the doctorate, characteristic of professional and research doctorates across all disciplines. The scholarly review of the literature conveys "strong and consistent messages of the discipline and the form of inquiry required in the discipline" (Johnson, Lee, and Green 2000, 287). The process of reviewing the literature affords a site where students continue to unpack and rehearse the secondary discourse of their disciplines. When doctoral students read themselves into their disciplines (McAlpine 2012; Wisker 2015), they learn to wrestle with the debates, alliances, and other contingencies communicated, subtly or overtly, through the literature (Kamler and Thomson 2006). Becky S. C. Kwan (2008, 42) identifies literature reviewing "as a strategic site of research" where doctoral reading, writing, and researching align. Such studies shape the body of inquiry regarding doctoral students' approaches to literature reviewing, wherein the act of reading and reading choices are socially mediated and disciplinary-specific.

Similar to the role of reading in the academic lives of music students, literature reviewing as a pedagogical feature in music specialisms has received little notice from the research community. One exception is the work of Patrick K. Freer and Angela Barker (2008), who explore reading and reviewing literature with their graduate music education students. Their practice-based investigation focuses on teaching and learning the literature review process; as I did, they guided their students' understanding of "the value of literature reviews" and experience with "how literature reviews can assist readers of research" (Freer and Barker 2008, 71). When student reviewers of literature read, write about, and critically synthesize scholarship, they encounter defining yet tacit discursive expectations. Course activities that guided literature-reviewing activities were aimed at strengthening literacy practices of DMA newcomers to the territory of music scholarship where they would eventually be situated. Literature reviewing provides students opportunities to reposition themselves as "agents who *use* and *evaluate* the research of others, in order to make a place for their own work" (Kamler and Thomson 2006, 35; emphasis in original).

The Course as Instructional and Research Site

By design, the Advanced Research and Writing course aimed to provide DMA students tools for developing and practicing scholarly reading, researching, and writing skills that supported original doctoral research topics. Each student applied the literature review to a proposal for her or his culminating DMA research project. Scaffolded activities and discussions often emphasized reading, with particular attention to reading for the purpose of writing a literature review. As Cynthia R. Haller (2013, 200) notes, "Generating reading-informed writing appropriately designed to reach academic readers is at the heart of academic discourse," and nowhere is reading-informed writing more evident than in the literature review. Reading, conceptualizing, and writing were approached as distinct yet coconstructed literacies endemic to literature reviewing. Because each student focused entirely on her or his own research interest, the course and course activities were framed as inquiry-based. Advanced Research and Writing provided the sort of structured and supportive setting that Sarah M. Urquhart et al. (2016) recommend, as musician-students learned to wrestle with reading in subdisciplines such as musicology, music theory, and music pedagogy.

The decision to feature doctoral reading practices and experiences in the Advanced Research and Writing course resulted from my ongoing interest in the role of academic reading in the lives of doctoral students (Green 2009). Consequently, the course afforded a site for an SOTL investigation into DMA students' reading practices and experiences when engaged in crafting literature reviews. The 2011–2018 research project described in this chapter was approved by the Institutional Review Board of Shenandoah University. To foreground academic reading, I routinely posed writing prompts to spark students' metacognitive awareness of their reading practices, positioning, and agency with text. Each cohort of DMA students submitted responses to three or more writing prompts concerning their reading strategies and reactions to academic reading. I gathered approximately 150 reflections of 200–250 words from 65 students throughout 2011–2018; not all students completed every prompt. In May 2018, I interviewed four students who successfully completed the course in 2016 and 2017. Excerpts of written (noted with a W) and interview (noted with an I) narratives from eighteen students appear throughout the chapter. Encouragingly, one student said, "Reading is so important to what we do, and I think it's not talked about enough" (I).

Thematic Sequencing: Reading-to-Write

Pedagogical principles of transparency and scaffolding underpinned the course. Because the "practices of teaching and learning are rarely transparent" (Gale and Golde 2004, 9), I appreciated that the students should understand not only what they were asked to do but also why. Therefore, I detailed the assignments as well as the rationale for staging assignments, the relevance of assignments, and each assignment's role in the course scheme. Knowing that academic reading and writing inevitably take longer than anyone anticipates, I asked them to start with small bits of reading and writing from their individual research readings. As their research projects evolved and their sense of agency grew, I provided less feedback and discontinued direct instruction. Most reading and writing assignments were scaffolded, allowing students to manage a few or only one learning task for a time, which facilitated increasing mastery (Burkholder 2011; Freer 2009; Pace 2004). Eventually, individual writing drafts contributed to final literature review drafts and research proposals. Each reading-to-write assignment was dependent on preceding assignments, and final writing projects were cumulative of earlier ones.

The next sections describe instructional reading-to-write activities and topics encompassed in the first several weeks of the course as students grappled with finding and reading text. During those weeks, students experimented with new reading strategies such as reading aloud, and they wrote abstracts, critiques, and annotated bibliographies. They also completed activities for conceptualizing and organizing bodies of literature.

By the last few weeks, they had developed reading-to-write tools and had become confident with several; they were self-directed in the final weeks and concluded the semester by integrating their literature reviews into research proposal drafts.

Making Reading Visible

During the first weekly session, we discussed the invisibility of academic reading (Baker et al. 2019; van Pletzen 2006), which elicited some surprise, as they were not accustomed to observing their own reading practices and had not necessarily considered the privileging of academic writing over reading. In all likelihood, their reading practices had not been assessed. We closed our first session by reading aloud Anne Lamott's "Short Assignments" (1994), an exercise meant to reintroduce them to a familiar and often effective strategy transferable to academic reading. In later reflections regarding their changing approaches to reading, two DMA students acknowledged the value of speaking text: "After a few paragraphs of practice, I started to get a little better . . . I read with greater attention, focus, and intensity" (W). Another student reported feeling silly at first, although reading aloud "made me read slower, and I found that . . . I needed to restate some sentences to truly understand what the author was trying to say" (W). Following Robert Scholes's advice (2002, 168), I could confirm that "reading aloud makes the reading process evident."

Each year, DMA students entered the course with individual topics of inquiry and immediately began gathering and sorting through readings relevant to their research. Realizing that their research must offer an original contribution to knowledge in their fields, students began reviewing the literature by aligning their thinking with other scholarship and identifying gaps and silences into which they could insert their own work. We reinforced the essential role and relative invisibility of academic reading in an examination of McAlpine's "Shining a Light on Doctoral Reading" (2012). After that session, a student wrote that the article struck "similarities in my own experiences to the narratives. Many of the [doctoral students] spoke of how they had difficulty with reading, feeling like they don't understand information that they think they should know" (W). This reflection resonates with other students' expressions of uncertainty and intimidation, which are explored later.

Reading is made visible when readers observe themselves. One's reading practices become public when others, such as peers, read and comment on texts that the reader has authored. Students in the course routinely received peer and instructor feedback (Pace 2004) on their writing, individually and in the whole-class setting. As a group, we sometimes critiqued individual students' writing, where, implicitly, reading practices were revealed. When academic reading is linked to academic writing, a student's reading, in some sense, becomes embodied through his or her writing. Mann (2000, 313) writes, "Thus when students engage in reading for academic purposes they are no longer engaging in a private activity undertaken for its own sake, but in an activity whose evaluated outcomes will—crucially—tell them something about themselves, and in particular something about themselves as students. It will tell them something about their worth in the eyes of others, and will have the potential to shape their changing image of themselves as university students."

As a whole-class exercise, students and I occasionally wordsmithed selected passages from their drafts. We offered suggestions, asked questions, and encouraged each writer to examine his or her writing through readers' eyes. Despite their profiles as accomplished musicians who performed in countless settings (Conkling 2003), public critique of their writing was unwelcome for some. Many students later said that the public wordsmithing sessions had been helpful, while others made clear that they preferred to keep their reading and writing private.

Practice, Practice: Writing Abstracts, Critiques, and Annotated Bibliographies

In the first weeks, students submitted formal statements of their proposed topics, supported by preliminary bibliographies of scholarly sources. While selecting initial sources, students became better acquainted with the form and function of abstracts, so we moved to abstract writing. They identified a scholarly source, usually a journal article, and read it closely in order to write from and about it. I challenged them to ignore authors' abstracts and write their own instead. Reading and writing were shaped by tasks of identifying research intent and focus, methods, findings, and, most important, rationale for the work—the "so what?"

This activity marked a shift from the familiar strategy of reading for in-class discussion, a pragmatic and short-term approach to reading for information and retention. Instead, I urged them to read as writers (Bunn 2011), to consider "the choices other writers have made in order to make their texts writerly" (Kamler and Thomson 2006, 128) by examining uses of organization, grammar, syntax, citation practices, and thesis development. Thus, students were required to read for more than content in this "taken-for-granted academic practice" exercise of abstract writing (Kamler and Thomson 2006, 85).

Then they built on abstracting by drafting critiques. To prepare, we unpacked Robert Christgau's "Writing about Music Is Writing First" (2005), a multilayered critique of popular music reviews. Richly nuanced, his appraisal of others' rock and popular music critiques required several passes for most of us as the students and I read for content, argument, and positioning. His confrontational posture emerged immediately: "This piece is designed to inspire and / or shame readers into paying closer attention to how they use language when they describe or analyze music" (Christgau 2005, 415). The students recognized that so provocative an approach might color or even bias a reader's interpretation of the piece.

As when writing abstracts, students critiqued a source from their expanding topical bibliographies, one that articulated an argument or a philosophical position substantiated by evidence and logic. They read critically and reviewed their readings guided by prompts such as, What claims does the author make? How is the argument framed? What is the work's place in scholarship? What contextual/sociocultural influences are at play? As Barbara Kamler and Pat Thomson (2006) observe, students can be reluctant to pass judgment on published scholars, and my students too were concerned that the act of critiquing was equivalent to criticizing. I emphasized the importance of differentiating critique from unmitigated criticism and explained that a well-conceived critical stance arises from reason and evidence, while criticism can be emotional in nature. By drafting critiques of works with which they were already familiar, they learned to temper subjective criticism with evidence-based critique and to consider the contributions of others' works as well as the shortcomings.

Hence, there arose "a possible connection between understanding text as discourse (rather than text as truth) and understanding that a text can be critically challenged" (Abbott 2013, 194–195). Reinforcing writing conventions of music scholarship for themselves and each other, they read their peers' critiques and offered feedback on the effectiveness of conveying and evaluating the work's overarching argument and use of evidence. This became an exercise in engaging critically with the authors of published works and with their peers as authors (Abbott 2013).

By writing critiques and assessing their peers' writing, they prepared for the next writing-from-reading assignment and drafted critical annotated bibliographies comprising several scholarly entries. They were expected to compose a coherent body of sources relevant to their research topics as the basis for their literature review drafts. Instructions for writing annotations were the same as those for writing critiques, with one addition. In order to draft well-conceived bibliographies of critical annotations, students were required to identify and articulate relationships among sources, effectively initiating a synthesis of the literature conceptually and in writing.

The activities of writing abstracts, critiques, and critical annotated bibliographies required repeated readings of the same works, affording students multiple opportunities to engage with their sources for different purposes. Over time, their understandings of texts became deeper, more selective, and increasingly effective (Wisker 2015). By returning to salient readings, one student recritiqued the works and self as reader: "In my recent reading experiences such as the texts for the annotated bibliography assignment, I find myself taking a moment to put things in perspective. By doing so, I am essentially 're-viewing' the text, acknowledging and factoring in historical and cultural circumstances. Then I ask myself the question of whether or not such factors alter my initial view of the text" (W). Such textual reengagements imbued the act of reading with "other forms of agency and action on the part of the reader," thus enabling the reader "to construct a relationship with . . . discourses of the text" (Luke and Freebody 1997, 215).

Rehearsals: Drafting Literature Reviews

The doctoral enterprise of any discipline requires that all members "enter into the discourse and commentaries surrounding the works of literature that have grown and evolved over time" (Golde 2007, 347). To foster a comprehensive (or integrative) view of the bodies of literature the students were reading, I presented two methods of reading for conversations in the literature: concept mapping and genealogical tracing. As Kamler and Thomson (2006) instruct, one point of departure for developing a well-synthesized literature review occurs when the reader-writer visualizes or maps ideas, theories, arguments, and the like.

Students found that creating a conceptual matrix of central themes across their sources was useful for contextualizing and envisioning associations among the works and the scholars who generated those works. "Mapping the field of knowledge production" (Kamler and Thomson 2006, 46) helped these doctoral reader-writers "identify connections between ideas and arguments and identify relationships that exist between individual pieces of work" (47). First, they established recurrent concepts or themes in a small group of sources that were particularly relevant to their topics. For one student, literature about the topic of memorizing a new piece of music revealed conceptual themes such as retrieval practice, memorization, performance, structure, and repetition. Charting themes and the sources associated with each theme helped the student visualize where and among whom particular discussions were conducted. According to another student, "Reading to write has changed my approach to reading in that I try to use the matrix to draw immediate comparisons in articles before I even read them" (W).

By reading extensively in their research fields, students were witnessing scholars' postures evolving through their publications. Crafting thematic matrices marked an important step for the students, when reading-to-write became a site of metacognitive awareness, not only of their own practices but also of disciplinary-specific literacies transmitted through reading and writing. They realized that texts were not necessarily "autonomous and authoritative, but contingent, open to critical examination, and connected with other texts in multiple ways within various communities of practice" (Haller 2013, 199).

I introduced another view on scholarship as a conversation by suggesting that they conceptualize bodies of literature in genealogical terms (Green 2009). First, students selected übersources, often-cited works regarded as seminal in their fields of inquiry. Consulting the works' bibliographies, we examined the sources that authors of these übersources used and explored the secondary sources as ancestors of the überworks. Next, we looked for descendants, other authors who referenced the überscholars' pieces. Although a simple activity, it stimulated tracing the debates, alliances, silences and dominances and seeking the conversations and voices in the literature. I charged them "to imagine the otherness of the text's author" (Scholes 2002, 166) and to remember that the works they were reading were generated by people, that the sources were not just words on pages.

Each writing-from-reading exercise set the stage for following activities. Abstract writing made each student the authority of one important source. Critique writing allowed students to analyze another meaningful source and to distinguish their own voices from the author's. They continued to rehearse critiquing and synthesizing by writing critical annotated bibliographies, which led to drafting literature reviews. In the last weeks of the semester, they submitted a series of three increasingly expanding literature review drafts. The drafts were staged throughout a few weeks, allowing students to engage in the recursive nature of interpreting and generating text (Wisker 2015). Process and product were inseparable.

Theme and Variations: Student Reflections on Reading-to-Write

Metacognitive Awareness

Metacognition is nominally referred to as thinking about thinking. DMA students, accustomed to reflecting on their artistic identities and skills, were eager to practice self-observation as doctoral learners, readers, researchers, and writers. I introduced them to metacognition as a means of activating deeper insights into their ways of reading, their reasons for reading, and their personal reactions to reading-to-write. I encouraged them to engage in metacognitive awareness (Flavell 1979), to examine their reading practices consciously, to observe their own reading strategies and purposes, and to notice their cognitive and emotional reactions to reading. In the process, students were constructing knowledge about themselves as readers and about "the reading strategies they are practicing and testing out on a range of texts" (Carillo 2017, 190–191).

Metacognitive awareness triggered "careful reflection" (Conor 2016, 18) on the interaction between the learners and activities inherent in the process of learning about themselves as academic readers. Some students easily located themselves as both readers and musicians, shown by this interpretation of the intrinsic association between reading musical scores (reading music) and reading about topics in music: "The parallels of reading music and reading prose are apparent. I notice that increased exposure to reading for certain weeks at a stretch correlates to greater speed and accuracy in sight-reading music.... I find myself spending equal amounts of time reading in the library and practicing in the practice room. The similarities between the two are obvious: [endless] hours of practicing are akin to [plodding] through pages and pages of readings" (W). Erin Conor (2016, 18) recommends helping students recognize, as this student did, and develop their "metacognitive capabilities" to strengthen "valuable skills that transfer to their creative lives."

I introduced the Metacognitive Awareness of Reading Strategies Inventory (MARSI; Mokhtari and Reichard 2002) as a tool for students to observe and assess their own methods of reading academically. The thirty-item instrument lists reading strategies, such as "I have a purpose in mind when I'm reading" and "I decide what to read and what to ignore," that readers rate on a scale of 1 to 5 (never to always). My purposes for asking them to take the inventory were threefold: to remind them to remain attuned to their reading practices, to assure themselves that they were using legitimate reading strategies already, and to introduce them to reading strategies they may not have considered. Shortly after being introduced to the MARSI, one student described two new techniques for absorbing textual landscapes that allowed more productive reading: reading "the abstract, introduction, and conclusion first to get the gist of the work" and, even more helpful, reading "the first 1–2 sentences under each heading" (W). At different points in the course, I urged interrogating their interactions with academic reading as a means of realizing "opportunities to learn *and* opportunities to be aware of learning" (Roldan and Turns 2018, n.p.).

Student narratives explored in this section exemplify further shifts in reading strategies and students' sense of themselves as scholarly readers. I gathered narratives from writing prompts designed to elicit metacognitive awareness of their reading practices and experiences and of themselves as readers of scholarship in music and associated disciplines. I also interviewed four students who had completed the course. When asked to reflect on the meaning of the act of reading academically and to describe themselves as academic readers, students often revealed a metacognitive attentiveness to their discursive actions and awareness of agency as increasingly competent readers. These exemplars illustrate students' ways of making reading visible for themselves and offer insights into doctoral reading for us as their readers. The following narrative excerpts are organized into two themes—"Shifts in Reading Practices," which centers on students' awareness of adjusting their reading strategies, and "Agency: DMA Students as Readers," which focuses on their sense of independence and competence.

Shifts in Reading Practices

Students' metacognitive explorations into their reading behaviors legitimized, enlightened, and made visible academic reading and writing. Observing the effects of and their reactions to reading, students became more attuned to their strategies, thereby self-validating their roles as academic readers. Like most doctoral students, those in the DMA course wrestled with practical matters such as the volume of reading and the fleeting amount of time allowed to accomplish reading tasks. After completing the course, one student described responding to these issues with self-discipline and reprioritization: "Honestly, I think that what I've had to learn is how to deal with the sheer volume of things that I have to read, figuring out how to budget time. You really do have to prioritize both time and mental energy. . . . Sometimes it's knowing when to put all the distractions away and just do it" (I). Another said simply, "I have learned that

I must budget myself more time to read such academic articles as they require more 'disciplined' reading strategies" (W). Academic reading and, subsequently, knowledge building require time (Golde 2007, 348); as musicians, performers, and teachers, the DMA students were tightly scheduled, yet they highly valued the time and energy necessary for learning to read and write as student-scholars.

Most were acutely aware of the privileged language of scholarship. The necessity to confront discursive expectations as readers and as writers who must replicate secondary discourse arose in several reflections. As one student wrote, "The material is often more dense than typical writing and clouded with sophisticated words, some of which I have never encountered before, forcing me to look up definitions" (W). Despite being obliged to adopt another practice, the reader acknowledged the necessity of using linguistic tools such as dictionaries. Others described the task of learning new language differently. One said that encountering a new word offered incentive to "look it up in the dictionary"; from this practice emerged the insight that "the act of doing that made me realize how good certain words are, how creative you can be with them" (W). Another reflected a similar realization of having successfully confronted rhetorical density: "Once you [get beyond] acquainting yourself with new vocabulary, you start reading more sensitively" (W). Reading properly in one's discipline means learning to read sensitively, critically, and with curiosity.

By metarecognizing and managing rhetorical and practical demands, students refined their reading techniques. They also recognized changes in their intellectual engagements with and approaches to text. One established an intentional reading style by first inspecting the landscape, exploring the author's intent and structure of the work, and then proceeding to a more detailed reading: "[I am] definitely much more analytical. . . . Before, I wouldn't really think about trying to analyze what is the author trying to say before I start reading—from the title, from the abstract, just having a skim over the sections. . . . But now I analyze it from that perspective—thinking about its structure [as I] read through" (I). Similarly, another student scoped the entire site of a work and then restructured its content to suit the doctoral focus: "Rather than simply listing the main ideas, I recompose them to form a new text. By discerning of only the most important ideas within a piece of writing, I am able to integrate the central ideas in a meaningful way. I notice that by using this strategy, I retain more of what I read" (W). By adjusting text, the student gained deeper understanding of the readings, a stage in preparing for dialogic entry into the discipline (Golde 2007, 348).

Near the end of the semester, one student pointed to the intersection of reading, writing, and thinking: "I find myself not just reading more for writing, but thinking more about the topic in hand. It has been [a relief] to know that my writing has been fueled by my reading, that ideas and words come quicker to the hand for writing" (W). A natural synergy among literacy practices and conceptualizing occurred as the students continued to practice reading-to-write, thereby authenticating their own voices as writers. As students moved through the exercises, their remarks signaled that they became more skilled and confident with disciplinary-specific ways of reading, writing, and creating knowledge.

Agency: DMA Students as Readers

The association of agency and metacognition became apparent as learners continued to bid for disciplinary positioning. Clay Walker (2015, 15) notes, "Agency invites a consideration of metacognitive activities, such as reflection and reflective writing that might generate opportunities for writers to compose new agencies." The first writing prompt instructed students to reflect on the meaning of the act of reading academically. One student wrote, "I find it fitting that you use the phrase 'act of reading academically,' rather than simply 'reading academically.' It is fitting because my understanding of reading is becoming oriented toward less of a passive action, but more of an action of agency" (W). I chose the wording of the prompt deliberately because I hoped it would engender responses to reading as "active transactions with text" (McAlpine 2012, 357).

Referencing van Pletzen (2006), McAlpine claims "that the reader is agentive while reading" (2012, 357). Furthermore, "reading involves bringing particular purposes to active transactions with text—text that invites different interpretations and reinterpretations—resulting in a changing reservoir of knowledge" (357). Some students found agency as doctoral readers, while others continued to encounter difficulties. Those who struggled expressed feeling intimidated because of the seemingly insurmountable challenges of academic reading. Sometimes, reading themselves into their discipline triggered students' concerns about their intellectual and creative abilities. Early reflections illustrated students' uncertainty about their abilities to meet textual demands; perspectives such as these were especially common in the first weeks: "Unfortunately, [reading] is a difficult skill and takes a lot of practice . . . [and] scholarly writings . . . can be even more difficult because of the language and rhetoric . . . being able to translate that sort of writing is even more difficult" (W). Despite the hint of lacking confidence, a bit of hopefulness was apparent too; with practice, reading without anxiety was possible (Roldan and Turns 2018, n.p.).

Another newcomer acknowledged the trajectory to disciplinary literacies while uncertain of her or his position in the discourse of the discipline. The student seemed to express a lack of entitlement (Fine and Wohl 2018) and of the ability to envision joining the scholarly conversations held in the literature: "These readings aren't vastly different from the writing that I will be doing, but often my 'imposter syndrome' sees these as far above my level" (W). Musicians cannot fake their musical abilities; in practice studios and on stage, DMA students know they cannot easily divert attention from mistakes. As mature musicians, they have a realistic awareness of themselves as artists, but that may not be the case in the academic realm; the imposter profile emerges. Even as the course was coming to an end, one student in particular revealed that the apprehension had not abated: "[When trying to engage] with the text, I feel this is where I fail. . . . I realize that I tend to create a . . . gap between myself and the author. . . . I feel a sense of unworthiness in the presence of the author" (W). For some, the act of reading did not come easily (Scholes 2002).

More commonly, their reflections indicated a turn toward becoming more experienced readers of scholarship. This reflection was a third and final prompted response, during the time when students were entirely self-directed readers and writers: "Perhaps the most important mental change from engaging with more scholarly articles on a regular basis is my lessening apprehension and fear when approaching these readings" (W). This passage contrasted directly with those that demonstrated anxiety; instead, reading had become an embodied experience through which tactics for complex discursive negotiations could be learned and applied (Walker 2015). The student went on, echoing an awareness of the interaction among academic literacies: "I am now understanding more about how these readings have been written, put together, and published, and that understanding leads to more confidence when reading, comprehending, and quoting" (W). As this passage indicates, the student realized that "reading, writing, and knowledge-making [are] interconnected practices," (Baker et al. 2019, 144), although often that association is not made visible.

Some narratives expressed a growing sense of empowerment and self-confidence. Asked about growth and changes experienced in the course, a former student expressed becoming more self-assured by "not being afraid just to go digging and not being overwhelmed by [reading new sources] and feeling like I would get there, even if today I didn't" (I). As the semester progressed and students gained more experience, several claimed their voices and recognized their strengths as readers and writers. One student reflected, "Negotiating my writing with the text I read is encouraging because again I see where I am going with what I am writing" (W). Others expressed pure excitement: "I get excited when I read something that is outside the box that I haven't read before but was already thinking myself" (W); "There's nothing more exciting than finding something that you've been looking for, finding a connection that you hadn't made before" (W).

These students were eager to explore the path that dovetailed reading and thinking. They realized the potential of aligning their research with existing knowledge, and they embraced the interwoven practices of reading, writing, and creating new knowledge. Another student implied that authentic engagement fostered agency and participation: "I find that in this stage of reading... I am more engaged in what I am reading because I feel like I have become familiar enough with certain people and topics to be allowed to insert my own opinion" (W). In the process of reading closely related disciplinary texts, a relationship between the reader and author emerged; critical engagement with reading also gave the reader the confidence to introduce his or her voice into a shared dialogue (Abbott 2013).

Coda: The Act of Reading

Constructing a literature review afforded rich opportunities to read intensively, conceptualize, and write from and about the literature. Given pedagogic support, DMA students found that the practice of literature reviewing gave them the means to decode troublesome literacy conventions of music scholarship. As one student wrote, "This class and the metacognition about reading have helped me understand that these scholarly articles are what I am working towards, and I should read them almost as inspiration instead of intimidation" (W). Disciplinary-specific reading and writing customs were unpacked, challenged, and attempted. By reading and producing texts, students learned to listen for scholarly conversations, negotiate "text within fields of text" (Haller 2013, 201), and develop their own informed perspectives (Abbott 2013). They were introduced to ways of operating as music researchers and scholars. While the course was not directed entirely toward doctoral reading, the act of reading was legitimized and made visible. When their journey from crafting abstracts, critiques, and critical annotations to creating scholarly reviews of literature had nearly ended, I asked students to reflect on their changes as doctoral readers. One wrote, "I am extremely proud [of] my awareness of my own changes" (W), indicating a shift from spectator to meta-aware academic reader prepared to create original scholarship.

Reviewing students' experiences has given me an opportunity to reconsider my own instructional practices; I have used this chapter to observe and interpret not only DMA students' perspectives but mine as well. I can affirm the significance of the work of others (for example, Abbott 2013; Baker et al. 2019; Mann 2000; Kamler and Thomson 2006; McAlpine 2012) who centralize academic reading and seek to demystify the act of reading. "Students benefit from systematic training in graduate level reading" (Wohl and Fine 2017, 226) and from guidance in decoding the linguistic norms of their disciplines. As Allison L. Harl (2013, 54) notes, "One important implication of the recent literature and theory suggests that we are all . . . responsible for . . . teaching reading and writing skills to our students, regardless of discipline."

As instructors, researchers, and engaged others, we can and should speak openly about the value of academic reading for doctoral students, for all students. We can choose to make a "pedagogic commitment" (Fine and Wohl 2018, 555) by acknowledging that doctoral students of all disciplines, at any stage of their studies, appreciate guidance with academic reading expectations. We are compelled to shine a light on reading as a powerful literacy practice.

References

Abbott, Rob. 2013. "Crossing Thresholds in Academic Reading." *Innovations in Education and Teaching International* 50 (2): 191–201. https://doi.org/10.1080/14703297.2012.760865.

Baker, Sally, Bongi Bangeni, Rachel Burke, and Aditi Hunma. 2019. "The Invisibility of Academic Reading as Social Practice and Its Implications for Equity in Higher Education: A Scoping Study." *Higher Education Research and Development* 38 (1): 142–156. https://doi.org/10.1080/07294360.2018.1540554.

Bunn, Mike. 2011. "How to Read Like a Writer." In *Writing Spaces: Readings on Writing*, vol. 2, edited by Charles Lowe and Pavel Zemliansky, 71–86. Anderson, SC: Parlor. https://wac.colostate.edu/docs/books/writingspaces2/bunn--how-to-read.pdf.

Burkholder, J. Peter. 2011. "Decoding the Discipline of Music History for Our Students." *Journal of Music History Pedagogy* 1 (2): 93–111.

Carillo, Ellen C. 2017. "Preparing College-Level Readers." In *Deep Reading: Teaching Reading in the Writing Classroom*, edited by Patrick Sullivan, Howard Tinberg, and Sheridan Blau, 188–209. Urbana, IL: National Council of Teachers of English.

Christgau, Robert. 2005. "Writing about Music Is Writing First." *Popular Music* 24 (3): 415–421. https://doi.org/10.1017/S0261143005000607.

Conkling, Susan Wharton. 2003. "Envisioning a Scholarship of Teaching and Learning for the Music Discipline." *College Music Symposium* 43:55–64.

Conor, Erin. 2016. "Engaging Students in Disciplinary Practices: Music Information Literacy and the ACRL Framework for Information Literacy in Higher Education." *Notes* 73 (1): 9–21. https://doi.org/10.1353/not.2016.0087.

Fine, Gary Alan, and Hannah Wohl. 2018. "Reading and Reputation: Sense, Sensibility, and Status in Graduate Education." *Qualitative Research* 18 (5): 554–564. https://doi.org/10.1177/1468794118778613.

Flavell, John H. 1979. "Metacognition and Cognitive Monitoring: A New Area of Cognitive-Developmental Inquiry." *American Psychologist* 34 (10): 906–911. https://psycnet.apa.org/fulltext/1980-09388-001.pdf.

Freer, Patrick K. 2009. "Focus on Scaffolding Language and Sequential Units during Choral Instruction." *UPDATE: Applications of Research in Music Education* 28 (1): 33–40. https://doi.org/10.1177/8755123309344327.

Freer, Patrick K., and Angela Barker. 2008. "An Instructional Approach for Improving the Writing of Literature Reviews." *Journal of Music Teacher Education* 17 (2): 69–82. https://doi.org/10.1177/1057083708317647.

Gale, Richard, and Chris M. Golde. 2004. "Doctoral Education and the Scholarship of Teaching and Learning." *Peer Review* 6 (3): 8–12.

Gee, James P. 1996. *Social Linguistics and Literacy*. London: RoutledgeFalmer.

Golde, Chris M. 2007. "Signature Pedagogies in Doctoral Education: Are They Adaptable for the Preparation of Education Researchers?" *Educational Researcher* 36 (6): 344–351. https://doi.org/10.3102/0013189X07308301.

Green, Rosemary. 2009. "American and Australian Doctoral Literature Reviewing Practices and Pedagogies." PhD diss., Deakin University. http://dro.deakin.edu.au/view/DU:30021275.

Haller, Cynthia R. 2013. "Reuniting Reading and Writing." In *Reconnecting Reading and Writing*, edited by Alice S. Horning and Elizabeth W. Kraemer, 192–219. Anderson, SC: Parlor. https://wac.colostate.edu/books/referenceguides/reconnecting/.

Harl, Allison L. 2013. "A Historical and Theoretical Review of the Literature: Reading and Writing Connections." In *Reconnecting Reading and Writing*, edited by Alice S. Horning and Elizabeth W. Kraemer, 26–54. Anderson, SC: Parlor. https://wac.colostate.edu/books/referenceguides/reconnecting/.

Hart-Davidson, Bill. 2015. "Genres Are Enacted by Readers and Writers." In *Naming What We Know: Threshold Concepts of Writing Studies*, edited by Linda Adler-Kassner and Elizabeth A. Wardle, 39–40. Logan: Utah State University Press.

Horning, Alice S., and Elizabeth W. Kraemer, eds. 2013. *Reconnecting Reading and Writing*. Anderson, SC: Parlor. https://wac.colostate.edu/books/referenceguides/reconnecting/.

Johnson, Lesley, Alison Lee, and Bill Green. 2000. "The PhD and the Autonomous Self: Gender, Rationality and Postgraduate Pedagogy." *Studies in Higher Education* 25 (2): 135–147. https://doi.org/10.1080/713696141.

Kamler, Barbara, and Pat Thomson. 2006. *Helping Doctoral Students Write: Pedagogies for Supervision*. London: Routledge.

Kwan, Becky S. C. 2008. "The Nexus of Reading, Writing and Researching in the Doctoral Undertaking of Humanities and Social Sciences: Implications for Literature Reviewing." *English for Specific Purposes* 27 (1): 42–56. https://doi.org/10.1016/j.esp.2007.05.002.

Lamott, Anne. 1994. "Short Assignments." In *Bird by Bird: Some Instructions on Writing and Life*, 16–20. New York: Pantheon Books.

Lea, Mary R., and Brian V. Street. 1998. "Student Writing in Higher Education: An Academic Literacies Approach." *Studies in Higher Education* 23 (2): 157–172. https://doi.org/10.1080/03075079812331380364.

Luke, Allan, and Peter Freebody. 1997. "Shaping the Social Practices of Reading." In *Constructing Critical Literacies: Teaching and Learning Textual Practice*, edited by Sandy Muspratt, Allan Luke, and Peter Freebody, 185–225. St. Leonards, Australia: Allen and Unwin.

Mann, Sarah J. 2000. "The Students' Experience of Reading." *Higher Education* 39 (3): 297–317. https://doi.org/10.1023/A:1003953002704.

McAlpine, Lynn. 2012. "Shining a Light on Doctoral Reading: Implications for Doctoral Identities and Pedagogies." *Innovations in Education and Teaching International* 49 (4): 351–361. https://doi.org/10.1080/14703297.2012.728875.

McMinn, Mark R., Anna Tabor, Bobby L. Trihub, Laura Taylor, and Amy W. Dominguez. 2009. "Reading in Graduate School: A Survey of Doctoral Students in Clinical Psychology." *Training and Education in Professional Psychology* 3 (4): 233–239. https://doi.org/10.1037/a0016405.

Middendorf, Joan, and David Pace. 2004. "Decoding the Disciplines: A Model for Helping Students Learn Disciplinary Ways of Thinking." *New Directions for Teaching and Learning* 2004 (98): 1–12. https://doi.org/10.1002/tl.142.

Mokhtari, Kouider, and Carla A. Reichard. 2002. "Assessing Students' Metacognitive Awareness of Reading Strategies." *Journal of Educational Psychology* 94 (2): 249–259. https://doi.org/10.1037//0022-0663.94.2.249.

Pace, David. 2004. "Decoding the Reading of History: An Example of the Process." *New Directions for Teaching and Learning* 2004 (98): 13–21. https://doi.org/10.1002/tl.143.

Roldan, Wendy, and Jennifer A. Turns. 2018. "'I Came in Thinking There Was One Right Practice': Exploring How to Help Graduate Students Learn to Read Academic Research." Paper presented at the ASEE Annual Conference and Exposition, Salt Lake City, UT, June 2018. https://peer.asee.org/29645.

Scholes, Robert. 2002. "The Transition to College Reading." *Pedagogy: Critical Approaches to Teaching Literature, Language, Composition, and Culture* 2 (2): 165–172. https://doi.org/10.1215/15314200-2-2-165.

Urquhart, Sarah M., Michelle A. Maher, David F. Feldon, and Joanna Gilmore. 2016. "Factors Associated with Novice Graduate Student Researchers' Engagement with Primary Literature." *International Journal for Researcher Development* 7 (2): 141–158. https://doi.org/10.1108/IJRD-11-2015-0029.

van Pletzen, Ermien. 2006. "A Body of Reading: Making 'Visible' the Reading Experiences of First-Year Medical Students." In *Academic Literacy and the Languages of Change*, edited by Lucia Thesen and Ermien van Pletzen, 104–129. London: Continuum.

Walker, Clay. 2015. "Composing Agency: Theorizing the Readiness Potentials of Literacy Practices." *Literacy in Composition Studies* 3 (2): 1–21. http://dx.doi.org/10.21623%2F1.3.2.2.

Wisker, Gina. 2015. "Developing Doctoral Authors: Engaging with Theoretical Perspectives through the Literature Review." *Innovations in Education and Teaching International* 52 (1): 64–74. https://doi.org/10.1080/14703297.2014.981841.

Wohl, Hannah, and Gary Alan Fine. 2017. "Reading Rites: Teaching Textwork in Graduate Education." *American Sociologist* 48 (2): 215–232. https://doi.org/10.1007/s12108-016-9322-0.

Rosemary Green is Graduate Programs Librarian and Adjunct Professor at Shenandoah University in Winchester, Virginia. Her teaching and research interests center on graduate students' reading, writing, and information literacies.

7

EMBEDDING SCAFFOLDED READING PRACTICES INTO THE FIRST-YEAR UNIVERSITY SCIENCE CURRICULUM

NEELA GRIFFITHS
YVONNE C. DAVILA

Why Should We Teach Reading to University Science Students?

Why should we teach reading to university science students? Because no one is born with the ability to read academic and discipline-specific literature. Critical reading of scientific texts is a key practice in science, as the primary literature constructs knowledge and communicates research in the field. To become members of and contribute to the scientific discourse community, university students need to start the journey toward mastery of the disciplinary discourses, including reading processes, which "are shaped by the epistemological values of the discipline" (Manarin, introduction to this volume). For many university students, this disciplinary mastery is difficult to achieve. Universities need to address this challenge and consider how best to support students to read effectively in their chosen field. A first step is to identify why so many students are experiencing challenges with the reading. In science, key factors may include the complexity of the scientific literature; students' unfamiliarity with the disciplinary discourses, which could lead to a lack in confidence; their perceptions of the role of reading; and the need to manage the burgeoning demands of digital literacy. Meanwhile, educators must adapt to working with an increasingly diverse student cohort and reconsider their potentially overoptimistic assumptions around students' ability to read and make meaning in the discipline.

In this chapter, we discuss the challenges with teaching reading to university science students and describe and evaluate our curriculum design initiative: an embedded and scaffolded series of learning activities that teach incoming first-year science students how to read and select relevant and reliable scientific primary literature.

What Are the Reading Challenges for University Science Students?

Many students studying science at university are surprised by the "centrality of reading" in the scientific field (van Pletzen 2006, 113) and do not understand the crucial role that scientific primary literature plays in constructing disciplinary knowledge. This misunderstanding may result in students questioning being asked to read and refer to the literature and in their being unprepared for and overwhelmed by the amount of reading they are expected to do (du Boulay 1999; Jolliffe and Harl 2008). A further challenge is that they are expected to read, evaluate, and cite the primary literature early in their university careers. This early exposure is an excellent way to introduce students to scientific reasoning (Muench 2000), to help them develop their scientific process skills (Brownell, Price, and Steinman 2013), and to give them "the tools and ways of thinking to build a robust conceptual framework" needed to gain expertise (Coil et al. 2010, 533). However, students may find the unfamiliar terminology and scientific jargon intimidating and incomprehensible (Round and Campbell 2013) and the academic vocabulary equally challenging (Patterson et al. 2018). In order to understand the texts, students need to learn to read two languages: field-specific technical language and the academic discourses of the scientific disciplines.

Overwhelmed by and underprepared for the unfamiliar disciplinary discourses and academic expectations, students may feel discouraged and lose confidence. Without support and guidance, they may never regain it; many science majors have reported feeling fearful of and intimidated by having to read and interpret the primary literature throughout their degrees (Smith 2001). Moreover, the ever-increasing availability of digital resources and wide-ranging and novel text types (e.g., hybrid genres) may compound this lack of confidence as students question their ability to critically read, comprehend, and evaluate these text types and effectively incorporate them into their assignments (Lea and Jones 2011).

A major challenge students face is that generally little to no guidance on how or why to read is provided in traditional university science teaching. Instead, disciplinary academics tend to make assumptions about their "novice" scientists' ability to read widely and interpret the literature

(Hunter and Tse 2013; Davies 2017). Consequently, when students fail to complete the expected reading, few academics attribute this incompletion to their students not knowing *how* to do the reading (Hamilton 2018). Along with the lack of guidance on how to read (Gillen, Vaughn, and Lye 2004), students rarely receive clarification about why it is important to understand the role that disciplinary reading processes play in meaning making (Brownell, Price, and Steinman 2013). If taught at all, reading tends to be presented as a study skill by academic support staff in supplementary skills workshops, while class time is devoted to disciplinary content (Coil et al. 2010). Using a generic study-skills approach may lead students to view the decontextualized learning materials presented in these workshops as irrelevant, optional, and "marginal to the curriculum" (Hunter and Tse 2013, 228).

Students' uncertainty about how to read in their disciplines is a growing concern for educators as university curriculum design needs to cater to an increasingly linguistically, culturally, and socially diverse student cohort. Curriculum designers need to adapt to students' potential lack of academic capital and ability to access "the academic knowledge community" (McKay and Devlin 2014, 959) and its reading conventions and to recognize that students bring their own "linguistic-experiential reservoir" (Rosenblatt 1994, quoted in van Pletzen 2006) with them. Other design considerations include the relative invisibility of students' reading processes and the need to support them in making the "epistemological shifts" (Manarin et al. 2015, 12) to read and make meaning in their discipline.

How Should We Teach Reading to University Science Students?

Having identified some of the reading challenges that science students often face in their tertiary studies, we need to consider the most effective ways to support them in developing their reading practices. The literature makes a case for teaching reading using an embedded, discipline-specific, scaffolded, and explicit approach. Arguably, "literacy in the discipline is the same as learning in the discipline" (Harper and Vered 2017, 697), and a contextualized and "visible" development of academic literacy practices, including reading practices, should therefore be embedded into the core curriculum (Amos and McGowan 2012; Wingate 2006; Jacobs 2005; Thies 2012). The reading process should be "overt and explicit" (Jacobs 2005; Jolliffe and Harl 2008) "so that students are aware of the particular skills being developed while they are engaging in . . . content-based activities"

(Baik and Greig 2009, 410). Students should be guided to read scientific literature using the same critical-thinking approaches as the disciplinary experts; that is, they need to learn to think like scientists. Thus, students are acculturated into the disciplinary community of practice and its language; they have opportunities "to use and explore that language, i.e. to read science, to discuss the meaning of its texts, to argue how ideas are supported by evidence and to write and communicate in the language of science" (Osborne 2002, 39), all of which build their capacity as trainee scientists (Burke et al. 2016).

Ideally, scaffolded immersion of novice students into the disciplinary community of practice (Vygotsky 1978) requires introducing them to foundational academic and disciplinary discourses early in the curriculum (Coil et al. 2010), preferably in the first semester of the first year. In addition, aligning these language- and literacy-focused teaching materials with assessment tasks helps students understand their relevance and application, which in turn means that they are more likely to be engaged. The participation of disciplinary academics in embedding reading practices is key (Wingate 2006; Hunter and Tse 2013). Disciplinary experts, the science practitioners, are ideally placed to induct students into the disciplinary discourses and make the reading process and the way scientific knowledge is constructed visible (Davies 2017).

Another argument for embedding these practices as an integral part of the students' course is that this approach is inclusive and confidence building. Significantly, embedded academic literacy design is not associated with remedial support but targets the student cohort (Nallaya and Kehrwald 2013) and recognizes that "all students, whether native or non-native speakers of English, 'non-traditional' or 'traditional' students, are novices when dealing with academic discourse in the disciplines" (Wingate and Tribble 2012, 484). Creating an equitable and confidence-building learning context allows "the acquisition of academic literacies in a non-threatening environment" (Nallaya and Kehrwald 2013, 81). This explicit teaching and visible curriculum helps build students' "confidence to contribute to existing discourse" (Hocking and Fieldhouse 2011, 45) and supports the development of effective reading practices.

Science education studies debate how early students should be exposed to the primary literature. Some science educators claim that students should be introduced to the primary literature from day one of their degree programs (see, for example, Coil et al. 2010; Muench 2000; Wenk and Tronsky 2011), whereas others suggest a more scaffolded and supported approach (Smith 2001; Hamilton 2018). Commencing students, particularly those who were trained in high school to read science textbooks as a list of facts to be read linearly, may attempt to read the primary literature in the same way. It is important to teach students that scientific journal articles are concrete examples of how scientific knowledge is generated through the scientific process (Gillen, Vaughn, and Lye 2004) and read as "a process of investigation, analysis, and discovery rather than simply a list of facts to be memorised" (Levine 2001, 122). A different reading approach is necessary because "primary research articles illuminate aspects of scientific inquiry that textbooks ignore, discussing the research question, the authors' hypotheses, the experimental design, and the results" (Wenk and Tronsky 2011, 60) and the authors' interpretations of these results (Round and Campbell 2013).

To ensure an inclusive learning design, our curriculum design initiative uses a flipped blended learning approach to introduce students to scientific reading practices. This approach aligns with recommendations for the effective design of science courses (Overton and Johnson 2016). In our initiative, students complete an online learning activity (bespoke interactive modules) before class and participate in collaborative exercises that apply their new knowledge in class. Presenting content online creates a technology-enhanced and student-centered learning environment, enhances accessibility and flexibility (Gunn, Hearne, and Sibthorpe 2011), and enables inclusivity (Devlin et al. 2012), as it supports students' learning in their own time and at their own pace. The active and collaborative application of the learning materials in a face-to-face class is essential as it enables students to practice the skills and highlights their importance in the discipline learning process (Chanock 2013). Using an interactive and active learning design also ensures that students engage with the content as opposed to sitting passively either at a computer or in a lecture (Gillen, Vaughn, and Lye 2004).

Learning Design

In this chapter, we describe our curriculum initiative design and students' learning journey. Our learning design was guided by our overall intention to induct incoming first-year science students into the science discourse community through introducing them to scientific reading practices and conventions, developing their reading strategies, and building their confidence in reading. We designed an embedded and scaffolded approach that explicitly teaches students how to read and select relevant and reliable primary scientific literature. This chapter also reports on our evaluation and investigation of the following research questions:

1. Do science students engage with learning activities targeting the development of reading practices?
2. What do students find most helpful about learning to read scientific texts using a flipped blended learning approach?
3. Does explicit teaching of reading practices improve students' confidence in their ability to read, understand, and use scientific journal articles?

Finally, we present our findings and their impact, and we discuss the key factors that have enabled the success of our initiative.

Context

Our public metropolitan university in Australia has seven faculties teaching undergraduate and postgraduate programs to approximately forty-five thousand students (on campus). In the Faculty of Science, a core first-year (FY) subject, Principles of Scientific Practice (PSP), introduces students to the major themes of contemporary science and inquiry-oriented experimentation with a focus on data handling, experimental design, and scientific argument. The majority of commencing FY science students (n ≈ 900) enroll in PSP in their first semester of study. This is the ideal subject in which to embed foundational reading practices, as the major assignment is a scientific report based on a laboratory experiment. Students are expected to read and cite the primary literature, which many find challenging, as they are unfamiliar with and lack confidence in reading scientific literature.

Curriculum Design

After considering our FY students' diversity and disparate learning needs, we selected Sally Kift's six interconnected organizing principles, known as the First Year Curriculum Principles of Transition Pedagogy (Kift 2009), as our curriculum design framework. These principles—transition, diversity, design, engagement, assessment, and evaluation and monitoring—are intended as a "guiding philosophy for intentional first year curriculum design and support that carefully scaffolds and mediates the first year learning experience for contemporary heterogeneous cohorts" (Kift 2009, 9). Following a student-centered approach, we identified the specific reading needs of our incoming science students. (For all stages in our learning design approach, see Davila and Griffiths [2016].) We aligned the basic reading practices and strategy design with three elements: the relevant subject learning outcomes, assignment requirements and criteria, and the associated Faculty of Science graduate attributes (communication and professional, ethical, and social responsibility). Our design also clearly articulates the elements of reading assessed in the scientific report assignment rubric, including the ability to retrieve and incorporate scientific literature and to interpret findings in relation to the literature.

As content in PSP is delivered using a flipped blended learning approach, we designed three interactive online modules (approximately ten minutes each) and a ninety-minute face-to-face workshop. An important consideration when designing and integrating academic language and learning practices into core curricula is to ensure that activities targeting discipline-specific language conventions do not take time away from content but constitute content (Hunter and Tse 2013; Wingate and Tribble 2012) and build process skills (Davies 2017). Thus, we carefully selected example scientific texts that matched the subject objectives, described experiments similar to the students' laboratory experiment, and followed a similar structure to that required in the assignment (Muench 2000). Our concern about students' fear of the primary literature also informed our learning design, and we chose accessible and manageable journal articles to provide a guided transition from textbooks to more complex texts (Hamilton 2018). At the same time, our aim was to demonstrate to students how scientific literature reflects the scientific process, meaning-making, and knowledge construction of the science discourse community (Patterson et al. 2018). Through judicious choices of the sample texts, we aimed to motivate novice scientists in training and enable students to "move from being passive recipients of scientific facts to active participants in a scientific discussion" (Gillen, Vaughn, and Lye 2004, 95).

To engage students, online learning activities need to be short, targeted, and contextualized. The modules are interactive and invite responses (e.g., questions, drag and drop, or mix and match), and they provide students with immediate feedback as to why their responses are correct or incorrect (Day et al. 2015; Lear, Li, and Prentice 2016). The interaction slides are interspersed throughout the modules and follow the information slides to help reinforce key concepts and ideas (fig. 7.1). It is also important that students' movement through the modules is controlled. For example, information slides are timed to match students' reading speed, and students have to respond to the interaction slides before they can progress (Gillen, Vaughn, and Lye 2004). As the materials are formative, the modules are available throughout the teaching session and can be revisited for "reference, practice and reinforcement" (Gunn, Hearne, and Sibthorpe 2011, 6).

Learning Journey—Online Modules and Workshop

Using the university's learning management system, PSP students are directed to complete the three modules in week 1 of the semester in preparation for the face-to-face workshop in week 2. This early scheduling ensures that students have enough time to practice their reading strategies, conduct research, and write the major assignment due at the end of the semester. The targeted student learning outcomes for these learning activities are:

1. Develop skills in reading and selecting appropriate scientific literature
2. Identify the content and function of each section in a scientific article

We "chunked" the module content into three skills groups to ensure incremental and progressive learning (Smith 2001) and balance across the subject learning objectives. The scientific reading practices introduced are:

- Module 1: Effective and efficient reading skills for university—introduces the overall structure of scientific articles and skimming and scanning techniques for effective and efficient reading of various sections of scientific journal articles.
- Module 2: Active reading for understanding at university—introduces the structure and purpose of scientific journal articles, strategies for choosing articles, and active reading techniques including asking questions, identifying discipline-specific language and technical terms, recording vocabulary, and highlighting and making notes.
- Module 3: Evaluating sources of information—introduces techniques for evaluating the scholarship, relevance, reliability, and currency of different sources of information including scientific journal articles, textbooks, industry reports, popular science texts, websites and blogs written by discipline experts, and Wikipedia.

The aligned ninety-minute face-to-face workshop "Reading and Evaluating the Scientific Literature" consolidates the materials presented in the online modules and enables students to test their understanding and practice applying their new knowledge in a supportive learning environment. The intentionally designed collaborative activities focus on building students' ability and confidence through the guided unpacking of a scientific article. The workshops are taught by disciplinary instructors who model reading scientific articles as a disciplinary specialist would, identifying the structure and communicative purpose of each section, its

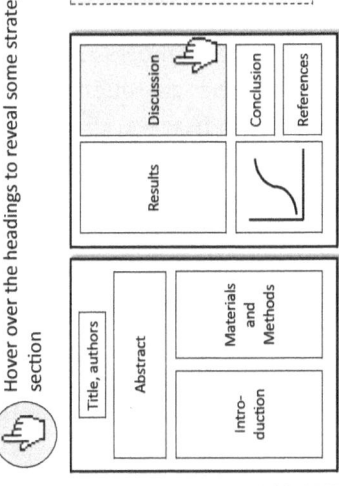

Fig. 7.1 Example of the blended learning reading practices resources. *Left*, an interactive slide on strategies for reading scientific journal articles (Module 2). Students hover over the headings to read pop-up information boxes. The discussion section pop-up is depicted here. *Right*, a workshop activity in which students identify, unpack, and discuss the different sections of a scientific journal article.

function, and its key points (fig. 7.1). The workshop finishes with a class discussion and question-and-answer session to foster peer learning and provide timely peer and instructor feedback. Using disciplinary instructors to facilitate the reading workshop in a regular class highlights to students the centrality of these practices in learning science. The instructors are trained and provided with a detailed lesson plan on how to facilitate the workshop activity, including prompts, questions, and suggested timing (Jacobs 2005).

EVALUATION AND ANALYSES OF THE CURRICULUM DESIGN INITIATIVE TEACHING SCIENTIFIC READING PRACTICES

We used a mixed-methods approach to evaluate students' engagement with and perceptions of the embedded reading practices learning activities. Using the learning management system, we tracked the completion of each online module by all students enrolled in the subject between 2015 and 2018 (there are two cohorts per year, eight semesters in total). This tracking gave us a measure of student engagement with the online reading modules. We used voluntary student surveys, which included closed five-point Likert scale and open-ended questions, to investigate students' experiences and perceived value of the learning activities. In 2015, we conducted a postactivity survey to explore students' experiences with the reading activities.

From 2016 to 2018, we conducted both pre- and postactivity online surveys to explore students' experiences with the reading activities and their potential changes in confidence in reading the scientific literature. Again, the survey consisted of closed five-point Likert scale questions. Students' responses to the pre- and postactivity confidence survey items were matched using student ID numbers and then recoded to restore anonymity. The data from the Likert scale questions were converted to ordinal data (1 = strongly disagree; 2 = disagree; 3 = neutral; 4 = agree; 5 = strongly agree). In 2016, 11/105 students completed both surveys; in 2017, 152/722 students completed both surveys; and in 2018, 91/694 students completed both surveys. The differences between pre- and postactivity responses were analyzed using a Wilcoxon signed-rank test (two-tailed) to investigate whether there was a change in the students' confidence in reading. Students' responses to the open-ended questions were manually coded, and broad themes were identified using a general inductive approach (Thomas 2006). The surveys had ethics approval, and students' consent was sought before their completion.

Findings from the Evaluation of the Curriculum Design Initiative

Do Students Engage with the Scientific Reading Practices Learning Activities?

Engagement with the preworkshop modules is essential for a successful flipped blended learning environment, as the modules provide students with their first exposure to key concepts. Many students commented that the modules "prepared me and made me think about the content which would be covered in the workshop" (2015 student survey). Notably, more students complete the first module than the second and third modules; on average from 2015 to 2018, 90.5 percent of students per semester completed Module 1, 82 percent completed Module 2, and 72 percent completed Module 3. We speculate that the students who do not attempt the modules tend to be those who think they already have strong reading strategies, or they pick the modules they think will be most useful for them personally rather than attempting all three. It is also possible that students may have "module fatigue" after completing one or two modules, leading to fewer students completing the third module.

What Do Students Think about Learning to Read Scientific Texts through Online Modules and an Interactive Workshop?

The postactivity surveys in 2015 evaluated students' experiences with the online modules and the workshop ($n = 142$ respondents). Most students (65 percent) strongly agreed or agreed that the online modules helped them develop efficient and effective reading practices. Similarly, over 55 percent of student respondents agreed that the modules helped them develop active reading practices. The majority of students (73 percent) reported using the reading strategies when finding and reading articles for their scientific report assignment, which suggests that our scaffolded learning materials successfully prepared students to apply them in the task. Unpacking the structure of an article in the workshop was extremely helpful for students when writing their own report, with 82 percent agreement. Furthermore, 89 percent of students indicated that they would use the reading practices in the future, which suggests that students saw the value in developing these strategies for their university studies and future career.

Four broad themes emerged from the responses to the open-ended survey question "What was most useful about the online modules and

Table 7.1 Summary of the main themes emerging from the 2015 student survey question "What was most useful about the online modules and workshop?"

Theme	Example student quotes
1. Development of skills for reading scientific articles	*Learning the techniques to be more efficient at reading articles such as scanning and making a list of questions as I read through an article.*
	Learning about the different ways I could actively read as I had little to no knowledge of these techniques.
2. Presentation of specific content on the structure and purpose of scientific articles	*Being able to break down the scientific articles into their various components and understanding what was involved in each.*
	I think it helps students familiarize themselves with the structure and function of each section in a journal article before they attempt to write something in that format themselves.
3. Accessibility and flexibility of the online modules	*The ability to complete them in our own time to gain a basic understanding of the workshop content. This allowed us a stress-free approach to learning.*
4. Opportunities for engaged learning (e.g., make comparisons, seek clarification, and revise and consolidate concepts)	*They we[re] easy and fast to understand, meaning it was easy to go back and find something to help if I didn't understand something.*
	Discussing [the article] with other people and the room to see everyone's take on it and helped me to notice things about the article that I didn't see before.

workshop?" (summarized in table 7.1). Students identified skills development and content, the accessibility of the content, and opportunities for collaborative learning as most useful. These themes provide further evidence of science students' perceptions of the effective learning value of the modules, the workshop, and the blended learning approach to developing reading practices. Students placed a high value on learning techniques for efficient and effective reading of scientific articles, such as active reading, to "understand how to retrieve relevant information from articles" (2015 student survey). Our reading activities "acted as a doable gateway to understanding how to go around [sic] reading these articles" (2015 student survey).

Students also identified an additional value of the reading practices learning activities—namely, that they could apply their improved understanding of how to read scientific articles to their scientific writing. One student commented that the reading practices had helped them learn to "retrieve relevant information from articles which helped me in forming my scientific article" and that "by reinforcing the knowledge on the specific sections in a scientific article, I was able to develop greater clarity [sic] how to write a scientific report for the practical" (2015 student survey).

Does Explicit Teaching of Reading Practices Improve Students' Confidence in Their Ability to Read, Understand, and Use Scientific Journal Articles?

In the 2015 postactivity surveys, 80 percent of students ($n = 123$) reported feeling confident in their ability to read the scientific literature more efficiently and effectively. Similarly, 80 percent of students felt confident that they could find and choose relevant journal articles for their assignment. Having developed their reading practices meant that students felt "less burdened when researching scientific articles" (2015 student survey).

In 2016, we introduced and conducted preactivity surveys to establish students' incoming (baseline) confidence levels at the beginning of their first semester of university and then repeated the survey postactivity (end of semester) to measure any change in confidence levels. Over three consecutive years, students reported significant increases in their confidence in their ability to find and choose relevant articles for their assignments (fig. 7.2). Students also reported improvements in their confidence in reading and understanding scientific texts, with the mean around 3 on the Likert scale (unsure) to 4 or above (agree or strongly agree that they are more confident) (fig. 7.2).

An important aspect of reading scientific journal articles is recognizing how they are structured and being able to identify and place information in the correct section. After completing the modules and workshop, there was a significant increase in students reporting that they were familiar with the structure of scientific articles (fig. 7.2). Similarly, students felt more confident placing information into the correct section of their reports. These results indicate that the explicit teaching of scientific reading practices significantly improves students' ability to recognize and distinguish specific sections of scientific text and thus increases their confidence in locating and retrieving information more quickly and efficiently.

Embedding Reading Practices Resources into Other Subjects

The impact of the reading practices curriculum initiative on student outcomes has extended beyond Principles of Scientific Practice. After their

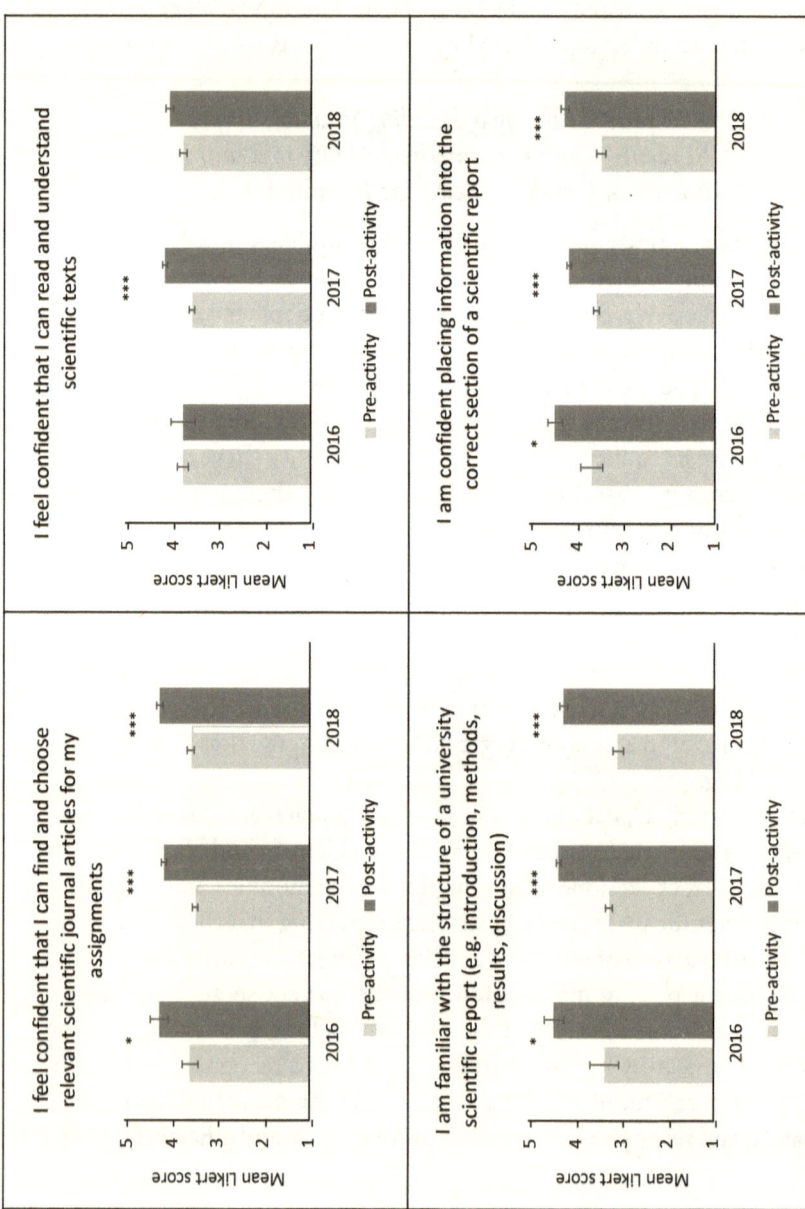

Fig. 7.2 Students' self-reported confidence in their reading skills before and after completing the modules and workshop. Mean ± standard error, five-point Likert scale: 1 = strongly disagree, to 5 = strongly agree. Wilcoxon signed-rank test on paired (pre- and postactivity) responses: *$P < 0.05$; ***$P < 0.001$. Sample size: $n = 11$, 2016; $n = 152$, 2017; $n = 91$, 2018.

success in PSP, we embedded the online modules into a core FY subject in another science degree course. The subject coordinator identified the reading practices modules as "perfect for use . . . as an interactive tool to introduce students to university reading" and reported that after one semester, "the majority of students found these modules helpful and learned useful skills from them (particularly in evaluating sources of information)" (2016 subject coordinator). Indeed, students pinpointed key skills that they developed: "I've been able to get a quick overview of different skills that I would need as both a student, and a researcher; such as how to read and dissect journal articles" (2016 subject feedback survey).

Discussion

The discipline-specific contextualized reading materials in the three online modules and the complementary workshop have been seamlessly embedded into a core first-year science subject. The overall aims of our curriculum design initiative were to develop science students' scientific reading practices and build their confidence. The evaluation data indicate that our initiative had a positive impact on students' perceptions of and confidence in their abilities to read scientific journal articles. Our embedded learning activities encourage students to read the primary scientific literature and provide them with strategies to be confident and efficient readers of science. As a result, our students are more effective and confident readers and more actively engaged with reading. They are also more prepared to conduct research and report their own experimental work for the major assignment. This is a marked improvement on earlier students' preactivity comments about scientific reading—for example, feeling "too 'scared' to approach" (2015 student survey), let alone read, peer-reviewed scientific journal articles, which "just seem daunting at first" (2015 subject feedback survey).

A major success of our curriculum design initiative is that the majority of FY students engage with the online modules and workshop each semester, as evidenced by students' positive feedback on their usefulness for learning to read science like a scientist. Two of the emerging themes from the open-ended survey question pinpoint this aspect of learning to read: Theme 3, accessibility and flexibility of the online modules; and theme 4, opportunities for engaged learning. Students appreciate having access to the instructional content online and the flexibility to complete the modules at a time, place, and pace that suits them. Paradoxically, although reading is often seen as a solitary pursuit, learning to read can clearly be achieved in an active and collaborative learning environment. For example, many students commented on the usefulness of discussing the sections of a scientific paper with their peers and sharing their ideas and interpretations—a distinct benefit of the follow-up collaborative face-to-face workshop (Chanock 2013; Burke et al. 2016). Without this opportunity to learn and apply purposeful and strategic reading practices or receive feedback, students' first encounter with scientific articles could be "to read a scientific article (with intention to drain all available information) . . . for an assessment task" (2015 student survey).

We found significant differences between the pre- and postactivity survey responses for confidence (2016 to 2018). In all cases, students reported increased confidence and familiarity in finding and choosing articles, reading and understanding scientific texts, placing information in a scientific report, and understanding the structure of scientific reports. This is an important result, achieved with confidence-building learning activities that follow a sequence of "modeling, practice and application" (Gillen, Vaughn, and Lye 2004, 96) of appropriate reading practices. Such modeling of effective reading practices (Muench 2000; Gillen, Vaughn, and Lye 2004) needs to go further than simply instructing students to identify specific sections of a document (see Hubbard and Dunbar 2017). Instead, students are shown how to read and evaluate the communicative purpose and function of each specific section. Carol A. Kozeracki et al. (2006, 344) commented that when students self-assessed as being "more comfortable" when reading scientific journal articles, this comfort level probably reflected their "gaining skill in these tasks but also becoming familiar with something with which they had previously had little experience." Our curriculum initiative works because it addresses this gap for FY science students, giving them more confidence in their "ability to complete academic work," an essential component in their growing academic capability (Burke et al. 2016, 56). Supporting FY students' foundational reading practices through explicit and targeted provision clearly has an impact.

Our results indicate that students in the first semester of their first year of university can make significant gains in their scientific reading practices. While previous studies have also shown improvements in undergraduate students' ability and confidence in reading and evaluating the scientific literature through targeted curricula (e.g., Kozeracki et al. 2006; Brownell, Price, and Steinman 2013; Wenk and Tronsky 2011), our curriculum design initiative has significantly impacted large, diverse first-year science cohorts (including life and physical sciences majors) over multiple years.

We have identified three key factors that have enabled the success of our initiative: our cross-disciplinary approach; an embedded, scaffolded, and explicit design targeting all students; and a flipped blended learning approach.

A Cross-Disciplinary Approach

Instrumental to the success of the curriculum design initiative has been our collaborative cross-disciplinary (academic language and literacy and science backgrounds) approach as we share our distinctly different expertise and act as critical friends. This cross-disciplinary "transaction space" (Jacobs 2005) enables us to design student-centered curricula grounded in science discourse. We work closely with the subject's head instructor in a collaborative "third space" (Briguglio 2014, 28) to design workshop activities that ensure that all aspects of the curriculum initiative are aligned and address the subject's intended learning outcomes. As the subject is taught by science faculty instructors, we ensure that they have the requisite reading strategies skills (Patterson et al. 2018) by providing a teaching manual and guidelines and organizing teacher training sessions on workshop facilitation. The role of disciplinary experts in the design and teaching of the materials is the key difference between our approach and a generic approach (Chanock 2013).

An Embedded, Scaffolded, and Explicit Design Targeting All Students

An inclusive design was critical to our curriculum initiative, as no one is born being able to read academic and discipline-specific literature. Using the primary literature and intentionally designing and embedding reading practices as "linguistically inclusive, integrated mainstream curricula" (Jacobs 2005, 476) targets all students and is an effective tool for increasing scientific literacy (Kozeracki et al. 2006), which in turn helps build the students' confidence (Kozeracki et al. 2006; Amos and McGowan 2012). Embedding reading practices also builds students' awareness of the role that reading plays in their field, highlights its centrality and relevance, and develops students' academic capability (Burke et al. 2016). Writing clearly articulated assessment criteria (Hunter and Tse 2013) of reading practices as part of the assignment rubric also demonstrates the important role that effective reading plays in students' ability to complete assignments and improve the quality of those assignments (du Boulay 1999; Manarin et al. 2015).

Our evaluation of students' levels of engagement with our reading practices learning activities showed a consistently high proportion of the student cohort completing the online modules before the workshop and active participation in the workshop. Students commented on how the learning activities supported their reading development (Theme 1, table 7.1). This finding is corroborated in the literature, which states that students want to be taught foundational practices early in their degrees (McKay and Devlin 2014) and value the learning of efficient and effective reading techniques. Our students' comments on learning these techniques were positive and also telling (Theme 1, table 7.1).

Our findings indicate that the explicit teaching of scientific reading practices significantly improved students' confidence in their ability to read, understand, and use scientific journal articles. Students commented that the attention paid to breaking down the structure of scientific reports (Theme 2, table 7.1), particularly in the face-to-face workshop, was confidence building. The guidance to and analysis of the communicative purpose and function of each section of a scientific report received many positive comments, and a number of students could see how improving their reading practices would impact their writing practices: "Overall, I had a great experience in analyzing academic article [sic] and this helped me to improve my academic writing and reading skills."

A Flipped Blended Learning Approach

Because we used a flipped blended learning approach to teach reading practices, students were able to complete the online interactive modules in their own time and at their own pace and then apply and consolidate their learning in the active and collaborative workshop. One of the four themes emerging from the students' survey comments focused on the role that such an approach played in their learning (table 7.1). Many students mentioned the accessibility and flexibility of the online modules (Theme 3, table 7.1), which enabled "a stress-free approach to learning." Students also commented very positively on the usability, usefulness, and relevance of the reading practices resources. Key to successful technology-enhanced learning is designing interactive resources that require students to engage with the material (Gunn, Hearne, and Sibthorpe 2011)—for example, built-in formative quizzes (Day et al. 2015). A teaching approach that provides materials such as guidelines or online videos that require no student engagement or input may engender passive learning. Our students' high levels of engagement (module completion) suggest that they recognize the significance and value of our learning activities to their disciplinary discourses and assessment tasks (Nallaya and Kehrwald 2013).

Another overall theme emerging from our evaluation was that students appreciated the engaged learning opportunities, specifically the peer interaction, and receiving timely clarification and feedback in the workshop (Theme 4, table 7.1). In addition, a number of students, including students with English as an Additional Language (self-identified), reported that they appreciated the opportunity to review the modules as many times as they needed. Providing the opportunity to revisit and review caters to the learning needs of our diverse student cohort (Devlin et al. 2012) and demonstrates that online learning can be confidence building, as it fosters academic literacy acquisition in "a non-threatening environment" (Nallaya and Kehrwald 2013, 81).

The advantages of using a flipped blended learning approach for our curriculum design, beyond the fact that today's students expect to learn online and benefit from the flexibility it brings, are that it provides an embedded, scaffolded, and explicit design that can be accessed by all students. Class time, including traditional-style lecture delivery, is freed up for students to participate in active learning exercises that build on the content introduced online. Importantly, when we use this approach, our students perceive academic and disciplinary discourses as content (see Hunter and Tse 2013; Wingate and Tribble 2012).

Developing Reading Practices beyond the First Year of Study

Students' evaluations of our foundational reading practices materials clearly show that, for most students, the online modules and workshop help develop their reading practices and build their confidence in using the scientific literature. However, reading is a dynamic and emerging practice (Manarin et al. 2015), and as educators, we need to encourage students to build on these basics throughout their degrees. Indeed, later-stage undergraduate and postgraduate students have reported a lack of confidence in reading research papers, an inability to identify papers of importance to their study area, and an inability to read and extract information efficiently (Hubbard and Dunbar 2017). Students need continued support to advance from confidently finding and citing a source and reading to understand, to developing the ability to critically evaluate and synthesize the source material.

Conclusion

In conclusion, through our cross-disciplinary partnership; an embedded, scaffolded, and explicit design; and an inclusive blended learning approach, our first-year science students receive a strong foundation in disciplinary reading and become confident readers. For readers wishing to implement a similar approach, we recommend the following actions: (1) design contextualized learning activities to teach students to read that meet their learning needs (i.e., that unpack the structures and conventions of scientific texts and provide strategies for reading to extract relevant information efficiently); (2) embed these activities into the core curriculum in the first semester of the first year, so that students can develop their strategies and use them in assignments across multiple subjects; (3) scaffold and support students' learning of disciplinary reading through formative, active, and collaborative learning activities and provide opportunities for practice and feedback; (4) make the teaching materials explicit and visible; and (5) use an inclusive and accessible teaching approach. Bringing academic and discipline-specific reading practices "to the fore in students' literacy practices" (Lea and Jones 2011, 390) from the first week of their university studies means that students "perceive them as an integral part of their developing knowledge and understanding" (Thies 2012, 16). Our role is to shift students from asking the "what" and "how" questions to asking "why" as they master increasingly complex and challenging critical reading practices while building their capacity to use these skills as trainee scientists.

Acknowledgments

This work was supported by a UTS Widening Participation Scheme First Year Experience grant in 2015, funded through the Australian Government Higher Education Participation Program. The surveys were conducted with human ethics approval: UTS HREC Ref. No. 2015000360 and ETH16-0614. Thanks to the subject coordinators, Associate Professor Alison Beavis and Dr. Scott Chadwick; our research assistant, Dr. Alan Kwok; and Dr. Adam Aitken and Mike Taylor for feedback on earlier drafts.

References

Amos, Kathryn, and Ursula McGowan. 2012. "Integrating Academic Reading and Writing Skills Development with Core Content in Science and Engineering." *Journal of Learning Development in Higher Education* (November). https://doi.org/10.47408/jldhe.v0i0.189.

Baik, Chi, and Joan Greig. 2009. "Improving the Academic Outcomes of Undergraduate ESL Students: The Case for Discipline-Based Academic Skills Programs." *Higher Education Research and Development* 28 (4): 401–416.

Briguglio, Carmela. 2014. "Working in the Third Space: Promoting Interdisciplinary Collaboration to Embed English Language Development into the Discipline." Final report for the OLT National Teaching Fellowship Program. OLT Resources. https://espace.curtin.edu.au/handle/20.500.11937/49479.

Brownell, Sara E., Jordan V. Price, and Lawrence Steinman. 2013. "A Writing-Intensive Course Improves Biology Undergraduates' Perception and Confidence of Their Abilities to Read Scientific Literature and Communicate Science." *Advances in Physiology Education* 37:70–79.

Burke, Penny Jane, Anna Bennett, Cathy Burgess, Kim Gray, and Erica Southgate. 2016. *Capability, Belonging and Equity in Higher Education: Developing Inclusive Approaches*. Newcastle, Australia: Centre of Excellence for Equity in Higher Education, University of Newcastle.

Chanock, Kate. 2013. "Teaching Subject Literacies through Blended Learning: Reflections on a Collaboration between Academic Learning Staff and Teachers in Disciplines." *Journal of Academic Language and Learning* 7 (2): A106–A119.

Coil, David, Mary Pat Wenderoth, Matthew Cunningham, and Clarissa Dirks. 2010. "Teaching the Process of Science: Faculty Perceptions and an Effective Methodology." *CBE—Life Sciences Education* 9 (4): 524–535. https://doi.org/10.1187/cbe.10-01-0005.

Davies, Laura J. 2017. "Getting to the Root of the Problem: Teaching Reading as a Process in the Sciences." In *What Is College Reading?*, edited by Alice S. Horning, Deborah-Lee Golinitz, and Cynthia R. Haller, 161–182. Fort Collins, CO: WAC Clearinghouse and University Press of Colorado.

Davila, Yvonne C., and Neela Griffiths. 2016. "Supporting Student Transition: Embedding Reading Practices into the First Year Science Curriculum." Paper presented at the STARS (Students Transitions Achievement Retention and Success) Conference, Perth, June 29–July 2, 2016.

Day, Trevor, Julie Letchford, Hazel Corradi, and Thomas Rogers. 2015. "Devising an Online Resource to Help Undergraduate Science Students Critically Evaluate Research Articles." *Journal of Academic Writing* 5 (2): 1–19.

Devlin, Marcia, Sally Kift, Karen Nelson, Liz Smith, and Jade McKay. 2012. *Effective Teaching and Support of Students from Low Socioeconomic Status Backgrounds: Practical Advice for Teaching Staff*. Sydney: Office for Learning and Teaching, Department of Industry, Innovation, Science, Research and Tertiary Education.

du Boulay, Doreen. 1999. "Argument in Reading: What Does It Involve and How Can Students Become Better Critical Readers?" *Teaching in Higher Education* 4 (2): 147–162. https://doi.org/10.1080/1356251990040201.

Gillen, Christopher M., Jasmine Vaughn, and Bethany R. Lye. 2004. "An Online Tutorial for Helping Nonscience Majors Read Primary Research Literature in Biology." *Advanced Physiology Education* 28 (3): 95–99.

Gunn, Cathy, Shari Hearne, and Julie Sibthorpe. 2011. "Right from the Start: A Rationale for Embedding Academic Literacy Skills in University Courses." *Journal of University Teaching and Learning Practice* 8 (1): 6.

Hamilton, John. 2018. "Academic Reading Requirements for Commencing HE students—a Professional Reflection on Whether Peer-Reviewed Journals Are the Right Place to Start: A Practice Report." *Student Success* 9 (2): 73–79.

Harper, Rowena, and Karen Vered. 2017. "Developing Communication as a Graduate Outcome: Using 'Writing across the Curriculum' as a Whole-of-Institution Approach to Pedagogy." *Higher Education Research and Development* 36 (4): 688–701.

Hocking, Darryl, and Wes Fieldhouse. 2011. "Implementing Academic Literacies in Practice." *New Zealand Journal of Educational Studies* 46 (1): 35–47.

Hubbard, Katharine E., and Sonja D. Dunbar. 2017. "Perceptions of Scientific Research Literature and Strategies for Reading Papers Depend on Academic Career Stage." *PLoS ONE* 12 (12): e0189753.

Hunter, Kerry, and Harry Tse. 2013. "Making Disciplinary Writing and Thinking Practices an Integral Part of Academic Content Teaching." *Academic Learning in Higher Education* 14 (3): 227–239.

Jacobs, Cecilia. 2005. "On Being an Insider on the Outside: New Spaces for Integrating Academic Literacies." *Teaching in Higher Education* 10 (4): 475–487.

Jolliffe, David A., and Allison Harl. 2008. "Studying the 'Reading Transition' from High School to College: What Are Our Students Reading and Why?" *College English* 70 (6): 599–617.

Kift, Sally. 2009. *Articulating a Transition Pedagogy to Scaffold and to Enhance the First Year Student Learning Experience in Australian Higher Education*. Final report for the ALTC Senior Fellowship Program.

Kozeracki, Carol A., Michael F. Carey, John Colicelli, and Marc Levis-Fitzgerald. 2006. "An Intensive Primary-Literature–Based Teaching Program Directly Benefits Undergraduate Science Majors and Facilitates Their Transition to Doctoral Programs." *CBE—Life Sciences Education* 5:340–347.

Lea, Mary R., and Sylvia Jones. 2011. "Digital Literacies in Higher Education: Exploring Textual and Technological Practice." *Studies in Higher Education* 36 (4): 377–393. https://doi.org/10.1080/03075071003664021.

Lear, Emmaline L., Linda Li, and Sue Prentice. 2016. "Developing Academic Literacy through Self-Regulated Online Learning." *Student Success* 7 (1): 13–23.

Levine, Elena. 2001. "Reading Your Way to Scientific Literacy." *Journal of College Science Teaching* 31 (2): 122–125.

Manarin, Karen, Miriam Carey, Melanie Rathburn, and Glen Ryland. 2015. *Critical Reading in Higher Education: Academic Goals and Social Engagement*. Bloomington: Indiana University Press.

McKay, Jade, and Marcia Devlin. 2014. "'Uni Has a Different Language . . . to the Real World': Demystifying Academic Culture and Discourse for Students from Low Socioeconomic Backgrounds." *Higher Education Research and Development* 33 (5): 949–961. https://doi.org/10.1080/07294360.2014.890570.

Muench, Susan B. 2000. "Choosing Primary Literature in Biology to Achieve Specific Educational Goals." *Journal of College Science Teaching* 29 (4): 255–260.

Nallaya, Shashi, and Jane Kehrwald. 2013. "Supporting Academic Literacies in an Online Environment." *Journal of Academic Language and Learning* 7 (2): A79–A94.

Osborne, John. 2002. "Science without Literacy: A Ship without a Sail?" *Cambridge Journal of Education* 32 (2): 203–218.

Overton, Tina, and Liz Johnson. 2016. *Evidence-Based Practices in Learning and Teaching for STEM Disciplines*. Occasional paper, Deakin University. http://www.acds-tlcc.edu.au/wp-content/uploads/sites/14/2016/07/ACDS-stem-principles-WEB.pdf.

Patterson, Alexis, Diego Roman, Michelle Friend, Jonathon Osborne, and Brian Donovan. 2018. "Reading for Meaning: The Foundational Knowledge Every Teacher of Science Should Have." *International Journal of Science Education* 40 (3): 291–307.

Round, Jennifer E., and A. Malcolm Campbell. 2013. "Figure Facts: Encouraging Undergraduates to Take a Data-Centered Approach to Reading Primary Literature." *CBE—Life Sciences Education* 12 (1): 39–46. https://doi.org/10.1187/cbe.11-07-0057.

Smith, Geoffrey R. 2001. "Guided Literature Explorations." *Journal of College Science Teaching* 30 (7): 465–469.

Thies, Linda. C. 2012. "Increasing Student Participation and Success: Collaborating to Embed Academic Literacies into the Curriculum." *Journal of Academic Language and Learning* 6 (1): A15–31.

Thomas, David R. 2006. "A General Inductive Approach for Analyzing Qualitative Evaluation Data." *American Journal of Evaluation* 27 (2): 237–246.

van Pletzen, Ermien. 2006. "A Body of Reading: Making 'Visible' the Reading Experiences of First-Year Medical Students." In *Academic Literacy and the Language of Change*, edited by Lucia Thesen and Ermien van Pletzen, 104–129. London: Bloomsbury.

Vygotsky, Lev. 1978. *Mind in Society*. London: Harvard University Press.

Wenk, Laura, and Loel Tronsky. 2011. "First-Year Students Benefit from Reading Primary Research Articles." *Journal of College Science Teaching* 40 (4): 60–67.

Wingate, Ursula. 2006. "Doing Away with 'Study Skills.'" *Teaching in Higher Education* 11 (4): 457–469.

Wingate, Ursula, and Christopher Tribble. 2012. "The Best of Both Worlds? Towards an English for Academic Purposes/Academic Literacies Writing Pedagogy." *Studies in Higher Education* 37 (4): 481–495.

Neela Griffiths is Senior Lecturer in the Academic Language and Learning Team at the University of Technology Sydney (UTS), Australia. Neela has been awarded an Australian Government Office of Learning and Teaching Citation for an outstanding contribution to student learning in undergraduate science, a UTS teaching and learning award, and two UTS citations for her work on developing academic literacies in the undergraduate science curriculum.

Yvonne C. Davila is Senior Lecturer in Higher Education Learning Design and Environmental Sciences in the Faculty of Science at the University of Technology Sydney, Australia. Yvonne has been awarded an Australian Award for University Teaching Citation for an outstanding contribution to student learning supporting student transition and success, and two UTS teaching and learning awards for her work on first-year university experience and developing academic literacies in the undergraduate science curriculum.

8

READING AND RELATIONSHIPS IN ORGANIC CHEMISTRY

BRETT MCCOLLUM
LAYNE MORSCH

Mastery of the language of chemistry often focuses on symbolic communication, as shown in figure 8.1. For more than 140 years, the symbolic language of chemistry has been instrumental to advances in the field (Goodwin 2008). Clarisse Habraken (2004, 90–91) describes the value of pictorial representations in chemistry as follows: "Chemists cannot talk to each other without the use of drawings and increasingly so, by using computer-generated pictures and molecular models. Because, in chemistry, the picture has become more than this; it has become a way of thinking and the dominant way of thinking.... The evolution from the first primitive drawings of 125 years ago to today's computer-generated drawings is a clear demonstration of the simultaneous evolution of a science and its scientific language." For many STEM fields, symbolic language has become the dominant form of written communication. Reading in these fields can be equated with the correct interpretation of the various representational systems. This explains the existing emphasis in higher education on understanding and communicating through the chemical symbolic language (Grove, Cooper, and Rush 2012; Flynn and Featherstone 2017).

Unfortunately, our focus on symbolic communication has resulted in neglecting the mastery of written and verbal modes of chemistry communication (Bhattacharyya and Bodner 2005). Without practice reading textual descriptions of chemical reactions, developing chemists are not familiar with the words to describe their field. Anecdotally, this can carry on into graduate school with doctoral candidates commonly struggling to describe their research without a paper and pen to symbolically represent what they cannot express in words.

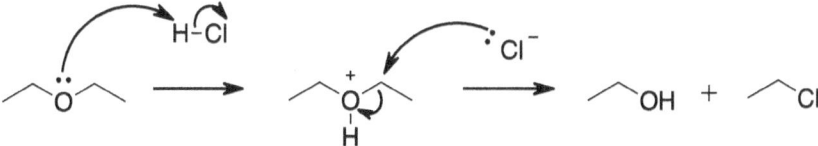

Fig. 8.1 An example of chemical symbolic language, using the skeletal formulae shorthand for structures and the electron-pushing formalization to illustrate the flow of electrons within the system.

The lack of practice with reading text in chemistry has even more concerning consequences. Gautam Bhattacharyya and George Bodner (2005) have observed that not only do novices struggle to benefit from the textual descriptions, students perform worse when written descriptions accompany the symbolic reaction schemes than when only the symbolic representation is presented! The text descriptions appear to confuse students, even though they are written in a similar manner to the verbal description an instructor would present in class. Furthermore, even though students are taught the nomenclature for chemical compounds, learners are unable to combine proper chemical terminology into sentences to accurately describe symbolic representations of reaction mechanisms to a peer. Instead, when students attempt to communicate using a new language, such as the professional language of chemistry, they often create a unique system. This distinct linguistic system that exists between the native and target languages is called an interlanguage (Selinker 1972). Interlanguage has been observed in science classrooms as students attempt to learn and implement disciplinary terminology and concepts (Lemke 1990). Groups of learners may then blend their individual interlanguages to form a local dialect that is functional between familiar individuals but is scientifically incorrect or unusable outside that local group.

Elaine Tarone (2014) has asked the question of what would happen if adult interlanguages fossilized, meaning that a learner stabilizes with an interlanguage short of full identity with the target language. We suggest that this could be a significant problem for an individual working in a professional field. After all, as Jay L. Lemke (1990, ix) said, "'Talking Science' does not mean simply talking about science; it means doing science through the medium of language." Learners that do not move beyond their interlanguage may struggle to communicate with others in a professional setting.

We propose that the inability of novices to describe chemical reactions or interpret written descriptions may be linked to insufficient practice with reading descriptions of chemical reactions in their textbooks and course materials. Insufficient engagement with learning materials may be related to learners' motivation. Aaron E. Black and Edward L. Deci (2000) used self-determination theory to explore self-regulation and learner motivation in organic chemistry. They classified the actions of the course instructor as either autonomy supportive or controlling, and individual students were identified as either autonomously and intrinsically motivated or extrinsically motivated. Black and Deci (2000) found that students who were intrinsically motivated at the start of the course were more likely to persist. Additionally, those that increased their intrinsic motivation during the course did not require instructor support or intervention to succeed. Importantly, this included students that were not intrinsically motivated at the beginning of the course. In contrast, those students that were extrinsically motivated strongly benefited from autonomy support situated within interpersonal peer interactions. While Black and Deci did not examine the impact of interpersonal learning interactions on engagement with learning materials, it is clear from their findings that faculty can support students that are not autonomously motivated in organic chemistry by adopting a pedagogy of interpersonal, autonomous learning experiences.

The processes of learners working together to build knowledge are described within social constructivism (Vygotsky 1978; Palincsar 1998). Inevitably, these interpersonal interactions lead to learners comparing their abilities with those of their peers. Social comparison theory has shown that students often compare themselves to others that are lower performing (downward comparison) or higher performing (upward comparison) than themselves. These comparisons can leave students with feelings of superiority or inferiority compared to others, but they can also lead to positive outcomes, including identifying a better-performing person as a model to aspire to (Festinger 1954; Dijkstra et al. 2008). Social comparison has also been shown to increase competition as students become more aware of their skill deficits related to others (Garcia, Tor, and Gonzalez 2006; Huguet et al. 2001). To encourage positive aspects of social comparison while avoiding some of the potential for negative results of this competition, such as lower levels of cooperation and problem solving (Orosz, Farkas, and Roland-Lévy 2013), a low-pressure environment that allows students to compare with one another without directly competing for higher grades would be ideal (Reeve and Deci 1996).

In this chapter, we describe the use of online collaborative learning (OCL) to facilitate autonomous interpersonal learning in organic chemistry based on peer relationships established across international borders.

OCL using synchronous communication methods is a relatively new area of study within teaching and learning research, emerging in tandem with advances in information communication technologies (McCollum 2020). Our intention of using OCL is to provide students the opportunity to contextualize reading assignments and course concepts as they collaboratively learn with a remote peer through video-conferencing software. We hypothesize that the autonomously supported peer relationships forged through online collaborative assignments (OCAs) motivate enhanced reading compliance similarly to oral performances in class (Nilson 2010, 211–222).

Context

We have previously reported on the importance of relationships in flipped learning (McCollum et al. 2017) as well as what constitutes a successful implementation of collaborative learning (Falcione et al. 2019). These studies revealed that peer relationships formed during active learning in the classroom were an important factor in motivating engagement in the processes of the active learning classroom, including reading preparation (McCollum et al. 2017). However, the development of relationships in the classroom had its own drawback. Interlanguage, the creation and use of terminology that is functional between familiar peers but scientifically incorrect, has been reported in university-level chemistry education (Bhattacharyya and Harris 2018) and was occurring in our classrooms. For example, students at Mount Royal University were using the term *moose antlers* based on an analogy taught by a tutorial instructor to describe the tertiary-butoxide moiety. The *moose antlers* substituent would not be understood by chemistry students who had not attended tutorials taught by this instructor. Interlanguage undermines a graduate's professionalism and should be minimized (Skagen et al. 2018).

We anticipated that communication between unfamiliar peers would limit the use of chemical descriptions unique to one classroom and thus inhibit interlanguage. Having identified our shared interest in promoting academic reading and using active learning strategies to empower learners, we worked together to design the OCAs. Among other goals, the OCAs between international student partners were explored as a means to further motivate improved reading habits and to minimize interlanguage. We anticipated that interactions between peers in a flipped classroom and between international peers for OCAs would provide practice with reading and explaining descriptions of chemical reactions that has been underemphasized in chemistry education. We aimed to identify a balance

Table 8.1 Number of study participants by year and institution.

	Fall 2016	Fall 2017
MRU	31	71
UIS	44	33

between students developing relationships that motivate good reading habits and students becoming so familiar that interlanguage develops.

Our research questions for this study are as follows: (1) How does student reading compliance in active learning classrooms change with the implementation of OCAs? (2) If an impact is detected, what factors motivate this change in reading compliance?

Study Participants

This study involved learners enrolled in Organic Chemistry I, a required second-year university course for students majoring in chemistry and life sciences. Although international standards for the curriculum in this course do not exist, there is significant overlap among most institutions in North America. Early in the design process, we examined the curricula at our two universities and made minor modifications to course content and learning outcomes to ensure that students could successfully contribute to the OCAs (McCollum et al. 2019). In the fall 2016 and 2017 semesters, students at Mount Royal University (MRU) in Calgary, Alberta, Canada, were each partnered with an international peer at the University of Illinois Springfield (UIS) in the United States. The number of participants is reported in table 8.1. Approval for the study was obtained from the Human Research Ethics Board (MRU HREB #2015-89 and #2016-51) or Institutional Review Board (UIS IRB #17-003 and AU IRB #2017-37-03) of each university. Ongoing informed consent was collected from the participants at each stage of data collection. Consent forms, surveys, and research interviews were managed by nonteaching members of the research team to avoid the potential conflict due to dual roles of course instructor and researcher.

Learners were semirandomly assigned to their partners. In 2016, partnerships were assigned based on similar levels of consent for the research study (Skagen et al. 2018). In 2017, partnerships were organized between international students by matching availability for online partnership meetings. Due to differences in the class sizes, some groups of three were formed. Student demographics of gender (approximately 70 percent female) and age (mean age of twenty-one years) were similar among all classes and both universities. Descriptions of the active learning methods used in these classrooms have been previously reported (McCollum 2016; McCollum et al. 2017; Morsch 2016; Skagen et al. 2018).

Online Collaborative Assignment Design

The OCAs were designed to encourage students to use proper chemistry terminology during their collaborative problem-solving meetings. Before online meetings, students were expected to individually complete their assigned readings and complete preparatory work on their half of each assignment, with partners given complementary assignments. The assignments required students to weave their work together, creating incentive for preparation. Students that did not do the work in advance of the meeting expressed regret and discomfort at making their partner wait while they completed their half of the preparation. An example question from one of the six OCAs is provided in figure 8.2 and table 8.2.

In this question, the MRU student was assigned the task of completing the reading assignment in order to be familiar with the necessary terminology and then constructing a description of the reaction mechanism using the terminology and concepts from the textbook. The partner (at UIS) was assigned the same preparation for the next question in the OCA. During their online meeting, the MRU student would read their prepared description to their partner, who would then attempt to sketch the original reaction mechanism based on the description. The UIS partner would show their sketch to the MRU student over the video chat, and the MRU student would verify if their sketch matched the original provided in the MRU assignment. If the student drawing and the original did not match, the MRU student would inform their partner. Without revealing the correct structure, the partners would discuss their work and identify any misconceptions on either side. After this question, the roles would be reversed, and a new question would be attempted. This did not guarantee that both learners acquired the same proficiency in the chemical language. For example, one partner may have become better at explaining or describing a structure, while the listener remained poor at interpreting the description to generate the corresponding symbolic representation. However, in this manner, the OCAs provided an environment for all students to apply the knowledge acquired from their course readings, enhancing their conceptual understanding of course content through social construction of knowledge and facilitating practice with problem-solving in organic chemistry.

Table 8.2 An example of a typical question style present in the OCAs.

MRU student version	UIS student version
Before meeting with your partner: • Prepare a description of the following reaction mechanism using language similar to that in the provided example. During your meeting: • Read your description to your partner and have them draw the mechanism based on your description. Don't show the mechanism to your partner. • Discuss if their drawing accurately represents what you described. If not, consider if they misunderstood what you asked them to draw, or if you described it incorrectly. Your reaction mechanism is (don't show it to your partner): (image shown in fig. 8.2).	During your meeting: • Your partner will read to you a description of a reaction mechanism. You will draw the mechanism based on their description. • Show your partner the mechanism you sketched. • Discuss if your drawing accurately represents what they described. If not, consider if you misunderstood what they asked you to draw, or if they described it incorrectly.

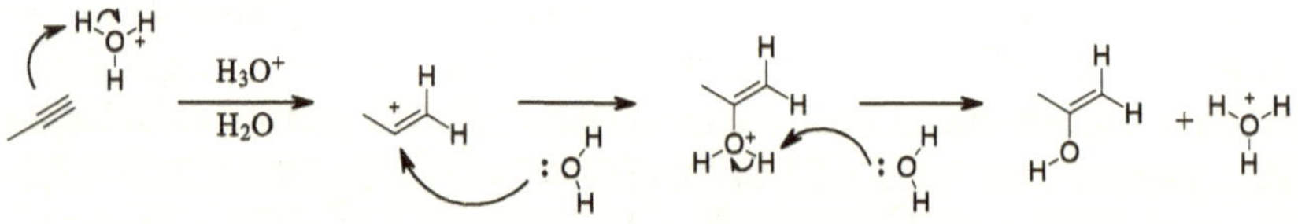

Fig. 8.2 Reaction mechanism drawing for a sample OCA assignment (see table 8.2).

OCAs were not graded for accuracy. Rather, students were informed that OCA assessment was based on completion and evidence of their collaborative problem-solving process. The intention of this design choice was to avoid students giving each other the answers (see fig. 8.2 and table 8.2) and bypassing the collaborative interactions.

Methodology

Mixed methods were used in this study, aligning with the nature of our two research questions. The first question relates to reading compliance and is inherently quantitative. The second question is about motivating factors, which requires qualitative approaches.

Quantitative Data and Methods

Data sources incorporated to assess quantitative impact included surveys and analytics data. Surveys were conducted with students from MRU, which included a question on reading compliance. Since the UIS class used an online textbook (Larsen et al. 2017), Google Analytics were available to quantify student usage. Welch's t-test (Welch 1947, 28) was used for statistical analysis of quantitative survey responses and textbook usage reports.

Qualitative Data and Methods

Qualitative data were necessary to understand changes in students' reading habits during the course. These data were collected via weekly reflections submitted online, surveys, and semistructured interviews. The weekly reflections were designed as an autonomous support providing an opportunity for students to be metacognitive about their learning in organic chemistry and their OCL experiences. As an example, one reflection prompted students to create a metaphor for OCL (Wentzel et al. 2019). The surveys included questions on oral and symbolic communication confidence in organic chemistry as well as the benefits and challenges of engaging in OCL (Skagen et al. 2018, 567).

Semistructured interviews were conducted by trained third- and fourth-year undergraduate research assistants. All interviews took place within the final two weeks of the semester. In total, individual or group interviews were conducted with fifty participants during fall 2016 and fall 2017. When possible, interviews were scheduled for groups of two or three participants (Morgan 1996, 29). This style of interview, a focus group, provides two primary benefits: (1) respondent's comments can generate reactions from other group members, and (2) when participants coinhabit the community explored by the focus group, each member functions as a check or balance to minimize false or extreme responses (Patton 2002). Some individual interviews were necessary due to scheduling issues. Interviews lasted between thirty and sixty minutes. The interview discussion prompts explored the student experience of OCAs.

Video recordings of students' online meetings were collected only in 2016. These recordings were used to evaluate the amount of correct chemical terminology relative to interlanguage used by the students in their conversations. The process of video recording for the students was determined to be a barrier to the collaborative activity for some students, as previously described (McCollum et al. 2019), and was removed from later iterations of OCAs.

Thematic analysis (Braun and Clarke 2006; Saldana 2009) of reflections, survey responses, and interviews was employed to analyze student perceptions. Independent parallel coding was completed by all team members on a subset of the transcribed interviews to generate initial codes. Discrepancies in coding by members across the multiuniversity team were resolved over video chat. Codes were grouped into themes and refined through an iterative process. Focused coding was then used to apply this code scheme to the remaining interviews and other qualitative data sources (Charmaz 1996; Thomas 2006), with each source assigned to two or more team members to ensure interrater reliability. The emergent themes were impact, barriers, resources, and collaborative learning approaches. We have previously reported on the barriers that students experienced in OCL and the strategies they developed for overcoming many of these barriers (McCollum et al. 2019). We have also found that OCL with an international peer led learners to develop greater communication confidence in chemistry, both oral and symbolic, as well as establish the foundation of their professional identity as an emerging scientist (Skagen et al. 2018, 567). We have not previously reported our analysis examining a possible link between student peer relationships, reading habits, and use of interlanguage.

IMPLEMENTING THE OCAS: ARE STUDENTS READING MORE?

Our first research question was, How does student reading compliance change with the implementation of OCAs? We answer this question by comparing quantitative metrics before the implementation of the OCAs and at the end of the 2017 semester (the second implementation of the OCAs). Due to the difference in data available for a print textbook (McCollum) as opposed to one online (Morsch), we explore the data for the two universities separately.

McCollum's organic chemistry students used a print textbook. He asked his students to self-report their reading compliance at the end of the semester using a scale from 0 (never) to 10 (always). Results for the OCA implementations in fall 2017 ($n = 71$, $M = 8.6$, $SD = 2.2$) were each compared to end-of-semester values from winter 2016, an active learning classroom before the OCAs ($n = 23$, $M = 8.0$, $SD = 2.1$). Welch's t-test with $a = 0.05$ was used for the comparison. A significant increase in reading compliance was observed ($t(94) = 1.18$, $P < 0.01$).

Morsch's use of an online textbook permitted him to track student reading, albeit at the class level. Page views per student increased by 41 percent, and time spent using the textbook increased by 25 percent from fall 2015 (active learning classroom before the OCAs) to fall 2017 (active learning classroom using OCAs). Thus, we see that the addition of the OCAs improved student reading compliance at the class level.

IMPLEMENTING THE OCAs: WHY ARE STUDENTS READING MORE?

In a previous study, we identified the importance of relationships in flipped learning (McCollum et al. 2017), showing that as students overcome their fears connected to social comparison theory (Festinger 1954) and develop peer relationships, they become more autonomous. Herein, we present evidence that implementing OCL as an autonomous supportive instructional method improved student reading habits. We must now ask, What is the impact of the OCAs on reading behaviors?

Students Are Forging International Relationships

The OCAs were deployed in our organic chemistry classes in the fall 2016 and fall 2017 semesters. Most partnerships functioned well. Not counting group changes due to students who dropped the course, only three groups out of seventy-four in fall 2017 required some level of instructor intervention. For both years of implementation, we gathered student feedback on the experience in many forms, including interviews, reflections, and surveys.

Analysis of data sources revealed a theme of establishment of trust and formation of a relationship between partners: "We would usually have a period of time, either before or after or sometimes both, when we weren't recording when we would just chat. [It] was fun because then we could compare what we were doing in class that week or sometimes like some personal stuff. Just like, uh yeah, some personal stuff." These partners were strangers from different countries who never met in person (only over video chat). The tone of this student's voice was particularly revealing, indicating that the personal conversation topics were private between the two students. While reflecting on those private conversations during the interview, the students weren't going to share details of those conversations with the interviewer.

Another participant described how they joined another group after their partner dropped the course and were witness to a relationship that had already formed between the two students from Calgary and Springfield: "My group of three was actually fun. They were a group before I joined them. They already had, like, a really close relationship. They would talk about each other's personal lives like they were friends! I was like, 'Aw, man, like, that's cool!' And then, they let me in, and then we became good friends." Keep in mind that the initial partnership had completed only two online meetings before this third member joined their group and that most meetings lasted less than an hour (based on submitted video recordings of the meetings). These students had established a relationship with their partner and had done so quickly.

International Relationships Are Improving Student Reading Behaviors

In their reflections and during the interviews, our participants repeated this observation: "It really does force you to just be familiar with the material and actually read it. You want to do well and you want to understand it because you don't want to look like an idiot. You don't want to look like an idiot so you're going to do it right. So, that's the main incentive, not really the points [grades]. It does make you understand the material." As described by this student (from 2017, without video recordings), the relationships that participants reported developing were an important motivator for reading the assigned material and becoming familiar with the course concepts. These relationships were important for reforming the reading compliance of extrinsically motivated learners. As Black and Deci (2000) note, pedagogy that is autonomous supporting through interpersonal peer interactions is even more important for students who were not initially autonomously motivated in organic chemistry. This change in behavior goes beyond mere reading compliance. This student did not say that they could avoid looking like an idiot simply by completing the readings. Rather, the main incentive for reading was a desire to perform well during the OCAs with their partner. This desired performance level required familiarity with and understanding of the material. Thus, the OCAs motivated students to engage with their reading for deeper learning, changing their reading behaviors relative to students that did not experience the OCAs.

Keep in mind that student partnerships had autonomy over when they met, whether they chose to compete the suggested preparatory work before meeting or during the meeting, and how much additional studying they engaged in individually before meeting. Although the student partners were not in direct competition for grades (being at different universities), the efforts of one partner would affect the experience of the other. Thus, to encourage positive aspects of the collaboration, we did not grade the OCAs for accuracy. Rather, students were assessed for evidence of a meaningful collaborative learning experience (e.g., documentation of the chemical symbolic communication used during the meeting and a narrative description of the process partners used to achieve a shared answer to each question). This design promoted a low-pressure environment similar to that described by Johnmarshall Reeve and Edward L. Deci (1996).

Another participant described how their partner and the assignments themselves kept them on task:

> It was really good. Like I said, there were a few things that were challenging about it, but we got through it. I think that was kind of the point, for it to be a bit challenging. It forced me to interact with material which I probably wouldn't have until later. You need to know this stuff by the time [of your meeting], it keeps you on track. Most college students don't study until there's an exam, but doing the [online collaborative] assignments you have to at least understand this portion of the material. You're never at the last minute like "Oh my God, I don't know anything" and then freaking out, because you have the assignments.

Although this participant also describes the peer interactions as a motivator for studying, they identify that the meeting with their partner creates a deadline for studying. Many students reported a realization that their partner is depending on them due to the complementary assignment design of the OCAs. Students appear to want to be reliable partners, perhaps because their partner has been helpful to them, working with them to overcome challenges. Surprisingly, none of the partnerships had two students that both consistently failed to prepare.

Online Collaborative Learning Inhibits Local Dialects

Previous to the use of OCAs, we had observed learner interlanguage resulting in the formation of local dialects between groups of students in our active learning classrooms. In contrast, review of the OCA meeting video recordings demonstrated that no "local" chemistry dialect emerged between remote partners during the six OCAs. Instead, during the limited number of interactions, students discovered how chemistry terminology is shared across international boundaries: "I was just expecting there to be more conflicts in the language. I know we both speak English, but with some of the terminology we use. There wasn't as many conflicts as

I expected considering we were in two different countries. We were on the same page." Several students reported being surprised at how chemistry is described using the same words in different countries, even though Canada and the United States are both English-speaking countries. Others expressed a realization that science is a global endeavor, and so it would be natural for experts to have shared terminology. A few students were amused by regional pronunciations of chemistry terms found in their textbooks, such as *nomenclature*: "No-men-cla-ture [/ˈnoʊmɛnˈkleɪtʃʊər/] versus nomen-clature [/noʊˈmɛɪŋ.ˌklahtʃʊər/]. We say 'nomenclature' or something. I don't know how he pronounces it. We say 'nomenclature,' and then they say something else that's like 'what?'" (The pronunciations in brackets for the previous quote are based on the International Phonetic Alphabet [International Phonetic Association, n.d.].)

Participants also reported that the OCAs resulted in greater confidence in reading and communicating in chemistry. Consider the following pair of quotes: "I've always felt more comfortable communicating chemistry through pictures, but the collaborative assignment forced me to explain things verbally. Although this was difficult, I think it made my understanding of the material better" and "Since beginning this semester, I feel as though my ability to accurately explain and describe chemistry concepts has greatly improved. I find that I have much more confidence, both talking about and understanding chemistry concepts while reading about chemistry." This improved confidence is an exciting result for us. One of the most common complaints about reading chemistry textbooks is that they are confusing and are packed full of unfamiliar terminology linked through an assortment of symbolic and graphical representations. It appears that a successful approach to help students overcome the challenge of reading a textbook full of new terminology is to connect them with an unfamiliar peer with whom they are required to practice using that terminology. The students shouldn't share a classroom experience, to prevent them from referring to examples from class as a terminology avoidance tactic.

We have often been asked why we don't simply have our own students engage in the same assignments as the OCAs locally, within our own classrooms—why do we have students doing the work online with a remote peer? Previous investigations revealed that students were less likely to complete their assigned readings before in-class collaborative assignments and thus less likely to be familiar with the necessary disciplinary terminology (McCollum 2015). The use of interlanguage was common, and the intended benefits of those activities were not realized. In contrast, students who have engaged with a remote partner to complete the OCAs are required to use proper disciplinary language in order to be understood and to understand their partner. Students reported instances of not knowing how to communicate a concept to their partner. Unable to draw on a shared classroom experience, the students reported opening their textbooks to find the appropriate terminology and phrases to express their chemical thinking. As previously reported, OCL enables growth in oral communication confidence to occur in parallel with improvements in symbolic communication confidence (Skagen et al. 2018). Therefore, while chemical symbolic language will continue to be a paramount way of thinking in the field (Habraken 2004), our focus on symbolic language training does not need to preclude expanded training opportunities that encourage practice with chemical speaking. Perhaps OCL is a solution to the unintended consequences reported by Bhattacharyya and Bodner (2005) of our overdependence on the symbolic aspect of chemical language.

Conclusions

Arthur Chickering and Linda Reisser (1993) have said that students must be exposed to culture, community, and diversity in order to have a successful university experience, involving a commitment from the students to engage with others and develop mature relationships. Collaborative learning, both in class through flipped learning and online through OCAs, provides students opportunities to experience different cultures and communities, thus combating the deficit in peer relationships occurring on university campuses.

While course-based reading assignments are a solitary activity, research participants described completing their reading in order to be viewed as reliable partners. Participants at both universities in our study reported increased reading compliance in an active learning class that used OCAs relative to active learning models without the OCAs. Collaborative learning, both in the classroom and online, can be used as a motivator for reading, in which students establish strong connections between the symbolic and the written forms of the chemical language. Through the interviews and reflections, students described a desire to be familiar with appropriate terminology and chemical concepts as a means to understand and be understood by their partner. Furthermore, these peer relationships resulted in greater confidence in reading comprehension, familiarity with chemical terminology, confidence in communicating in chemistry, and awareness of regional pronunciations of shared terms.

This link between peer relationships in OCL and reading habits has impacts for all disciplines. No matter what course a student is taking, when interacting with their peers, students rank their abilities relative to those of their peers (Festinger 1954). By facilitating interpersonal learning interactions within a reward system that functions closer to the highly autonomous end of the continuum (Deci, Nezlek, and Sheinman 1981), faculty can better support students that are not intrinsically motivated at the beginning of the course (Black and Deci 2000). Our OCAs are based on interpersonal learning interactions, empower student pairs with significant autonomy, and use a reward system that is autonomous. As a result, students focus on the peer interactions and the relationship building rather than grades. Our students have reported wanting to be competent, or at least appear competent, in front of their peers. Thus, when faculty create the conditions for peer interaction, they are stimulating a desire in their students to appear knowledgeable. Ideally, this aspiration also results in a desire to learn, encouraging students to become more autonomously motivated than at the start of the course. When faculty go one step further and explicitly bring the textbook into those peer interactions, they are establishing this link between the peer interactions and reading habits. By carefully designing our instructional style and employing a series of online collaborative assignments to connect international peers for course-based problem solving, we have found that peer relationships are more influential in incentivizing good reading habits than the course content.

Acknowledgments

We thank Darlene Skagen, Tonda Chasteen, Brandon Shokoples, and Lauren VanderWal for their contributions to this project. Funding was provided to McCollum by the Petro-Canada Young Innovator Fund and a Mount Royal University Internal Research Grant. Funding was provided to Morsch by a UIS College of Liberal Arts and Sciences Scholarship Enhancement Grant, a Charles V. Evans Research Grant, the UIS Center for Online Learning Research, and the Service Faculty Fellows program.

References

Bhattacharyya, Gautam, and George Bodner. 2005. "'It Gets Me to the Product': How Students Propose Organic Mechanisms." *Journal of Chemical Education* 82 (9): 1402–1407.

Bhattacharyya, Gautam, and Michael Harris. 2018. "Compromised Structures: Verbal Descriptions of Mechanism Diagrams." *Journal of Chemical Education* 95 (3): 366–375. https://doi.org/10.1021/acs.jchemed.7b00157.

Black, Aaron E., and Edward L. Deci. 2000. "The Effects of Instructors' Autonomy Support and Students' Autonomous Motivation on Learning Organic Chemistry: A Self-Determination Theory

Perspective." *Science Education* 84 (6): 740–756. https://doi.org/10.1002/1098-237X(200011) 84:6<740::AID-SCE4>3.0.CO;2-3.

Braun, Virginia, and Victoria Clarke. 2006. "Using Thematic Analysis in Psychology." *Qualitative Research in Psychology* 3 (2): 77–101.

Charmaz, Kathy. 1996. "Grounded Theory." In *Rethinking Methods in Psychology*, edited by Jonathan Smith, Rom Harré, and Luk Van Langenhove, 27–49. London: Sage.

Chickering, Arthur, and Linda Reisser. 1993. *Education and Identity*. San Francisco: Jossey-Bass.

Deci, Edward L., John Nezlek, and Louise Sheinman. 1981. "Characteristics of the Rewarder and Intrinsic Motivation of the Rewardee." *Journal of Personality and Social Psychology* 40 (1): 1–10.

Dijkstra, Pieternel, Hans Kuyper, Greetje van der Werf, Abraham P. Buunk, and Yvonne G. van der Zee. 2008. "Social Comparison in the Classroom: A Review." *Review of Educational Research* 78 (4): 828–879. https://doi.org/10.3102/0034654308321210.

Falcione, Sarina, Eleanor Campbell, Brett McCollum, Julia Chamberlain, Miguel Macias, Layne Morsch, and Chantz Pinder. 2019. "Emergence of Different Perspectives of Success in Collaborative Learning." *Canadian Journal for the Scholarship of Teaching and Learning* 10 (2). https://doi.org/10.5206/cjsotl-rcacea.2019.2.8227.

Festinger, Leon. 1954. "A Theory of Social Comparison Processes." *Human Relations* 7:117–140. https://doi.org/10.1177/001872675400700202.

Flynn, Alison, and Ryan Featherstone. 2017. "Language of Mechanisms: Exam Analysis Reveals Students' Strengths, Strategies, and Errors when Using the Electron-Pushing Formalism (Curved Arrows) in New Reactions." *Chemical Education Research and Practice* 18:64–77.

Garcia, Stephen M., Avishalom Tor, and Richard Gonzalez. 2006. "Ranks and Rivals: A Theory of Competition." *Social Psychology Bulletin* 32:970–982. https://doi.org/10.1177/0146167206287640.

Goodwin, William. 2008. "Structural Formulas and Explanation in Organic Chemistry." *Foundations of Chemistry* 10:117–127.

Grove, Nathaniel, Melanie Cooper, and Kelli Rush. 2012. "Decorating with Arrows: Toward the Development of Representational Competence in Organic Chemistry." *Journal of Chemical Education* 89 (7): 844–849.

Habraken, Clarisse. 2004. "Integrating into Chemistry Teaching Today's Student's Visuospatial Talents and Skills, and the Teaching of Today's Chemistry's Graphical Language." *Journal of Science Education and Technology* 13:89–94.

Huguet, Pascal, Florence Dumas, Jean M. Monteil, and Nicolas Genestoux. 2001. "Social Comparison Choices in the Classroom: Further Evidence for Students' Upward Comparison Tendency and Its Beneficial Impact on Performance." *European Journal of Social Psychology* 31:557–578. https://doi.org/10.1002/ejsp.81.

International Phonetic Association. n.d. "The International Phonetic Alphabet and the IPA Chart." Accessed May 20, 2017. https://www.internationalphoneticassociation.org/content/ipa-chart.

Larsen, Delmar, Ronald Rusay, Robert Belford, Dietmar Kennepohl, Dianne Bennett, Allison Soult, Brett McCollum, Samuel Keasler, Joshua Halpern, Tim Soderberg, Kristie Kosti, William Stockwell, Kathryn Haas, and Layne Morsch. 2017. "Come Join the Party! Recent Progress of the Community Based LibreTexts (neé ChemWiki) Project." *Committee on Computers in Chemical Education Newsletter*, Spring 2017, paper 5. https://confchem.ccce.divched.org/2017SpringCCCENLP5.

Lemke, Jay L. 1990. *Talking Science: Language, Learning, and Values*. Norwood, NJ: Ablex.

McCollum, Brett. 2015. "Exploring the Role of Instructional Styles on Learning Experiences in a Technology-Enhanced Classroom with Open Educational Resources." Paper presented at the 2015 Symposium on Scholarship of Teaching and Learning, Banff, Alberta, November 12–14, 2015.

———. 2016. "Improving Academic Reading Habits in Chemistry through Flipping with an Open Education Digital Textbook." In *Technology and Assessment Strategies for Improving Student Learning in Chemistry*, edited by Madeleine Schultz, Siegbert Schmid, and Thomas Holme, 23–45. Washington, DC: American Chemical Society Symposium Series.

———. 2020. "Online Collaborative Learning in STEM." In *Active Learning in College Science: The Case for Evidence-Based Practice*, edited by Joel J. Mintzes and Emily M. Walter, 621–637. New York: Springer-Nature. https://doi.org/10.1007/978-3-030-33600-4_38.

McCollum, Brett, Cassidy Fleming, Kara Plotnikoff, and Darlene Skagen. 2017. "Relationships in the Flipped Classroom." *Canadian Journal for the Scholarship of Teaching and Learning* 8 (3). https://doi.org/10.5206/cjsotl-rcacea.2017.3.8.

McCollum, Brett, Layne Morsch, Brandon Shokoples, and Darlene Skagen. 2019. "Overcoming Barriers for Implementing International Online Collaborative Assignments in Chemistry." *Canadian Journal for the Scholarship of Teaching and Learning* 10 (1). https://doi.org/10.5206/cjsotl-rcacea.2019.1.8004.

Morgan, David. 1996. "Focus Groups." *Annual Review of Sociology* 22 (1): 29–152.

Morsch, Layne. 2016. "Flipped Teaching in Organic Chemistry Using iPads." In *The Flipped Classroom Volume 1: Background and Challenges*, edited by Jennifer Muzyka and Christopher Luker, 73–92. Washington, DC: American Chemical Society Symposium Series.

Nilson, Linda B. 2010. *Teaching at Its Best: A Research Based Resource for College Instructors*. San Francisco: Jossey-Bass.

Orosz, Gábor, Dávid Farkas, and Christine Roland-Lévy. 2013. "Are Competition and Extrinsic Motivation Reliable Predictors of Academic Cheating?" *Frontiers in Psychology* 4 (87): 1–16. https://doi.org/10.3389/fpsyg.2013.00087.

Palincsar, A. S. 1998. "Social Constructivist Perspectives on Teaching and Learning." *Annual Review of Psychology* 49:345–375.

Patton, Michael. 2002. *Qualitative Research and Evaluation Methods*. Thousand Oaks, CA: Sage.

Reeve, Johnmarshall, and Edward L. Deci. 1996. "Elements of the Competitive Situation that Affect Intrinsic Motivation." *Personality and Social Psychology Bulletin* 22 (1): 24–33. https://psycnet.apa.org/doi/10.1177/0146167296221003.

Saldana, Johnny. 2009. *The Coding Manual for Qualitative Researchers*. Los Angeles: Sage.

Selinker, Larry. 1972. "Interlanguage." *International Review of Applied Linguistics in Language Testing* 10 (1–4): 209–232.

Skagen, Darlene, Brett McCollum, Layne Morsch, and Brandon Shokoples. 2018. "Developing Communication Confidence and Professional Identity in Chemistry through International Online Collaborative Learning." *Chemical Education Research and Practice* 19:567–582. https://doi.org/10.1039/C7RP00220C.

Tarone, Elaine. 2014. "Enduring Questions from the Interlanguage Hypothesis." In *Interlanguage: Forty Years Later*, edited by Zhaohong Han and Elaine Tarone, 7–26. Philadelphia: John Benjamins.

Thomas, David. 2006. "A General Inductive Approach for Analyzing Qualitative Evaluation Data." *American Journal of Evaluation* 27 (2): 237–246.

Vygotsky, L. S. 1978. *Mind in Society: The Development of Higher Psychological Processes*. Cambridge: Cambridge University Press.

Welch, B. L. 1947. "The Generalization of 'Student's' Problem when Several Different Population Variances Are Involved." *Biometrika* 34:28–35.

Wentzel, Michael, Isaiah Ripley, Brett McCollum, and Layne Morsch. 2019. "Practicing Multi-modal Chemistry Communication through Online Collaborative Learning." In *Communication in Chemistry*, edited by Richard Sinsinger and Amanda Koenig, 57–74. Washington, DC: American Chemical Society Symposium Series. https://doi.org/10.1021/bk-2019-1327.ch005.

Brett McCollum is Professor of Chemistry at Mount Royal University. He researches effective uses of technology for student learning and is a 3M National Teaching Fellow, Canada's most prestigious teaching award in higher education.

Layne Morsch is Professor in the Department of Chemistry at the University of Illinois Springfield. An Apple Distinguished Educator, he has received many teaching awards.

9

TEACHING ANALYTICAL READING IN PSYCHOLOGY AT ALVERNO COLLEGE

JOYCE TANG BOYLAND
KRIS VASQUEZ
JORDAN R. DONOVAN
RACHEL M. HENRY

Alverno College, the home of *Learning That Lasts* (Mentkowski 2000), is an alternative, Catholic, women's college, with workshop-style classrooms and no grades, designed for active, self-reflective, intrinsically motivated learning. Like many small private colleges, Alverno works hard to retain and graduate the students that it attracts. Well over two-thirds of our students are first-generation college students (Allen 2016). On many counts, we have been wildly successful. Nevertheless, we continue to seek and find gaps to fill in our students' education. Assumptions that held forty years ago about the skills our students come with no longer hold. As evidenced by a steadily increasing percentage of students being placed into our lowest-level first-year communication course, disparities in students' high school preparation are growing, yet all difficulties with reading are diagnosed and addressed only on an individual basis, an increasingly heavy burden for the staff. Since our mission remains to welcome all comers to the rewards—and joys—of higher education, we needed to take bold steps to manage gaps in student preparation.

STUDENTS AND FACULTY FACED DILEMMAS

In the psychology department, students were flustered by the senior empirical research project course, in which they conceptualize, carry out, and write up an original experiment; they wished they had more time to read the literature and discern the gaps that their research was supposed to fill. They had precious little experience reading the scholarly literature at all, let alone reading or writing through the lens of psychological science.

Analogous problems arose with the capstone seminar, in which students compose a full-length theoretical review paper.

At the same time, we faculty found ourselves facing a moral dilemma: more and more students were reaching their senior year without the discipline-specific reading skills to navigate the scholarly literature necessary to competently complete those courses. More frequently than was palatable, we needed to choose between failing students who were about to reach the end of their financial aid and passing students who were not as ready to graduate as we would have liked. When we present our psychology graduates to the world, we are certifying that they can read primary sources and keep up with new knowledge in the discipline. Our students need proficiency in academic language—language used in academic settings whose grammatical features are unfamiliar and typically require more effort and working memory to process than the language that students pick up in everyday life. An inability to process academic language is a barrier to advancement. To close achievement gaps, students need competence in academic language.

Faculty considered creating a preexperimental psychology course so that students would have more time to do the required literature review and theoretical framing of their experimental project, but we worried about burdening students with yet another graduation requirement. Eventually, students themselves brought up the possibility of creating a course to help them through the senior-level onslaught of scholarly reading, at which point the decision was made to go ahead and develop such a course: Analytical Reading in Psychology.

Four Cornerstones for Building Students' Scholarly Abilities

As we put together the new course, we drew both on our team's disciplinary training in linguistics, cognition, and development and on our institutional heritage in the scholarship of teaching and learning, including metacognition and motivation.

Cornerstone One: Explicit Task Analysis to Align Learning Goals

Alverno's outcome-based curriculum is framed by eight intellectual abilities, each broken down to different subskills to work on at different levels of intellectual maturity. These detailed ability statements serve to focus student and faculty attention, as they provide pictures of what successful performance could look like. Each assignment's outcomes are explicitly linked to course outcomes, in turn linked to departmental and college-wide outcomes, which were developed with a view toward creating value for professionals in their disciplines. Thus, we make explicit for students and external audiences the value of a liberal arts education in the professional world. This general orientation toward identifying and making explicit for students their path toward progress underlies our overall approach to the course we created.

Cornerstone Two: Grammar as Ally, Not Nemesis

We arrived as outsiders, not literacy experts, to the old debate about the value of teaching grammar (Hartwell 1985). Given reports of how traditional grammar is sometimes taught, we could understand views of grammar-teaching as a nemesis that stymies students' progress, as well as our colleagues' skepticism of our plans. Nevertheless, we were even more sympathetic to a position paper by the Assembly for the Teaching of English Grammar (ATEG), which points out facts such as "if [students] know how to find the main verb and the subject, they have a better chance of figuring out a difficult sentence" (Haussamen 2002). The sophomore-to-junior leap from textbook to scholarly literature brings an onslaught of difficult sentences, including many that do not (correctly) yield to default strategies learned in K-12 education (Beck, McKeown, and Kucan 2002, 3–6).

Morton Ann Gernsbacher's (1990) classic theory of language comprehension as structure building lays out an elegant account of the mental processes and representations that take a reader from passing eyes over script into a coherent comprehension of extended text (Gernsbacher and Kaschak 2013). Extensive psycholinguistic research shows that a foundational step in this process is building a grammatical representation of sentences—integrating words into phrases and clauses, then clauses into sentences, and so on up the hierarchy to a discourse model (Gernsbacher 1990; Christiansen and Chater 2016). In proficient expert reading, creation of grammatical structure and necessary shifts of attention proceed automatically, but when the challenge level is high, conscious effort may be required. Ying Guo, Alysia D. Roehrig, and Rihana S. Williams (2011) demonstrate empirically that morphological and syntactic awareness significantly predicts reading comprehension in adults. Given this situation, we wanted to give students grammatical tools to figure out difficult sentences. Furthermore, helping students attend to and integrate phrases into clauses and into coherent sentences supports their efforts to attend to and integrate higher-level text structures into coherent wholes. But is this a realistic hope?

Some fear that grammar is too difficult to learn, not only for the student but also for the teacher. However, grammatical analysis is much less monolithic and more adaptable than commonly assumed (Aarts and Haegeman 2006; Müller 2018). In particular, there is no need to teach traditional prescriptive grammar or any other kind of grammar as an end in itself, especially not in the form of definitions or rules. Students need only just enough ability to detect linguistic structure to build the foundation for their mental models of what is expressed by the text. Thus, rather than grammars heavily reliant on abstruse definitions and rules, the models of language that will serve best to ground the teaching of reading are ones that highlight the structural patterns that writers (and speakers) use (Boyland 2009; Tyler 2010; Diessel 2019). A substantial portion of our course is devoted to helping students practice grouping a sentence's words into constituent phrases correctly enough to do things such as connect a subject with its verb and a verb with its arguments. We aimed to craft a system that would help students find subjects and predicates without fear and then go on to dig into scholarly reading in the disciplines, complex embedded sentences and all. The goal is for students to use these tools to gain mastery over and appreciation of the disciplinary material that they are reading.

Cornerstone Three: Cognition for Language

Reading well requires well-developed mental representations that span levels of analysis. At the level of vocabulary, David Braze et al. (2007) show that adults' reading comprehension depends both on their decoding ability and on "lexical quality." Those adults whose knowledge of words included knowledge of pronunciation, roots and affixes, acceptable syntactic contexts, and semantic nuances generally understood more of what they read than readers with thinner lexical representations. Indeed, adults with little exposure to passive sentences show surprising difficulty comprehending even simple passive sentences (Street and Dabrowska 2014). Higher-order text structures—sentences, paragraphs, sections—also need to be represented (Wang 2009). The more connected each structure is to others, the richer the representation (Bybee 2010). Cognitive psychology gives similar accounts of the value of robustly connected representations of structures at multiple levels of analysis (Kintsch 1988; Gernsbacher 1990; Christiansen and Chater 2016).

The cognitive skill of reading well requires not just representations that become elaborated but also mental processes that become automatized skills through repeated active experience—processes such as translating letters to sounds, noticing Greek and Latin roots and affixes, grouping words into common phrases, parsing sentences into subjects and predicates, or finding the topic sentence of a paragraph (Hendrix and Griffin 2017; Seidenberg and MacDonald 2018). For example, "repeated exposure to specific syntactic constructions, such as relative clauses, will make them easier to process, and allow for more chunks to be kept in memory" (Christiansen and Chater 2016, 174). As students automatize low-level reading skills, they can increasingly devote attentional resources to higher-level comprehension, such as appreciating the big picture and making connections as new information comes in (Kintsch 1988; Ellis 2015). Fluency research highlights the role of enriched word knowledge and increasingly effort-free lower-level decoding processes that allow readers to shift attention to comprehension of larger structures (Samuels 2006).

Cornerstone Four: Metacognition in Support of Meaning-Making

Because academic language is so unfamiliar to students, teaching must address head-on the specific challenges and opportunities that academic language presents (Snow and Uccelli 2009). Giving students metacognitive tools supports them as they make meaning of texts and as they begin, through reading, to try on a new scholarly identity.

Gerald Graff and Cathy Birkenstein's (2010) *They Say / I Say* (*TSIS*) introduces students to the idea of scholarship as a conversation and provides word-for-word sentence frames that represent different rhetorical moves typically made by scholarly authors in the act of expressing a response to someone else's position. Although *TSIS* is primarily a composition textbook, it brings metacognition to the reading classroom in very helpful ways. To begin with, it alerts students to rhetorical structure, so that they begin to see the interplay of different voices in a single scholarly text. It goes on to elaborate explicitly for students what rhetorical moves might look like, complete with variations and slots and fillers, so that students develop lexically and grammatically concrete mental representations of a variety of rhetorical moves.

A second tool for the metacognitive toolbox is to recognize that texts reflect the values of the discipline and that both authors and readers have dynamic personal relationships with texts (Nowacek 2011; Rose 2015). Scholars not only produce texts but also consume them, and they do so selectively, according to their purposes. Opening students to this possibility not only improves the purposefulness and efficiency of their reading but also gives them a tangible sense of joining those in the know and building their identities as beginning scholars (Haas 1994; Nowacek 2017).

Self-assessment is a third angle on metacognition for the sake of meaning-making. Alverno emphasizes self-assessment as a powerful ingredient in lifelong learning. Ellen C. Carillo (2017) makes explicit what our students have always learned: self-assessment not only consists of evaluating what one is "good at" and "not good at" but also involves becoming aware of one's purpose for reading and planning to meet those goals. Beyond this, we aim for students to be prepared for the difficulties and emotions associated with difficulty.

Finally, cognitive psychologists (Bjork 1994; Soderstrom and Bjork 2015) have firmly established that optimal and lasting learning requires appropriate difficulty. A challenge for teaching is how best to maintain students' motivation in order to power their persistence through difficulty. Fortunately, simply being aware that intelligence improves with practice actually significantly improves persistence (Yan, Thai, and Bjork 2014; Yeager et al. 2016).

IMPLEMENTING ANALYTICAL READING IN PSYCHOLOGY

Our students come to Analytical Reading in Psychology as first-semester juniors, newly admitted to the major. Although they have taken lower-level college-wide requirements covering general reading strategies, they have little to no experience reading scholarly research articles. In this course, then, we point students toward skills and strategies that allow us to make progress even when conditions are not ideal and reading is not fluent.

The assigned readings are scholarly sources, including empirical articles, theoretical review papers, book chapters, and short reports. Some assignments focus on fine-grained analysis of language or disciplinary content; others ask students to paraphrase or summarize passages or articles or to infer authors' goals. The midterm and final exams ask students to browse donated hard-copy journals and individually select articles of personal or professional interest. Students then use their articles to address a gamut of varied questions.

Implementing Cornerstone One: Explicit Task Analysis to Align Learning Goals

We developed Analytical Reading in Psychology in accordance with Alverno norms: doing a task analysis of what students needed to learn, making those abilities explicit, and giving formative feedback according to stated outcomes. At the top level, we made it clear that reading in the discipline fits squarely into our departmental advanced outcomes. At a very concrete level, we instructed students in specific skills and, when practicing them together, explained how these skills allow them to carry out the activities that will eventually be expected of them in Experimental Psychology and in the Senior Seminar. In-class activities are formally linked to top-level outcomes, not just through in-person and written instructions but also through our course rubric. We use the metaphor of the classroom as a gym and the professor as a personal trainer to describe the work of the teacher in explicitly identifying and addressing fine-grained improvements that students can make to improve their work in the long term.

Implementing Cornerstone Two: Grammar as Ally, Not Nemesis

Counteracting the common student narrative of "I don't do grammar," we turned grammar into our ally. As we read scholarly sources together in our course, students quickly encounter sentences that they do not know how to process. Sometimes the apparent problem is unfamiliar vocabulary. However, getting a definition might not solve the actual problem, which is often syntactic in nature. Instead of simply guessing the meaning of unfamiliar words from context (much less possible in scholarly reading than in narrative reading [Graves 2007])—or simply ignoring those words and attempting to comprehend the sentence by rearranging the known words in a way that seems to make sense—we gave students grammatical structure as a more reliable way to understand difficult sentences.

Our attempts to give students a grammatical framework were motivated by our observations that students' attempted paraphrases of complex sentences often revealed not only a complete misunderstanding of the intended meaning of the sentence but also hints as to strategies that students were attempting to use. One typical student, for example, took the sentence "Our results provide strong support for models in which action intentions (in addition to movement intentions) play a crucial role in the observation and understanding of other people's actions" and paraphrased it as "Action intention models support people's actions by observing and understanding the role they play." Many students have picked up a strategy of responding to material they do not understand by taking hold of whatever words they understand and making as much sense as they can of them, relying on context. Such miscomprehensions are by no means uncommon, but they become visible only when students' reading is assessed at the level of sentences (Mulroy 2003).

To begin to build students' facility with the syntactic structures common in academic language, exercises early in the semester present simple sentences as samples to analyze for subject versus predicate + complement—for example, "The dog (subject) || chased (predicate verb) + the cat (complement)." Then, students are asked to construct their own simple sentences and identify the subjects and predicates. Soon, we ease students into compound and complex sentences by offering examples and asking them to expand their own simple sentences in different ways: first by adding adverbials in different places, then by adding modifiers to the subject and to the complement. Eventually, we model the process of analyzing difficult sentences and then ask students to try their hand at analyzing with classmates and on their own.

For written work, we specify a color-coding scheme: red for subjects, green for predicate verb groups, blue for complements, and yellow for adverbials. When they are ready, we provide red, green, blue, and yellow sticky notes on which they write the respective parts of a sentence, which they then stick together in a column, each succeeding colored square below each preceding square. Modifier phrases are marked with a highlighter: modifiers of the subjects are marked orange ("like red but a bit yellower than red"), while modifiers of the complements get marked turquoise ("like blue but a bit yellower than blue"). Notably, all this work can be done without any grammatical terminology, perhaps a relief to students and instructors alike.

We might, for example, attack a sentence such as "Also, individuals who feel pressured to suppress prejudice may experience psychological reactance" (Miller et al. 2011, 580).

1. Red: We would start with "Who (or what) blankety-blanked?" to break the simple sentence into the subject half ("What or who is blankety-blanking? *Individuals*") versus the predicate half ("They're ___-ing or they ___-ed? *May experience*") and find the break between *prejudice* and *may*.
2. Green: At the next step, they examine the predicate half, finding the predicate verb cluster (main verb *experience* with any "helping verbs" *may*) versus the rest of the predicate half.
3. Blue: If "the thing blankety-blanked something," we have found a complement ("They blankety-blanked what? *Reactance*").
4. Yellow: If "the thing did so in some way," we have an adverbial ("They blankety-blanked where/when/why/how? *Also*").
5. Orange: If we find out "which or what kind of thing blankety-blanked someone?" ("What kind of individuals? Individuals *who feel pressured to suppress prejudice*"), we have a modifier of the subject.

6. Turquoise: If we find out "which or what kind of thing got blankety-blanked?" ("What kind of reactance? *Psychological* reactance"), we have a modifier of the complement.

To simplify complex sentences, we ask students to substitute placeholders if there are long word groups, resulting in sentences like "In this way, this XYZ action blankety-blanked that ABC situation," or in this case, "People like X might do Y."

Sources of difficulty could be long phrasal sequences modifying a subject or complement (Biber and Gray 2016), which would get marked orange or turquoise. Or they could be embedded clauses (Snow and Uccelli 2009), which we could mark up lightly as "minisentences." Or they could be lists, whose grammatically parallel items could be marked A, B, C or 1, 2, 3 (Sturt, Keller, and Dubey 2010).

Implementing Cornerstone Three: Cognition for Language

Given the degree to which reading is a cognitive act, we draw on cognitive psychology to deepen students' mental representation of some aspect of the text, starting with words, or to increase the range or fluency of the processes students use to build their representations of the text. That is, we help students understand words, sentences, paragraphs, and sections, and we ask them to practice the cognitive processes necessary for building and using their understanding.

We Strengthen Linguistic Representations

We begin the semester by collectively reading aloud the introduction of a journal article; the first obstacles that students notice are unfamiliar vocabulary items. Lacking alternatives, students often fall back on strategies that were taught to them in earlier years in the context of reading children's or young adult stories, such as seeking semantic context clues, which are of limited value for reading difficult technical material (Anderson and Nagy 1992; Beck, McKeown, and Kucan 2002). To multiply the speed of vocabulary acquisition, we practice looking up etymologies so that frequently encountered roots and affixes will be reinforced and become islands of familiarity as students continue to encounter new words composed of roots and affixes.

A second strategy to increase retention of new vocabulary words is to practice pronunciation one syllable at a time, so that students gain multiple accurate mental representations of the new word in different modalities (Rosenthal and Ehri 2011). We also listen to online pronunciations to identify lexical stress patterns, a form of phonological representation relevant to adult reading (Breen and Clifton 2011; Kentner 2012). We explain that both of these habits were designed to make vocabulary learning longer-lasting and more effective, since simply attaching a dictionary definition to a string of letters that they cannot pronounce or reproduce will not create lasting memory traces.

As for rhetorical structures, the college composition literature on academic discourse as a conversation was enormously helpful in class. We referred frequently to Graff and Birkenstein's *They Say / I Say* (2010) to ask students if they were reading a "they say" or an "I say" and to attend to the relations between the "they say" (the sources to which the authors were responding) and the "I say" (the authors' own points). Students thus elaborated their mental representation of the ideas in the article by filling in the sources of the ideas.

We also taught students to attend to text structures, in particular the hierarchical representation of sections, subsections, and subsubsections, so that their mental maps of the text would better match the text. To help students represent hierarchical structure, we have used simple outlines, diagramming software, mind-mapping software, and most recently (and most effectively), free folding outliner software such as FoldOut (for PC) and OutlineEdit (for Mac).

Maintaining a multilevel hierarchical representation rather than flattening hierarchical text structures is difficult for some students. Much of the value of hierarchical text structure involves reducing working memory load by taking masses of content and allowing a reader to focus on only a few things at a time, either by taking a high-level view of just major sections or by zooming in and looking at just the subsubsections within a single subsection. Every semester, however, we have had students who reduced working memory load not in one of those two ways but by maintaining only two levels of analysis in mind at a time—section (top-level) and subsection (bottom-level). For these students, when the text's actual structure had three or more levels, their mental representation of the structure was distorted, leading to an inaccurate mental map of the text. The folding outliners have worked well because they dynamically represent the component > subcomponent relationship by allowing the user to play with folding up subcomponents inside the higher-level components or opening out components to reveal the subcomponents within. Then, there is no mistaking which is the larger overarching unit and which is the smaller component. Seeing the multilevel part-whole relationships allows these students to create more accurate mental models of the text.

We Ask Students to Practice Mental Processes Allowing Them to Build and Use Their Understanding

Keeping track of rhetorical and textual structures is how a reader stays oriented to both the big picture and the particulars of what they see in front of their eyes. If an article is seen as an undifferentiated mass of words, a long article can become an endless, unmotivating morass. Thus, when students begin to encounter longer, more advanced papers, we give them experience in chunking material into coherent bundles that take up less working memory than heaps of miscellaneous words. We give them model texts (Bunn 2013) of empirical articles, theoretical review articles, articles from adjoining disciplines, scholarly book chapters, and credible but nonscholarly sources.

Such practice in extracting voices and in folding and unfolding textual structures is an example of a general principle—namely, achieving fluency (broadly defined) through practice. We repeatedly spent flipped class time finding authors' and sources' voices, breaking down words and putting them together, and breaking down and putting together phrases, clauses, sentences, paragraphs, sections, and articles. Students learn to create one-sentence-per-paragraph summaries to gain a bird's-eye view of an article. We teach students to figure out why one author cited another and to figure out how the results they summarized address gaps in the literature, thus linking sentence-level understandings to a grasp of the whole. We consider how certain sentence structures are typically used in certain parts of an article, and we consider how different article structures are associated with different genres and different disciplines. Such practice in mindfully shifting attention from level to level smooths the process of creating coherence by integrating low-level information into higher-order understanding.

Implementing Cornerstone Four: Metacognition in Support of Meaning-Making

Successful reading of difficult text depends heavily on being able to derive meaning from text—both literal semantic meaning and human meaning. Psychology majors usually arrive on campus with a desire to "help people," which is construed largely as listening well with interpersonal sensitivity. Courses on research can seem like artificial obstacles in the way of accomplishing good in the world. In our analytical reading course, we aim to show students an alternative view of research as a way to broaden their view of helping people and increase their effectiveness in doing so.

Social psychology suggests that a sense of purpose and social belonging (Walton and Cohen 2011) improves engagement with material and persistence through difficulties. We chose articles to assign that bear on issues with social impact to build a sense of purpose as students connect the empirical literature with issues in their daily lives. The midterm and final are detailed analyses of articles that they select, according to their own interests, from among hard-copy journals donated by faculty; these assessment activities are presented explicitly as an opportunity to further their success in senior-level project courses and in graduate school by increasing their level of skill at deciphering the scholarly discourse around topics of particular interest, as well as by increasing their social impact. In these assessments, students share their analyses of their chosen articles, building camaraderie by seeing classmates like themselves beginning to take on a fledgling scholarly identity. Because a great deal of class time involves working through difficulties together and conversing about faculty experiences in working through unfamiliar material, students recognize that reading complex material is hard for many people, support each other through the challenges, and see that "people like them" can gradually develop strategies to work through even the densest prose.

On the first day of class, I (Joyce) relate to my students how I, as an undergraduate, used to consider my responsibilities satisfied when I had passed my eyes over an assigned reading from beginning to end. We go on to talk about what I had to learn, through experience, about how professionals read—nonlinearly, using headings and subheadings as guideposts to glean just what is needed for our purposes. Students enter the course intimidated by scholarly reading; the first assignment, a baseline check of their ability to read a journal article, reinforces the expectation of difficulty. After a few weeks, they are assigned a classic book chapter that specifically lays out the evidence for "desirable difficulties" in producing lasting learning (Bjork 1994). Very few students spontaneously make the connection between the content of the article and their own learning and self-assessment. Instead, as Michael Bunn (2013) points out, the applicability of the reading to their other work must be made plain. For many, this is an "aha" moment where they encounter the evidence that learning is hard, but the difficulty has rewards. Extended nonacademic discussion then ensues, where students emotionally process the implications of these findings. On the last day of class, I relate how I do not have a green thumb and have killed many plants. Then, each student receives a baby aloe plant. I explain that these were not propagated due to natural talent; rather, simple but steadfast watering led to incremental growth that is not visible day by day. Now here they are, a testament to what grows out of faithful attentiveness.

Impacts of Analytical Reading in Psychology

While this chapter is primarily a show-and-tell demonstrating the feasibility of an approach to teaching reading, we do have encouraging data to share. We begin with some quantitative data on student learning and retention and conclude with excerpts of qualitative data collected.

Quantitative Data

Because the analytical reading course was developed in response to our students' struggles in Experimental Psychology, we measured the value of Analytical Reading in Psychology by comparing pass rates in Experimental Psychology before and after its introduction as a departmental requirement. We excluded students in the transitional semesters who took the nascent course as an elective, since many of them were recommended for the course due to low reading skills. From fall 2012 on, eighty-two students took Experimental Psychology before they had the opportunity to take Analytical Reading. Of these, fifteen dropped, withdrew from, or failed Experimental Psychology, for an 18.3 percent noncompletion rate (81.7 percent successful completion). Beginning in the academic year 2016–2017, students have taken Analytical Reading as a prerequisite to Experimental Psychology. Since that time, seventy-eight students have taken Experimental Psychology. Of these, five dropped, withdrew, or failed, and seventy-three passed, for a 6.4 percent noncompletion rate (93.6 percent successful completion rate). A chi-squared test shows that there was a significant relationship between taking Analytical Reading and passing Experimental Psychology (χ^2 [1, N = 160] = 5.16, P = 0.021). The odds ratio for passing Experimental Psychology based on taking Analytical Reading is 3.27 (95 percent confidence interval [1.13, 9.48]). Thus, the students who took Analytical Reading had three times the odds of passing Experimental Psychology compared to those who did not take Analytical Reading.

Qualitative Data

Boyland (2017) reported on data we had available at the time, two semesters after instituting Analytical Reading in Psychology as a departmental requirement. Students finishing the Experimental Psychology course were asked to reflect on how they got through the semester, a sort of written exit interview. The qualitative observations we discuss below come from a variety of sources: student work samples, student reflections written while taking the class, student reflections while taking subsequent classes, alumni reflections, and faculty observations in this and subsequent classes. These comments and other observations have been gathered as part of the normal educational process over the eight semesters that the course has been taught, as well as through targeted data collection from alumni between May 2018 and January 2019, all of which was either approved or exempted by Alverno's Institutional Review Board. Across these data sources, we noticed significant themes: grammatical and rhetorical awareness, strategies for vocabulary, and meaning-making and identity.

Grammatical and Rhetorical Awareness

Faculty noted that students who took the class showed better comprehension and awareness of main points in the papers they read. While many factors besides grammar contributed, substantial improvements in students' paraphrasing of isolated sentences demonstrate that grammatical awareness contributed substantially to overall comprehension: "What's different is the quality of the summarizing and paraphrasing they do. I used to get a hodgepodge of ideas from the article and a Mad Libs style paraphrase (what's another word for 'hypothesis?' I'll put 'guess.')." Students and alumnae also noted improved comprehension: "I was always wondering why we did this but as time went on I figured out that it is a useful tool to be able to break down sentences. Breaking down sentences allows you to fully understand what the sentence is about and the important parts of it." Similarly, another alumna said,

> When I was in 200-level courses, I remember skimming over a lot of articles or reading them but not fully understanding what they were saying or trying to prove with the experiments. I think that after I took [the] class in Analytical Reading, I really noticed in Senior Seminar how much different an article looked to me. I wouldn't just skim it anymore. I always read it, broke it down not only by paragraphs, but even to sentences to fully understand what the article was saying. That was when I realized that I had changed the way that I saw and read an article and that I used to not understand what I was reading fully until after I took [the] class.

Another alumna specifically called out grammar practice: "Learning how to break down these articles helped the best, including breaking down individual sentences that may be complex or confusing."

Analyzing sentences into their functional constituents remains a laborious task for most students. But they almost universally report that when they encounter sentences that they do not understand, it is the most effective way to get the most accurate understanding of what is going on in the sentence. These would be sentences that they formerly would try to understand through contextual inference, word rearrangement, or thesaurus substitution—or that they would simply skip over. Through doing these exercises, students see that attending to grammatical structure is a support to reading comprehension, not a nemesis.

Faculty consistently noted students' improved grasp of the structure of arguments, leading to better understanding of articles and substantial improvement in the quality of the resulting writing. One comment connected *TSIS* (Graff and Birkenstein 2010) with improved coherence of students' reading: "Students are better able to identify central themes of the articles (instead of latching onto sentences in sort of haphazard ways and quoting them at me in case the sentences were important). They are able to separate the authors' ideas from claims that authors bring up to refute, which was a problem before we started this class. They understand how the structure of an argument proceeds. They can, when they need to, skim more efficiently because they are better able to locate clues as to what is being discussed." Furthermore, they "are better able to articulate their own interpretations and claims and link to supporting evidence than they used to be."

Students also appreciated *TSIS* for giving them an understanding of who is saying what in an article. Students and alumnae were almost unanimous in their enthusiasm for the one-sentence-per-paragraph technique. Many students, though only a few alumnae, reported on how thinking in terms of hierarchical structure brings out relationships between ideas: "One clue that I use to identify how different ideas in a research paper relate to one another is using hierarchal structure headings and subheadings." In any case, many students remarked on a new sense of coherence and mastery when reading scholarly articles, likely due to a combination of *TSIS*, extensive reading leading to fluency, and practice in linking lower-level structures into higher-order wholes. Student comments support this interpretation: "When I completed each subtopic paragraph I would pause, process what I just read and jot down a few notes in the space around it. Once I began doing this, over time these practices became second nature to me, and I found myself comprehending much more of what was being read."

Strategies for Vocabulary

Students have reported that learning pronunciation is a surprising but effective strategy for increasing vocabulary learning. Learning word roots was also valued, as in these two students' responses to a prompt asking for what strategies were most helpful: "Finding the meaning and origin, help me understand the sentence better and by learning the origin of the word, it is easier to understand why the word was chose [sic]," and "The way in which I looked up words before was not to the same extent as now that I've taken the class. Before the class I only looked at the definitions, but now I know to look up the etymology as well as the pronunciation."

Meaning-Making and Identity

Faculty note that students now "ask specific, directed questions about what I want in article summaries. They seem much more aware that reading is part of being a scholar." Identity as a scholar, furthermore, includes scholarly purpose: "[Previously,] there was no sense of student purpose in even the good paraphrases. Now I regularly get 'here's what they said, focusing on what's most useful for me, and my impressions about how strong this evidence is.' I get better summaries from the 'average' student now than I used to get from the students at the top of the class." Faculty teaching the senior capstone wrote, "Students often refer to the literature they looked at ... and it's clear that they do so with an understanding that they've delved into a real literature and that the experience of having done that work puts them in a very different position from having merely talked about some topic in some course." These comments speak to students' growing belongingness in the discipline.

Students' immediate and visible sense of release upon receiving "permission" to read articles nonlinearly according to their own purposes was palpable. Before receiving this permission, reading articles was often a task assigned to them that they were duty bound to complete on someone else's account. Afterward, it became an activity that they engaged in to accomplish specific goals for the near-term and long-term future, whether that be seeking an overview of a research area or preparing for graduate school or a career.

Many alumnae report delayed appreciation of the work that was done in the reading class. A representative comment is "Although I struggled most of my college years trying to understand the purpose of the assignments, or in general the material I was reading, I look back now and understand that it helped me stretch my thinking, look for the deeper intentions of what writers are implying and has helped me, per say [sic], 'connect the dots' when reading." One alumna has even offered to send a picture of their now-grown aloe plant.

Other alumnae comments related to becoming disciplinary readers: "I would dread when an instructor would mention even needing to include one scholarly article in a paper. The more practice I had, the more confident I felt. Currently, I am a graduate student and I use scholarly literature with virtually every assignment. I am confident that the work I put in in my undergraduate years has paid off." Similar comments were expressed even by alumnae who didn't remain in academia: "Although I am not currently enrolled in school, I still read scholarly articles in my personal research rather than shying away from them." The sense of identity and belonging that comes from mastery of reading is hard to miss: "I would often feel like I wasn't fully comprehending what I read. I remember feeling so different when I would read the articles, I would find for my senior seminar paper because I felt like I knew what I was doing. I felt like I had finally learned how to properly read an article and be able to fully understand it without any confusion and it felt amazing."

Overall Lessons Learned and Recommendations

Our experience of teaching Analytical Reading in Psychology has been overwhelmingly positive and continuously stimulating. Given our experience, we recommend the following: Do not take any ability for granted; address and assess basic-level skills explicitly as skills for lifelong learning without shame, and be willing to teach, model, and reinforce skills that students might possess but do not yet exercise fluently. Frequent low-stakes practice builds students' intuitions. Early wins feed motivation for practice, which feeds competence, which feeds positive affect, which feeds more practice in a virtuous cycle. Practice in low-level skills, if clearly connected to students' personal goals, has strong positive effects.

Helping students gain a sense of belonging in the discipline pays off in an increased sense of professional identity, whether by sharing our respective experiences and strategies as readers, by sharing something as lowly as used hard copies of journals previously thumbed by faculty, or by pointing out the alignment between what they do in class and their growing ability to continue learning independently as professionals in psychology. Reminding students of how far they have come in one semester helps students see that they can do something that they might have imagined was out of reach; they can attach an alternative meaning to "XYZ is something I was never good at." Even if they were never "good at" XYZ, if they keep nourishing their skills, their skills will grow, they will read psychology more effectively, and they will be able to use the knowledge they gain to help others.

Summary

We found that requiring a focused analytical reading class for first-semester juniors in the major benefited students regardless of their background or the strength of their abilities. Even if not appreciated right away, these benefits were both cognitive and affective, and they resulted in behavioral changes that increased learning and success further along in the curriculum; this benefits the institution as well as the students. We found success by ensuring that activities were well aligned with desired outcomes, by being unafraid to examine and intervene in students' ability to parse and interpret individual sentences, by spending a great deal of time practicing skills together, and by encouraging metacognitive reflection.

Students do not magically learn, at college matriculation, skills that they were not taught in their K-12 education. As society pushes for increased college enrollment, we face a situation where the same students who were underprepared in high school now face even more difficult hurdles that will leave them with crushing debt but no degree, if they fail to learn to read fluently. Our experience with this course has shown that it is realistic for departments to increase content learning while addressing basic skills that serve students both in and out of the discipline.

References

Aarts, Bas, and Liliane Haegeman. 2006. "English Word Classes and Phrases." In *The Handbook of English Linguistics*, 116–145. Malden, MA: Blackwell.

Allen, Carrie. 2016. "Alverno College: Lessons from an Assessment Pioneer." NILOA Examples of Good Assessment Practice. https://www.learningoutcomesassessment.org/wp-content/uploads/2019/08/AlvernoCaseStudy.pdf.

Anderson, Richard C., and William E. Nagy. 1992. "The Vocabulary Conundrum." *American Educator* 16 (4): 14–18, 44.

Beck, Isabel L., Margaret G. McKeown, and Linda Kucan. 2002. *Bringing Words to Life: Robust Vocabulary Instruction*. New York: Guilford.

Biber, Douglas, and Bethany Gray. 2016. *Grammatical Complexity in Academic English: Linguistic Change in Writing*. Cambridge: Cambridge University Press.

Bjork, Robert A. 1994. "Memory and Metamemory Considerations in the Training of Human Beings." In *Metacognition: Knowing about Knowing*, edited by Janet Metcalfe and Arthur Shimamura, 185–205. Cambridge, MA: MIT Press.

Boyland, Joyce Tang. 2009. "Usage-Based Models of Language." In *Quantitative and Experimental Linguistics*, edited by David Eddington, 351–419. Munich: Lincom.

———. 2017. "Addressing College Retention by Teaching Diverse Students to Read Scholarly Articles." Paper presented at the 29th Annual Convention of the Association for Psychological Science, Boston, MA, May 25–28.

Braze, David, Whitney Tabor, Donald P. Shankweiler, and W. Einar Mencl. 2007. "Speaking Up for Vocabulary: Reading Skill Differences in Young Adults." *Journal of Learning Disabilities* 40 (3): 226–243.

Breen, Mara, and Charles Clifton. 2011. "Stress Matters: Effects of Anticipated Lexical Stress on Silent Reading." *Journal of Memory and Language* 64 (2): 153–170.

Bunn, Michael. 2013. "Motivation and Connection: Teaching Reading (and Writing) in the Composition Classroom." *College Composition and Communication* 64 (3): 496-516.

Bybee, Joan. 2010. *Language, Usage and Cognition.* Cambridge: Cambridge University Press.

Carillo, Ellen C. 2017. *A Writer's Guide to Mindful Reading.* Fort Collins, CO: WAC Clearinghouse.

Christiansen, Morten H., and Nick Chater. 2016. *Creating Language: Integrating Evolution, Acquisition, and Processing.* Cambridge, MA: MIT Press.

Diessel, Holger. 2019. "Usage-Based Construction Grammar." In *Cognitive Linguistics—a Survey of Linguistic Subfields*, 295–321. Berlin: de Gruyter.

Ellis, Nick. 2015. "Implicit and Explicit Language Learning: Their Dynamic Interface and Complexity." In *Implicit and Explicit Learning of Languages*, edited by Patrick Rebuschat, 3–23. Amsterdam: John Benjamins.

Gernsbacher, Morton Ann. 1990. *Language Comprehension as Structure Building.* Hillsdale, NJ: L. Erlbaum.

Gernsbacher, Morton Ann, and Michael P. Kaschak. 2013. "Text Comprehension." In *The Oxford Handbook of Cognitive Psychology*, edited by D. Reisberg, 462–474. London: Oxford University Press.

Graff, Gerald, and Cathy Birkenstein. 2010. *They Say / I Say: The Moves That Matter in Academic Writing.* New York: W. W. Norton.

Graves, Michael. 2007. "Conceptual and Empirical Bases for Providing Struggling Readers with Multifaceted and Long-Term Vocabulary Instruction." In *Effective Instruction for Struggling Readers, K-6*, edited by Barbara M. Taylor and James Ysseldyke, 55–83. New York: Teachers' College Press.

Guo, Ying, Alysia D. Roehrig, and Rihana S. Williams. 2011. "The Relation of Morphological Awareness and Syntactic Awareness to Adults' Reading Comprehension." *Journal of Literacy Research* 43 (2): 159–183.

Haas, Christina. 1994. "Learning to Read Biology." *Written Communication* 11 (1): 43–84.

Hartwell, Patrick. 1985. "Grammar, Grammars, and the Teaching of Grammar." *College English* 47 (2): 105.

Haussamen, Brock. 2002. "Some Questions and Answers about Grammar." https://ncte.org/statement/qandaaboutgrammar/.

Hendrix, Rebecca A., and Robert A. Griffin. 2017. "Developing Enhanced Morphological Awareness in Adolescent Learners." *Journal of Adolescent and Adult Literacy* 61 (1): 55–63.

Kentner, Gerrit. 2012. "Linguistic Rhythm Guides Parsing Decisions in Written Sentence Comprehension." *Cognition* 123 (1): 1–20.

Kintsch, Walter. 1988. "The Role of Knowledge in Discourse Comprehension: A Construction-Integration Model." *Psychological Review* 95 (2): 163–182.

Mentkowski, Marcia. 2000. *Learning That Lasts: Integrating Learning, Development, and Performance in College and Beyond.* San Francisco: Jossey-Bass.

Miller, Carol T., Kristin W. Grover, Janice Y. Bunn, and Sondra E. Solomon. 2011. "Community Norms about Suppression of AIDS-related Prejudice and Perceptions of Stigma by People with HIV or AIDS." *Psychological Science* 22 (5): 579–583.

Müller, Stefan. 2018. *Grammatical Theory: From Transformational Grammar to Constraint-Based Approaches.* 2nd ed. Berlin: Language Science Press.

Mulroy, David. 2003. *The War against Grammar.* Portsmouth, NH: Heinemann.

Nowacek, Rebecca S. 2011. *Agents of Integration: Understanding Transfer as a Rhetorical Act.* Carbondale: Southern Illinois University Press.

———. 2017. "Building Mental Maps: Implications from Research on Reading in the STEM Disciplines." In *Deep Reading: Teaching Reading in the Writing Classroom*, edited by Patrick Sullivan, Howard B. Tinberg, and Sheridan D. Blau, 291–312. Urbana, IL: National Council of Teachers of English.

Rose, Shirley. 2015. "All Writers Have More to Learn." In *Naming What We Know: Threshold Concepts of Writing Studies*, edited by Linda Adler-Kassner and Elizabeth Wardle, 59–61. Boulder: University Press of Colorado.

Rosenthal, Julie, and Linnea C. Ehri. 2011. "Pronouncing New Words Aloud during the Silent Reading of Text Enhances Fifth Graders' Memory for Vocabulary Words and Their Spellings." *Reading and Writing* 24 (8): 921–950.

Samuels, S. Jay. 2006. "Reading Fluency: Its Past, Present, and Future." In *Fluency Instruction: Research-Based Best Practices*, edited by Timothy V. Rasinski, Camille L. Z. Blachowicz, and Kristin Lems, 7–20. New York: Guilford.

Seidenberg, Mark S., and Maryellen C. MacDonald. 2018. "The Impact of Language Experience on Language and Reading." *Topics in Language Disorders* 38 (1): 66–83.

Snow, Catherine E., and Paola Uccelli. 2009. "The Challenge of Academic Language." In *The Cambridge Handbook of Literacy*, edited by David R. Olson and Nancy Torrance, 112–133. Cambridge: Cambridge University Press.

Soderstrom, Nicholas C., and Robert A. Bjork. 2015. "Learning versus Performance: An Integrative Review." *Perspectives on Psychological Science* 10 (2): 176–199.

Street, James A., and Ewa Dabrowska. 2014. "Lexically Specific Knowledge and Individual Differences in Adult Native Speakers' Processing of the English Passive." *Applied Psycholinguistics* 35 (1): 97–118.

Sturt, Patrick, Frank Keller, and Amit Dubey. 2010. "Syntactic Priming in Comprehension: Parallelism Effects with and without Coordination." *Journal of Memory and Language* 62 (4): 333–351.

Tyler, Andrea. 2010. "Usage-Based Approaches to Language and Their Applications to Second Language Learning." *Annual Review of Applied Linguistics* 30:270–291.

Walton, Gregory M., and Geoffrey L. Cohen. 2011. "A Brief Social-Belonging Intervention Improves Academic and Health Outcomes of Minority Students." *Science* 331 (6023): 1447–1451.

Wang, Danhua. 2009. "Factors Affecting the Comprehension of Global and Local Main Idea." *Journal of College Reading and Learning* 39 (2): 34–52.

Yan, Veronica X., Khanh-Phuong Thai, and Robert A. Bjork. 2014. "Habits and Beliefs That Guide Self-Regulated Learning: Do They Vary with Mindset?" *Journal of Applied Research in Memory and Cognition* 3:140–152.

Yeager, David S., Gregory M. Walton, Shannon T. Brady, Ezgi N. Akcinar, David Paunesku, Laura Keane, Donald Kamentz, Gretchen Ritter, Angela Lee Duckworth, Robert Urstein, Eric M. Gomez, Hazel Rose Markus, Geoffrey L. Cohen, and Carol S. Dweck. 2016. "Teaching a Lay Theory before College Narrows Achievement Gaps at Scale." *Proceedings of the National Academy of Sciences* 113 (24): E3341–E3348.

Joyce Tang Boyland is Associate Professor of Psychology at Alverno College, Milwaukee, and Adjunct Assistant Professor of Linguistics at the University of Wisconsin, Milwaukee. Her UC Berkeley dissertation applied cognitive and developmental psychology principles to present a usage-based explanation of historical linguistic phenomena and language development through the life span.

Kris Vasquez is Chair of the Psychology Department at Alverno College. Her research interests include prejudice, morality, and behavioral economics. Her teaching focuses on research methods and detection of pseudoscience.

Jordan R. Donovan is a behavioral treatment therapist at Autism Treatment for Children, where she oversees applied behavioral analysis therapy for children with autism. She has a BAS in psychology with an emphasis in dance and theater from Alverno College.

Rachel M. Henry is a recent graduate of Alverno College and currently works at the Medical College of Wisconsin as a research coordinator. Their interests are in neuroimaging and applications of neuroscience in spaceflight.

10

STRATEGIES TO PROMOTE READING COMPLIANCE AND STUDENT LEARNING IN AN INTRODUCTORY CHILD DEVELOPMENT COURSE

TRENT W. MAURER
CATELYN SHIPP

Like so many scholarship of teaching and learning (SOTL) projects, this one began with a teaching "problem" (Bass 1999). Over the objections of the faculty in the program, an administrator had imposed a curricular redesign on our introductory-intermediate child development course sequence, ostensibly because our existing sequence was not "cost efficient." Previously, the two courses in the sequence each enrolled around twenty to thirty students in each section, with multiple sections of each; each course included hands-on laboratory components where the students got the opportunity to interact directly with young children in the university laboratory childcare facility; and each course covered only half of child development from conception to six years. Now, the introductory course in the sequence would have no hands-on laboratory components, would have to cover all of the developmental content material from both courses, and would have triple the enrollment of the prior courses. As a result of this imposed redesign, the introductory course became much more textbook dependent, and student comprehension of the assigned readings became essential for their mastery of the course material. At the time this decision happened, I (Trent) had volunteered to be the faculty member to undertake the redesign because I had the most experience teaching both courses in the original sequence.

In my first semester teaching this newly redesigned class, I actually encountered two "problems," both of which were related to student reading of the assigned textbook: (1) very few of the students were consistently doing all of the assigned reading by the date it was due, and (2) when students did complete the assigned reading on time, most of them didn't seem to be able to identify the central ideas that were necessary to participate in the learning activities I facilitated in class. Initially, I noticed that student scores on the daily reading quizzes were frequently below passing, but it wasn't until I asked for anonymous midsemester feedback from the students that I was able to discern that both of these factors were contributing. So, I did what SOTL scholars do when they encounter such problems: I turned to the experts (i.e., the SOTL literature on the subject and an instructional designer at our Center for Teaching and Learning).

This chapter presents the end result of those efforts to solve this teaching "problem": a case study of my approach to promote student learning in this context, grounded in the SOTL literature. However, this chapter provides more than just my perspective as the instructor of the course. In an effort to include a student perspective and voice and to engage a student as a meaningful partner in the teaching and learning inquiry process (Felten 2013; Felten et al. 2013; Werder and Otis 2010), I am cowriting this chapter with a former student of mine who was enrolled in this course after I had made all the revisions and who experienced my approach firsthand. To ensure clarity and best distinguish between our voices and perspectives, the remainder of this chapter is written as a dialogue between Trent (the instructor) and Catie (the former student and current research collaborator). We also acknowledge and wish to make transparent to the reader the status imbalance and power differential between the two of us on this project as part of providing a full context for our work (Felten 2013). To that end, although I have chosen to self-identify as "Trent" in this paper, it was Catie's choice to refer to me as "Dr. Maurer."

TRENT: It would probably be helpful to start with a general overview of the institution and then describe how the redesigned course now works. At the time of the redesign, the institution was a public Carnegie Doctoral/Research University (subsequently R3) with an enrollment of approximately twenty thousand students on a single campus. Roughly 90 percent of those students were undergraduates, and many of them were first-in-family to higher education.

The course meets twice a week for fifteen weeks. Class periods are seventy-five minutes each. Students may choose either an electronic or a paper copy of the textbook. Students are assigned to complete readings from the textbook (approximately half a chapter, roughly fifteen to thirty pages, per period) along with a reading guide (between twenty-five and fifty factual knowledge questions) in preparation for each class period. Consistent with prior research, students are not given answers to the reading guide questions to check their work (Helms and Helms 2010; Horning 2007; Maurer and Longfield 2015). Before coming to class, students complete a sixty-minute, five-question, open-book, multiple-choice online quiz on the reading material through the course management software. Students are given sixty minutes to reduce time pressure anxiety, to allow plenty of extra time for students with documented disabilities that necessitate additional time, and to encourage students to check their answers against both the reading and their reading guides before submitting them. At the start of class, students complete a five-minute, five-question, closed-book, multiple-choice and fill-in-the-blank quiz via clickers on the same reading material. I then adjust the lesson and activities for the class period based on student responses to the online and in-class quizzes.

CATIE: I remember that during the first few days in the Child Development course, it appeared very intensive and even quite overwhelming. Dr. Maurer was very up-front about the importance of staying on top of all assigned reading and assignments in order to obtain optimal performance and learning outcomes in the course, and his honesty and encouragement early on were very effective in preparing me for the coursework ahead. Furthermore, the assigned reading and quizzes preemptively prepared me to stay on top of the material.

TRENT: The approach I use in this course synthesizes what is known from the SOTL literature about four different topics that intersect with reading: (a) student reading compliance, especially of textbooks and in introductory courses; (b) student study behaviors, especially as they relate to reading; (c) reading guides as methods to promote effective and timely reading of assigned texts; and (d) just-in-time teaching and contingent teaching as methods for customizing daily interactive classroom sessions to best address student misconceptions and misunderstandings of the assigned readings and expand students' abilities to apply the material from the readings.

The average college student in the United States spends between twelve and fifteen hours per week on all academic work combined, only some of which is reading (Arum and Roksa 2011; Pascarella et al. 2011). This amount is less than half of what the United States Department of Education Office of Postsecondary Education mandates that a student taking a fifteen-credit hour semester course load should be spending (US Department of Education 2011). Data from our own Georgia Southern University students on the 2015 National Survey of Student Engagement (NSSE; Georgia Southern University, n.d.) revealed that only 6 percent of first-year students and 8 percent of seniors reported spending the mandated amount of time out of class on academic work. The modal student was spending less than one-third of the required time on all out-of-class academic work (i.e., six to ten hours).

Further research has revealed that student reading compliance is as low as 20 percent (Burchfield and Sappington 2000). Large majorities of college students attend class without first completing assigned readings (Nathan 2005). Locally, NSSE data have revealed that 82 percent of both first-year students and seniors at Georgia Southern University reported at least sometimes attending class without having completed readings or assignments (Georgia Southern University, n.d.). Students in introductory courses read less than a third of the assigned pages at all (Gurung and Martin 2011). Much of this data relies on student self-reporting, and there is evidence that as many as 70 percent of college students claim to have completed assigned readings that they haven't actually done (Sappington, Kinsey, and Munsayak 2002), which suggests that reading compliance may be even lower than these numbers reflect.

Failure to complete assigned readings presents at least two significant problems for student learning. First, as one might expect given the frequent connection between assigned readings and course assessments, students who have not completed the readings are unlikely to have learned the material over which they will be summatively assessed: reading compliance significantly predicts students' exam scores (Sappington, Kinsey, and Munsayak 2002). Second, course instructors cannot reliably build on student knowledge from assigned readings during subsequent classroom sessions if students haven't learned the material from those readings. If students have not completed the assigned reading, they cannot meaningfully participate in class discussions or other active learning activities about that material designed to facilitate critical and analytical thinking (Koontz and Plank 2011; Willingham 2014). After all, as I tell my students, "all new learning requires a foundation of prior knowledge" (Brown, Roediger, and McDaniel 2014, 5), and "one cannot apply what one knows in a practical manner if one does not know anything to apply" (Sternberg, Grigorenko, and Zhang 2008, 487).

Furthermore, students often wait until just before an exam to complete assigned readings, if they complete them at all, and then reread the material multiple times, despite the relative ineffectiveness of this action as a study strategy (Gurung and Martin 2011; Hartwig and Dunlosky 2012; Karpicke, Butler, and Roediger 2009; McDaniel and Callender 2008; Persky and Hudson 2016; Putnam, Sungkhasettee, and Roediger 2016; Roediger and Karpicke 2006). This approach to studying is known as "massed practice" in the literature or "cramming" by students. It is not only both common and ineffective, but there is evidence that even when students participate in a demonstration of the greater effectiveness of spaced practice over massed practice *on their own learning*, students still mistakenly rate massed practice as a more effective study strategy (Kornell and Bjork 2008). Old habits die hard.

So the question then becomes, What can I do as the course instructor to nudge students toward consistently completing the readings on time and spacing their study of the course material instead of cramming (Nilson 2016)? The literature suggests that brief quizzes on assigned readings at the start of class can promote timely reading compliance (Maki and Maki 2000; Maurer and Longfield 2015). Specifically, short quizzes at the start of class, when paired with prompt feedback, are an effective teaching strategy (Connor-Greene 2000), and students are more likely to complete assigned readings if there is an external incentive to do so, such as a graded quiz (Nilson 2016; Ruscio 2001). However, my own prior research with first-year students in another course at this university revealed that there was no difference in student attendance between sections where there were no reading quizzes, low-value reading quizzes, and high-value reading quizzes, and student self-reported reading compliance did not vary significantly across the sections (Maurer 2010, 2011). Additionally, some of my earlier research had suggested that under some circumstances, quizzes on course material may not enhance student learning (Maurer 2006). So, I started by creating reading quizzes for students to complete both online through the course management system and in class via clickers, but I was mindful that this approach might not be particularly effective with this population and therefore would need to be only a first step in the process.

CATIE: The quizzes assigned outside of class and at the start of class encouraged me to not only read and comprehend the chapters but also utilize my recall study strategies repeatedly throughout the unit. I took each half-chapter assignment seriously by preparing for each class day as if I were preparing for an exam, because I knew that my performance on the quizzes would be crucial to my final grade. Therefore, to obtain optimal mastery of the material for these graded assignments, I would complete the reading and the reading guide, and I would also engage in a study session based on recall strategies before each class period. As a result, I became very familiar with the material in the half-chapter assigned before each class period, which led to optimal performance on these quizzes and a gradual accumulation of the necessary knowledge in smaller increments across time. Furthermore, my preparation before each class period allowed me to gain an even greater understanding in the application-based classroom experience. For example, my confidence in the concrete definitions and explanations provided by the textbook encouraged me to participate in class and generate my own real-world examples, which greatly improved my ability to bring the words of the textbook to life. I thoroughly enjoyed each class period because I was seeing the tangible effects of what I was studying at home, and I was seeing how I would be able to apply all of this information both in my future coursework and in my future career. As a result of these tools that encouraged me to mold my study strategies in the most effective ways, I was well prepared with a mastery of the material come exam time.

It's important to note that I similarly studied and completed assignments in previous courses; however, this course solidified my belief in the effectiveness of the strategies I was using. The Child Development course was denser than most of the courses I had taken previously, and it required more time and effort than some of those courses. As a result of using the reading guides and other strategies in this course, I was later able to tackle more challenging courses with increased confidence and success.

Trent: Catie's thorough preparation and firm grasp of the assigned material was obvious to me each class period. Unfortunately, most of my students aren't as motivated or metacognitively aware as Catie. For many of them, just because they are doing the readings on time doesn't mean they are learning what they need to from them. Some students lack the necessary skills to read effectively (Kaback 2012), and others may simply struggle with unfamiliar concepts and material.

Here is where reading guides come in, as Catie mentioned. Reading guides model how to select what to focus on in textbook material and help students determine meaning and achieve basic comprehension and vocabulary (Helms and Helms 2010; Horning 2007). Reading guides have the added benefit of helping ensure that students complete the reading on time (Horning 2007). Students themselves even believe that if faculty provided reading guides, it would increase reading compliance (Brost and Bradley 2006). The basic idea behind reading guides is that I, as an expert in the field, know what is most important for students to get from that particular set of readings, so I create a set of questions for the students to complete about the readings *as they do the readings*. If students complete the reading guide for a class period and study that material, then they know that they are reasonably prepared for that class period. The online preclass quiz then serves as a check for students on their understanding of the material. I explain all of this information to students during the first week of class when I introduce them to the reading guides before the assigned readings and quizzes begin. As part of an overview on how to be successful in this course (and other courses), I discuss the expectations for study time mentioned above and note that it should not take more than two to three hours per class period to complete the readings and reading guides, study the material, take the online quizzes, and restudy the material based on what they missed. I invite students to come see me during office hours if they find that it regularly takes them longer than three hours to complete the assigned work for each class period; no student ever has.

An example of a question from a reading guide is, "Define 'marasmus' and 'kwashiorkor' (p. 175). How are they different (be sure to look at the pictures)? How can people tell them apart?" In this example, I am directing students to pay specific attention to differences between two dietary diseases and focus on information that would help students tell the two diseases apart. Techniques as simple as defining new terms or comparing and contrasting related terms or concepts are vital for reading comprehension of introductory textbooks, but for students who have never been taught these reading strategies, this information may not be obvious. The reading guides, through scaffolding this process, help make it obvious.

Catie: I know most students, including myself, have the mindset that the content covered by the professor in class is the most important material for upcoming assignments or exams. So, when assigned textbook reading, it's almost an automatic process to skim the text to gather a general idea of the topic but then turn to the professor for more specific, detailed information. That is why the reading guides are such an amazing tool to help students realize that the professor is using what is in the textbook in addition to what is discussed in class. Successful learning requires a student to critically think about more than one source of material, but that can be overwhelming without a tool to pinpoint where students should be focusing their attention while engaging with multiple sources. This insight is such an important thing to understand, because when students feel overwhelmed, it can often result in avoidant behaviors (e.g., avoiding the textbook).

Therefore, the reading guides provide an effective tool that encourages students to both space out their studying and center their attention on the most important information in the text. For instance, with the guides provided, I could study one-half of the chapter in-depth and continually add on to and master the material as the unit unfolded. In this way, I was not overwhelmed with large amounts of material right before the exam. It kept me on my toes as I was constantly studying, but it also led to less stress and anxiety come exam time. By the next scheduled exam, I felt very confident in my comprehension of the material. As a result, I did not feel overwhelmed as the exam date neared, for I had studied little by little through the half-chapter assignments and did not have to relearn an entire unit, as may be the case in classes that do not provide such guidance.

The reading guides also prepared me for the types of questions that I could expect on the exam, which centered my focus on the most important topics. Furthermore, the text for the class could be an overwhelming read, but the reading guides were helpful in maintaining my attention while reading. I noticed that the reading guides emphasized main, crucial content that aligned neatly to both what we covered in class and what appeared on the exam. After completing the reading guides, I felt confident to participate in the daily activities, which further enhanced my understanding of the material, as we often focused on how to apply those key concepts of the text to real-world examples. My ability to actively engage with these application-based activities greatly helped me grasp even the most difficult concepts. Overall, these reading guides streamlined my studying and really encouraged my learning and interest in the content. Throughout this course, I did not experience the overwhelming feeling of studying without knowing what I should or should not focus on.

One reviewer of an earlier draft of this chapter asked how a more "average" student in the course might have responded to the reading guides and the approach taken. I do believe that most students are motivated to do well, but if they don't have the knowledge or resources to succeed, it can be easy to feel overwhelmed. The approach taken in this course serves as a way to encourage students that spending the time required to complete the readings and reading guides will help immensely both in this course and in others like it.

TRENT: Again, unfortunately, many of my students don't always approach the reading guides like Catie. The reading guides are only a tool and need to be used properly for maximum effectiveness. Simply completing the reading guide doesn't mean that the students have learned everything important from the assigned reading. Some students may complete the reading guide but not study it, especially if they wait until the last minute to do the readings or are unwilling or unable to devote enough time to the task. Indeed, I have gotten a fair number of complaints on my student evaluations of teaching that completing the assigned readings and reading guides requires too much time and that it interferes with the other demands on students' time (e.g., other courses, work, and social activities). Other students may spend significant time studying the reading guide but study ineffectively or stumble over common misconceptions or misunderstandings, which may also cause them to question the value of the time they have devoted to completing the reading guides.

Here is where just-in-time teaching (JiTT) and contingent teaching come in. JiTT is a teaching and learning approach that integrates web-based study assignments and subsequent classroom instruction that the instructor adjusts based on student responses on those assignments (Novak et al. 1999). As described by Gregor Novak (2006, para. 1), "the heart of JiTT is the 'feedback loop' formed by students' outside-of-class preparation that fundamentally affects what happens during the subsequent in-class time together." For this course, I use JiTT as one component to customize the learning activities for each class period. For each seventy-five-minute period, I typically create two to three hours' worth of learning activities to focus on different core concepts, theories, or issues from the assigned readings. I use student responses to the preclass online quiz on the readings to initially narrow down the range of activities to pick from before I go to class.

In class, I use contingent teaching based on the student responses to the in-class quiz on the readings to finalize the selection of learning activities for the day. Contingent teaching allows instructors to respond in the moment and vary what teaching activities and approaches they will use depending on the students' demonstrated mastery of the material rather than adhering to a predetermined sequential lesson plan (Draper and Brown 2004). This approach is particularly valuable when students' responses demonstrate lack of understanding or misunderstanding of the course material, because instructors can provide additional instruction and explanation for the material in question (Kay and LeSage 2009). Furthermore, this approach helps model some of the very constructivist theories of learning that I teach in the course (Vygotsky 1978), focusing on learning that occurs in the gap between what students can do unassisted and what they need additional structure or scaffolding to learn

(Freeman and Vanden Heuvel, 2015). However, rather than focusing solely on student errors or misconceptions, I also use this approach to expand on what students have learned well to help them go beyond the material for the day and see new applications for that material.

In this way, I tailor the lessons for each day to work on specific areas of strength and weakness in student understanding of the day's assigned readings. Typically, I select as the first learning activity of the day something that most of the students "got" from the readings (i.e., correctly answered a quiz question about on the online quiz, in-class quiz, or both). That way, we are always starting from a point of strength and building on it, expanding what students can do with material they have mastered, and reinforcing the idea that completing the readings before class will make further learning possible. This approach differs somewhat from typical applications of JiTT or contingent teaching, which tend to focus more on student deficits than strengths. Next, I move on to a learning activity that's connected to something that most of the students "missed" from the readings (i.e., incorrectly answered a quiz question about). Some days, these two learning activities consume the entire class period. Other days, we may do as many as five learning activities. It really just depends on how long it takes to help the students work through the material, but in all cases, every learning activity we do is directly connected to the assigned reading for the day.

In fact, I now try to always explicitly link the learning activity to the exact reading guide question or questions it addresses (e.g., "RG Questions #13 & #14") when I introduce the learning activity. This was not my initial approach. At first, I simply selected the learning activity, explained how my choice was connected to their quiz performance, and reiterated that the activity would be based on or building on the assigned readings for the day. However, in my first few semesters, I received feedback from several students on my anonymous, informal midsemester course feedback form that without an explicit connection between the activities we did in class and the reading guides, they didn't see the value in doing the reading guides. I had failed to connect enough of the dots for them to understand what I was doing. To address this issue, I conducted a follow-up in-class discussion about various ways to help students during which I tried to engage the students as meaningful partners in the teaching and learning process (Felten 2013; Felten et al. 2013; Werder and Otis 2010). As a result of the discussion, the students and I decided that simply referencing the exact reading guide question(s) for each activity would be sufficient scaffolding for them to see the connection.

I should also note that one reviewer of an earlier draft of this chapter suggested that students may respond positively if they are aware that an instructor is taking more risks with a teaching method such as contingent teaching than would be typical with more traditional didactic lecturing. I have not collected any data to directly evaluate this possibility, but my anecdotal experience suggests that student responses may be more mixed. I have received feedback from students on both my midsemester feedback forms and end-of-semester evaluations that suggests that some students do recognize and appreciate this risk-taking, whereas others would strongly prefer didactic lecturing. However, it is not clear to me whether those who stated a preference for lecturing were reacting to the contingent teaching itself or the fact that it required them to complete the assigned readings before class.

CATIE: At first, I was not fully aware of Dr. Maurer's adjusted lessons. I originally thought that the in-class quizzes were designed solely to keep us reading and studying the material throughout the unit. I know that many of my fellow classmates complained of the quizzes given before class because they were not used to a college course holding them accountable for assigned textbook readings, especially in a way that does not allow for optimal performance to come from merely skimming the text. Despite these complaints, I eventually began to notice that the content we, as a class, may have misunderstood or needed to revisit was explained in-depth during class time. It was not a lecture-based class that merely repeated what we studied in the text; it was an interactive class that proved to be helpful with application and comprehension of the material that we might not have grasped from reading the text. In this way, Dr. Maurer was extremely responsive to our academic needs. He always noted that a quiz question we may have collectively missed would be covered in greater detail during class.

Overall, this course helped me reflect on my own study strategies. When I tell other students about my study strategies, they think I'm crazy for the number of days I put into the process. However, I end up studying for significantly less time right before the test, which results in much less anxiety than those who engage in massed-practice strategies in an effort to relearn the content before an exam. Staying on top of the material throughout the unit leads to increased confidence and an ability to approach exams with a positive mindset. Overall, the design of the course encourages a successive relearning study strategy (Rawson, Dunlosky, and Sciartelli 2013), which, based on personal experience, is by far the most effective technique for mastery of new material.

TRENT: That's a great transition to where we are now in thinking about and designing this course. Recently, Catie and I began a new SOTL project to explore how to most effectively teach students to adopt the successive relearning study strategy. That strategy has the advantage of being not only one of the best-supported strategies from the SOTL literature (Rawson, Dunlosky, and Sciartelli 2013) but also one that requires students to complete the assigned readings in a timely fashion. We are hopeful that this project will give us a better understanding of yet another way to encourage and increase student learning from the readings.

Additionally, in my own prior work, I have encouraged SOTL scholars to explicitly include "student collaborators' own learning from the process"

(Maurer 2017, 5) in the final product when they engage in collaborative faculty-student projects like this one. Catie, what have you learned from the process of cowriting this chapter?

CATIE: The opportunity to cowrite this chapter allowed me to see the crucial role research plays in our everyday lives. I attended Dr. Maurer's Child Development course without really realizing that the material I was learning in the class was not the only aspect of the course based on research. The backbone of the course's schedule, assignments, quizzes, exams, in-class activities, and professor-student relations also relied heavily on intensive research. This understanding increases my respect for the courses I am currently taking and will take in the future, and it also increases my drive to become a more avid consumer of research so that I, like Dr. Maurer, am able to base my work on what other scholars across a variety of disciplines have discovered. Furthermore, this project showed me how interactive the scholarly community truly is. Remaining within a single discipline will not allow you to fully understand the inner workings of many areas of research. I have been able to see how scholars from a variety of fields are coming together to gain optimal insights within a shared area of interest. Overall, this project has expanded my understanding of the research process, and it has allowed me to see how applicable the research process can be.

TRENT: One of the reviewers of an earlier draft of this chapter suggested we close this chapter by returning to the information that opened the chapter and the decision to make the significant structural changes to this course. As the reviewer noted, the decision "necessitated a great deal of heavy lifting from both instructor and students on the textbook front." I couldn't agree more, which is why the faculty objected to the imposed redesign in the first place. As luck would have it, as I am writing these words, we have just been given another administratively imposed redesign for the course. This time, we have to expand the age range from conception to eight years, representing a substantial further increase in the content we must cover in this course. However, unlike the last redesign, this time we have what we have learned from the first redesign to assist us in the process, and I am hopeful that we can extend our approach to better promote student reading and student learning in the new course.

References

Arum, Richard, and Josipa Roksa. 2011. *Academically Adrift: Limited Learning on College Campuses.* Chicago: University of Chicago Press.

Bass, Randy. 1999. "The Scholarship of Teaching: What's the Problem?" *Inventio* 1 (1): 1–10.

Brost, Brian D., and Karen A. Bradley. 2006. "Student Compliance with Assigned Reading: A Case Study." *Journal of Scholarship of Teaching and Learning* 6 (2): 101–111.

Brown, Peter C., Henry L. Roediger III, and Mark A. McDaniel. 2014. *Make It Stick: The Science of Successful Learning.* Cambridge: Belknap.

Burchfield, Colin M., and John Sappington. 2000. "Compliance with Required Reading Assignments." *Teaching of Psychology* 27 (1): 58–60.

Connor-Greene, Patricia A. 2000. "Assessing and Promoting Student Learning: Blurring the Line between Teaching and Testing." *Teaching of Psychology* 27 (2): 84–88. https://doi.org/10.1207/S15328023TOP2702_01.

Draper, Stephen W., and M. I. Brown. 2004. "Increasing Interactivity in Lectures Using an Electronic Voting System." *Computer Assisted Learning* 20 (2): 81–94. https://doi.org/10.1111/j.1365-2729.2004.00074.x.

Felten, Peter. 2013. "Principles of Good Practice in SOTL." *Teaching and Learning Inquiry: The ISSOTL Journal* 1 (1): 121–125. https://doi.org/10.2979/teachlearninqu.1.1.121.

Felten, Peter, Julianne Bagg, Michael Bumbry, Jennifer Hill, Karen Hornsby, Maria Pratt, and Saranne Weller. 2013. "A Call for Expanding Inclusive Student Engagement in SOTL." *Teaching and Learning Inquiry: The ISSOTL Journal* 1 (2): 63–74. https://doi.org/10.20343/teachlearninqu.1.2.63.

Freeman, Traci, and Brian Vanden Heuvel. 2015. "Who's in the Room? Using Clickers to Assess Students' Needs, Attitudes, and Prior Knowledge." In *Clickers in the Classroom: Using Classroom Response Systems to Increase Student Learning*, edited by David S. Goldstein and Peter D. Wallis, 23–34. Sterling, VA: Stylus.

Georgia Southern University. n.d. "NSSE 2015: Frequencies and Statistical Comparisons." Accessed October 19, 2018. http://em.georgiasouthern.edu/osra/nsse/.

Gurung, Regan A. R., and Ryan C. Martin. 2011. "Predicting Textbook Reading: The Textbook Assessment and Usage Scale." *Teaching of Psychology* 38 (1): 22–28. https://doi.org/10.1177/0098628310390913.

Hartwig, Marissa K., and John Dunlosky. 2012. "Study Strategies of College Students: Are Self-Testing and Scheduling Related to Achievement?" *Psychonomic Bulletin Review* 19 (1): 126–134. https://doi.org/10.3758/s13423-011-0181-y.

Helms, Josh W., and Kimberly T. Helms. 2010. "Note Launchers: Promoting Active Reading of Mathematics Textbooks." *Journal of College Reading and Learning* 41 (1): 109–119. https://doi.org/10.1080/10790195.2010.10850338.

Horning, Alice S. 2007. "Reading across the Curriculum as the Key to Student Success." *Across the Disciplines* 4 (1). http://wac.colostate.edu/atd/articles/horning2007.cfm.

Kaback, Suzanne. 2012. "Getting Students to Read: Anticipation Guides as Tools to Encourage Engagement with Academic Texts." *AILACTE Journal* 9:19–33.

Karpicke, Jeffrey D., Andrew C. Butler, and Henry L. Roediger. 2009. "Metacognitive Strategies in Student Learning: Do Students Practise Retrieval when They Study on Their Own?" *Memory* 17 (4): 471–479. https://doi.org/10.1080/09658210802647009.

Kay, Robin M., and Ann LeSage. 2009. "Examining the Benefits and Challenges of Using Audience Response Systems: A Review of the Literature." *Computers and Education* 53 (3): 819–827. https://doi:10.1016/j.compedu.2009.05.001.

Koontz, Tomas M., and Kathryn M. Plank. 2011. "Can Reading Questions Foster Active Learning? A Study of Six College Courses." *Journal on Excellence in College Teaching* 22 (3): 23–46.

Kornell, Nate, and Robert A. Bjork. 2008. "Learning Concepts and Categories: Is Spacing the 'Enemy of Induction'?" *Psychological Science* 19 (6): 585–592. https://doi.org/10.1111/j.1467-9280.2008.02127.x.

Maki, William S., and Ruth H. Maki. 2000. "Evaluation of a Web-Based Introductory Psychology Course: II. Contingency Management to Increase Use of On-line Study Aids." *Behavior Research Methods, Instruments, and Computers* 32:240–245. https://doi.org/10.3758/BF03207789.

Maurer, Trent W. 2006. "Daily Online Extra Credit Quizzes and Exam Performance." *Journal of Teaching in Marriage and Family* 6 (1): 227–238.

———. 2010. "Incentive-Based Reading Compliance." Paper presented at the SOTL Commons Conference, Statesboro, GA, March 9–12, 2010.

———. 2011. "Incentive-Based Reading Compliance: Part II." Paper presented at the SOTL Commons Conference, Statesboro, GA, March 9–12, 2010.

———. 2017. "Guidelines for Authorship Credit, Order, and Co-inquirer Learning in Collaborative Faculty-Student SOTL Projects." *Teaching and Learning Inquiry: The ISSOTL Journal* 5 (1): 1–17. http://dx.doi.org/10.20343/teachlearninqu.5.1.9.

Maurer, Trent W., and Judith Longfield. 2015. "Using Reading Guides and On-line Quizzes to Improve Reading Compliance and Quiz Scores." *International Journal for the Scholarship of Teaching and Learning* 9 (1): 6. http://digitalcommons.georgiasouthern.edu/ij-sotl/vol9/iss1/6.

McDaniel, Mark. A., and Aimee A. Callender. 2008. "Cognition, Memory, and Education." In *Cognitive Psychology of Memory*, vol. 2 of *Learning and Memory: A Comprehensive Reference*, edited by Henry L. Roediger, 819–843. Oxford: Elsevier.

Nathan, Rebekah. 2005. *My Freshman Year: What a Professor Learned by Becoming a Student*. Ithaca, NY: Cornell University Press.

Nilson, Linda. 2016. *Teaching at Its Best: A Research-Based Resource for College Instructors*. 4th ed. San Francisco: Jossey-Bass.

Novak, Gregor. 2006. "What Is JiTT?" Web Physics IUPUI. http://webphysics.iupui.edu/jitt/what.html#:~:text=Novak%2C%20gnovak%40iupui.edu,and%20an%20active%20learner%20classroom.

Novak, Gregor M., Evelyn T. Patterson, Andrew D. Gavrin, and Wolfgang Christian. 1999. *Just-in-Time Teaching: Blending Active Learning and Web Technology*. Saddle River, NJ: Prentice Hall.

Pascarella, Ernest T., Charles Blaich, Georgianna L. Martin, and Jana M. Hanson. 2011. "How Robust Are the Findings of *Academically Adrift*?" *Change* 43 (3): 20–24. https://doi.org/10.1080/00091383.2011.568898.

Persky, Adam M., and Shelby L. Hudson. 2016. "A Snapshot of Student Study Strategies across a Professional Pharmacy Curriculum: Are Students Using Evidence-Based Practice?" *Currents in Pharmacy Teaching and Learning* 8 (2): 141–147. https://doi.org/10.1016/j.cptl.2015.12.010.

Putnam, Adam L., Victor W. Sungkhasettee, and Henry L. Roediger. 2016. "Optimizing Learning in College: Tips from Cognitive Psychology." *Perspectives on Psychological Science* 11 (5): 652–660. https://doi.org/10.1177/1745691616645770.

Rawson, Katherine A., John Dunlosky, and Sharon M. Sciartelli. 2013. "The Power of Successive Relearning: Improving Performance on Course Exams and Long-Term Retention." *Educational Psychology Review* 25 (4): 523–548. https://doi.org/10.1007/s10648-013-9240-4.

Roediger, Henry L., and Jeffrey D. Karpicke. 2006. "The Power of Testing Memory: Basic Research and Implications for Educational Practice." *Perspectives on Psychological Science* 1 (3): 181–210. https://doi.org/10.1111/j.1745-6916.2006.00012.x.

Ruscio, John. 2001. "Administering Quizzes at Random to Increase Students' Reading." *Teaching of Psychology* 28 (3): 204–206. https://doi.org/10.1207/S15328023TOP2803_08.

Sappington, John, Kimberly Kinsey, and Kirk Munsayac. 2002. "Two Studies of Reading Compliance among College Students." *Teaching of Psychology* 29 (4): 272–274. https://doi.org/10.1207/S15328023TOP2904_02.

Sternberg, Robert J., Elena L. Grigorenko, and Li-fang Zhang. 2008. "Styles of Learning and Thinking Matter in Instruction and Assessment." *Perspectives on Psychological Science* 3 (6): 486–506. https://doi: 10.1111/j.1745-6924.2008.00095.x.

US Department of Education. 2011. "Content Details: 34 CFR 600.2—Definitions." US Government Printing Office. http://www.gpo.gov/fdsys/granule/CFR-2011-title34-vol3/CFR-2011-title34-vol3-sec600-2.

Vygotsky, Lev S. 1978. *Mind and Society*. Cambridge, MA: Harvard University Press.

Werder, Carmen, and Megan M. Otis, eds. 2010. *Engaging Student Voices in the Study of Teaching and Learning*. Sterling, VA: Stylus.

Willingham, Daniel T. 2014. *Why Don't Students Like School? A Cognitive Scientist Answers Questions about How the Mind Works and What It Means for the Classroom*. San Francisco: Jossey-Bass.

Trent W. Maurer is Professor of Child and Family Development and Director of the School of Human Ecology Undergraduate Research Program at Georgia Southern University. He teaches courses in family science, child development, and the University Honors Program.

Catelyn Shipp was an undergraduate student at Georgia Southern University and a member of the University Honors Program. In 2019, she graduated with a major in psychology and a minor in child and family development.

11

READ LITERATURE, READ THE WORLD

Teaching and Learning the Interpretive
Strategies of Literary Studies for Transfer

ANGELA J. ZITO
JAKOB T. ZEHMS

> You're teaching [students] to read both literally—you know, looking at the words on the page and thinking about what they mean—and then figuratively toward bigger cultural, critical, and conceptual ideas that are functioning in our world today. So, I'm teaching [students] to read the world by exploring and practicing methods of analysis in some of the most complex and sophisticated forms of cultural expression we can encounter. You get good at that, you get good at reading the world.
> —"Cameron," faculty instructor of introductory literature

As part of her dissertation research, Angela conducted a series of interviews with introductory literature course (ILC) instructors at the University of Wisconsin–Madison through the fall and spring semesters of 2016–2017. The main purpose of these interviews was to explore to what extent this diverse community of instructors shared common student learning goals, pedagogical approaches, and assessment strategies across their independently designed courses and discussion sections. The idiosyncratic nature of ILCs at her institution would suggest, she hypothesized, that any shared goals, philosophies, and practices among them might point to foundational habits of mind around which this teaching community cohered—whether they realized it or not.

Reading lay at the center of the commonalities she discovered through two cycles of process coding (Saldaña 2009) and close reading analysis (Bass and Linkon 2008) of the interview data. Universally, these eighteen instructors prioritized the teaching and learning of what they variously described as "close," "critical," "empathetic," and "analytical" reading. This is perhaps unsurprising—one naturally expects students to read (and to read a lot) in a literature course. What she found interesting, however, was how their characterizations of reading as an ILC learning goal tended to negotiate two interconnected but distinct permutations: *reading literature* and *reading the world*. This community of ILC instructors perceived the reading done in their courses to be both distinct from other ways of reading (captured in the permutation *read literature*) and simultaneously transferable to other contexts (captured in the permutation *read the world*). In short, they seemed to share the hypothesis—articulated by "Cameron" in the epigraph above—that if you get good at reading literature, you get good at reading the world.

These instructors' perception raised several questions: Do undergraduate students perceive literary reading practices to be transferable to other contexts? How might literary reading practices be taught more effectively for transfer as well as for discipline-specific learning? What might new knowledge about the transferability of literary reading contribute to reading instruction in other disciplines?

Angela designed the study presented here to address these questions, striving not only to cast light on what works in teaching literary reading for transfer but also to outline a new conceptual framework for thinking about the place of reading in instructors' teaching practices (Hutchings 2000). Through the academic year 2017–2018, she led two iterations of an Intermediate Composition course that explicitly invited students to take up the question, Do the reading strategies of literary study help us read more carefully and critically in other contexts? At the conclusion of these courses, she collected and analyzed student artifacts and self-reports and gained a research partner and coauthor in the process. Jakob, who took the course in spring 2018, volunteered to assist in the analysis of student surveys and the development of this essay's argument. While Angela designed the course and the parameters of the study before his participation, Jakob's contributions and perspective as a student partner are integral to this chapter.

For those readers who may not be familiar with literary studies' disciplinary approaches to the complex act of reading, we linger for a moment over the two categories of reading identified (reading literature and reading the world) before moving on to a fuller presentation of the study design, analysis of student artifacts, and discussion of results.

Read Literature

Throughout Angela's dissertation interviews, it was clear that *what* literature is read in ILCs was less important to participating instructors than *how* it is read. Similar observations about the goals of literary learning are made in SOTL research within this disciplinary context (Chick, Hassel, and Haynie 2009; Linkon 2011; Tinkle et al. 2013).

Because of historical contentions between the fields of composition and literature within English studies, scholarship in the teaching and learning of reading in this area appears across and often straddles both fields. Perhaps no scholars do so more explicitly than writing in the disciplines (WID) researchers Joanna Wolfe and Laura Wilder. Having studied the rhetorical conventions most prevalent in published literary studies scholarship (Wilder 2005, 2012), as well as the rhetorical maneuvers that literature faculty most value in student writing (Wilder and Wolfe 2009; Wolfe 2003), Wolfe and Wilder (2016) curated their collective WID research into an introductory literature textbook, *Digging into Literature*. In it, they identify several distinct but interrelated interpretive strategies for reading and writing about literature that resonate with the "methods of analysis" identified by the ILC instructors who participated in Angela's dissertation research. In this project, we focus on four strategies: surface/depth, patterns, context, and genre (Wolfe and Wilder 2016).

Surface/Depth

The surface/depth interpretive strategy is, as Wolfe and Wilder (2016) note, "the most central" to literary reading because it captures a foundational assumption in the discipline: texts and their meanings are complex (40). In contrast to fields that might subscribe to the principle that the simplest solution is likely the right one, literary studies assumes that what appears to be simplest (or on the "surface") never fully captures the significance of the object under study (Chick, Hassel, and Haynie 2009; Linkon 2011; Wilder 2012). Literature scholars assume that attentive reading and careful analysis can unravel multiple strands of meaning from any individual text, some more complex or compelling than others (Corrigan 2017).

This mindset—that is, an openness to complexity and engagement with multiple possible meanings—has occupied literary theorists for generations. Louise M. Rosenblatt, among the most influential of these theorists in the teaching of English, proposed that readers approach texts always from some point on a continuum between what she termed *efferent* and *aesthetic* stances—or, a stance from which the reader's purpose is to "retain the information that will serve her practical purpose," in the former case, and, in the latter, a stance from which the reader's purpose is to "pay attention to the associations, feelings, attitudes, and ideas that [the] words and their referents arouse within [her]" (Rosenblatt 1994, 24–25). While a reader may approach a text, literary or otherwise, with a purpose falling anywhere between and incorporating elements of both the efferent and aesthetic stances, Rosenblatt holds that literary texts present a "more complex, more nuanced, more intense" experience for aesthetic reading than do other texts (e.g., newspapers and scientific reports) because literary texts are themselves linguistically and conceptually complex (34). Full participation in literary reading, according to Rosenblatt, requires that readers shift their attention beyond the practical information found at the "surface" of the text toward a "deeper" interrogation of the self and one's experience of the world through the text.

Recently, some literary theorists have become critical of any surface/depth approach to reading literature, arguing that such an approach too frequently adopts a stance of suspicion, in which "what a text seems to be saying is either distracting or deceptive" and in which the text's "subterfuges must be resisted, its superficiality proclaimed" (Felski 2015, 56). Regardless of whether the tension across a text's multiple meanings is complementary or combative, however, attending to complexity remains the cornerstone of literary reading.

Patterns

Wolfe and Wilder's (2016) remaining interpretive strategies grow out of and feed into the disciplinary assumption of complexity in texts' meaning. The patterns strategy involves calling attention to recurring images, concepts, linguistic features, or other formal elements as a means of discovering and articulating deeper meanings beyond the surface of a text. The patterns strategy resonates with what literary scholars refer to as "close reading," wherein interpretive claims are grounded in textual evidence found in the individual work under interpretation. Close reading—or attending to linguistic and formal patterns—is the predominant mode of analysis taught in undergraduate literature courses and practiced professional publications. While close reading is most often practiced in combination with other interpretive strategies (such as attending to context and genre, discussed below), its primary characteristic in isolated practice is its focused, sustained attention to the text at hand—its form, syntax, use of literary devices, evocation of images and concepts, and so on.

Context

Unlike the patterns strategy, which attends to linguistic and formal elements within the text itself, the context strategy purposefully looks outside the text to consider the interpretive significance of its historical, cultural, and social environments. Many subfields of literary scholarship adopt context as their defining mode of analysis. For instance, feminist criticism and queer theory consider literary texts' representation or reproduction of gendered social structures and power dynamics, and multiculturalism considers the influence of race and ethnicity in the construction and consumption of literature. Scholars and students alike rarely use the context strategy alone in developing complex interpretive claims; far more often than not, it is incorporated into the close reading of texts.

Genre

Like the context strategy, the genre strategy looks outside the literary work at hand to discover or support complex interpretive claims. Genre takes a narrower approach, though, in that it considers specifically a text's categorization according to its form, audience, purpose, style, or mood (e.g., fairy tale, lyric, or pastoral). We might view the genre strategy as a large-scale version of patterns as well as a specific application of context in that it is most effective when it discovers complexity in a text's deviation from established conventions (e.g., patterns in form and style). As with the consideration of context, interpretive strategies targeting genre are most often incorporated in a close reading of the text.

By parsing these approaches to teaching and learning literary reading, we do not mean to suggest that close, critical reading of literature is reducible to a set of easily consumable skills. To the contrary, literary reading encompasses affective as well as cognitive engagement, such that students learn to adopt new lenses for seeing the world outside as well as within literary texts (Zito 2019).

READ THE WORLD

Every participant in Angela's dissertation interviews talked at some length about a desire to see students make connections between how they interpret literary texts and how they interpret the world in which they live: "The kind of reading that you do in [an ILC], when you look closely at a text, is a sort of reading I think is important in reading situations in real life—but also in reading a history text, reading a psychology text. . . . Because it's so easy to just read through and find facts and facts and facts, but if we're not questioning the results, then we're just sort of immediately taking things that are thrown at us. We're not questioning, we're not considering other ideas" ("Lacy," graduate teaching assistant [GTA] instructor of introductory literature). In most cases, these instructors wanted students to come to view the world as itself a text demanding of careful reading—a complex, often ambiguous text that is generative of many possible meanings.

Scholarship on literary learning similarly posits that literature is analogous to the world it either represents or imagines, specifically through their shared traits of ambiguity, multiplicity, complexity, and difficulty (Bruns 2011; Linkon 2011; Rosenblatt 1995; Salvatori and Donahue 2005; Zunshine 2006). As Nancy Chick (2017) wrote in response to Wolfe and Wilder's (2016) introduction to the interpretive strategies of literary study,

> It is not that we see reading as a scavenger hunt designed by a text's author—it is how we see, period. We see texts as, for instance, multilayered, full of patterns both meaningful and ambiguous, inextricably grounded in a variety of contexts, and tested and understood through varied perspectives. We also read and reflect on what we have read as part of our lifelong process of understanding ourselves, others, and the world around us, which we also see as multilayered, full of patterns both meaningful and ambiguous, inextricably grounded in a variety of contexts, and tested and understood through varied perspectives. (567)

"Lacy," the GTA instructor quoted above, echoes this sentiment when she describes the importance she sees in the learned recognition that everything we encounter can and should be read beyond its surface meaning ("facts and facts and facts") by considering diverse interpretive possibilities ("questioning" and "considering other ideas").

Significantly, Lacy was not alone in including texts specific to other academic disciplines ("a history text . . . a psychology text") within the "situations in real life" that can and should be read using literary strategies. The majority of interviewees (fourteen of eighteen) expressed a belief that the critical reading and writing taught in their classes was broadly applicable to other academic contexts. "Jesse," for instance, a faculty interviewee, contended vigorously that "the principles are exactly the same" between the process of closely reading *A Raisin in the Sun* and students' reading practices as future medical professionals or engineers.

Scholarship in writing transfer and writing in the disciplines observes a similar tendency among literature instructors to assume that their disciplinary practices in writing are universal across fields (Wardle 2009; Wilder 2012; Wolfe, Olson, and Wilder 2014). This assumption does not seem to hold up to scrutiny, however, as research across writing studies demonstrates that writing conventions rather shape and are shaped by disciplinary identities and practices (Adler-Kassner and Wardle 2015). Indeed, recent studies in the transfer of learning about writing suggest that explicit instruction in disciplinary conventions *as* disciplinary (rather than universal) actually encourages transfer by requiring students to think reflectively and metacognitively about the abstract principles that guide their writing in specific contexts (Anson and Moore 2017; Horning, Gollnitz, and Haller 2017; Sullivan, Tinberg, and Blau 2018; Wardle 2009).

There is the distinct possibility, then, that explicit instruction in literary reading strategies—especially the central principle that assumes "there's more significance here than meets the eye"—could improve not only students' performance in literary reading but also their judicious application of literary reading practices in other contexts. Perhaps if students learn to use careful, attentive reading as a method for constructing meaning of complex literary texts, then they will be more likely to consciously employ careful, attentive reading in real-world contexts. The present study pursues this hypothesis through a course designed around explicit instruction in literary interpretive strategies and guided experimentation with its application in other academic and nonacademic contexts.

Course and Study Design

As a PhD student in English at the University of Wisconsin–Madison, a top-tier public research university in the United States, Angela was able to design and teach sections of Intermediate Composition. Intermediate Composition emphasizes the four modes of literacy (reading, writing, speaking, and listening) as well as advanced techniques in academic research. This course invites students of all majors to enroll; across the eight to ten individual sections offered every semester, we see a variety of students from sophomore to senior standing majoring in STEM, social sciences, and arts and humanities disciplines. This course maintains a low enrollment cap of nineteen students for each section, providing space for students to engage in multiple rounds of drafting, feedback, and revision.

Individual sections of Intermediate Composition differ significantly in curricular design, as the instructors frame their sections around their own pedagogical strengths and scholarly interests. Angela designed her section around the questions arising from her dissertation research pertaining to the hypothesized transfer of literary reading practices. Following Peter Felten's (2013) principles of good practice in SOTL, she wanted to pursue these questions in partnership with students—specifically, with students much like those who might enroll in an ILC (that is, of diverse majors, interests, and experiences with academic writing and reading). To do this, she framed the course around the concept of interpretation, approaching the concept as a process shaped by reading, writing, and conversation across social as well as academic communities. She structured the course in three five-week units focused on interpretive practices in (1) literary studies, (2) public discourse, and (3) students' major disciplines.

The first unit introduced students to the four literary interpretive strategies outlined above. Students practiced using these strategies to interpret short works of fiction in a series of low-stakes writing assignments and peer-review class activities. In her handouts and class discussions around these assignments and activities, she foregrounded the surface/depth, patterns, context, and genre strategies specifically within the literary studies academic context. The unit culminated in a graded portfolio containing revised versions of both writing and audio-recorded speaking assignments. She purposefully did not assign traditional literary analysis writing assignments in this course. Rather, she crafted close-reading assignments that asked students to explain how they went about developing complex and plausible interpretations of their chosen texts. In their portfolios, students also submitted a short reflective essay on their experience using these interpretive strategies in reading, writing, and conversing throughout the unit.

Throughout the second and third units of the course, students were prompted to recall the surface/depth, patterns, context, and genre interpretive strategies with regard to their reading of public-facing nonfiction genres and diverse academic genres. Assignments and activities throughout these units prompted students to describe the interpretive strategies they saw at work in these genres and to reflect on their intersection (or lack thereof) with the interpretive strategies of literary study. As with Unit 1, portfolios for Units 2 and 3 contained revised versions of both writing and speaking assignments as well as short reflective essays on their reading and writing experiences throughout the unit.

Roughly three months after the conclusion of each iteration of the course in fall 2017 and spring 2018—after all assignments were completed, grades submitted, and Institutional Review Board exemption confirmed—students were invited via email to participate in this study. When Angela requested that they participate in an anonymous survey and allow her to analyze their course writing, many were enthusiastic to do so (including Jakob, who asked to contribute to the analysis of data).

Of thirty-six students across the two semesters, seventeen agreed to participate in the study (nine from the fall semester and eight from the spring). This is not a large sample, to be sure, but the breadth of data for each student is significant: Likert scale and write-in responses in the survey, as well as three reflective essays for each student.

Data Analysis

In this section, Jakob and Angela analyze two sources of data: (1) anonymous student survey responses submitted after the course's completion and (2) students' reflective writing from the three units in the course. The survey data provide a view into students' own perceptions of the transferability of literary reading practices, while their essays provide evidence of the effectiveness with which those practices were transferred across course units.

We acknowledge that, as the instructor and a single student of this course, our analysis is necessarily limited by our respective perspectives and biases. We do believe, however, that through our ongoing discussions of each component of the data, we were able to effectively recognize and distance ourselves from our assumptions coming into the project. More importantly, through our collaborative effort to persuasively interpret the data for an interdisciplinary SOTL audience, we hope to contribute to the growing body of literature acknowledging and celebrating the benefits of student-instructor partnerships in SOTL work. In what follows, Jakob takes the lead in presenting an analysis of the student surveys. Angela then follows with a complementary analysis of the reflective essays.

Survey Responses

Survey data were collected from seventeen students who completed Intermediate Composition in the 2017–2018 academic year. The questions in the survey asked students to rate the degree of transfer they saw between the interpretive strategies presented in the course and their own academic and extracurricular lives.

Student responses indicate that, on a broader scale, they felt that there was a great degree of transfer between the interpretive strategies they developed and contexts outside of Intermediate Composition. When asked, "Have you consciously used any of the interpretive strategies practiced in this class (surface/depth, patterns, context, genre) in one or more of your other classes?" sixteen out of seventeen respondents strongly agreed. Interestingly, when asked, "Looking back, do you think you may have used any of these interpretive strategies without realizing it?" sixteen out of seventeen students strongly believed they had also used one or more of these interpretive strategies unconsciously in other academic and extracurricular activities. In their write-in responses, many of these students discussed how they found themselves using interpretive strategies as methods of interpreting films and literature that were not assigned in an academic context, with one respondent finding that he or she could use these tools to interpret "art and writing or reading on [her/his] own, and particularly when reading news stories." When asked, "Do you think you'll use any of these interpretive strategies in the future?" all seventeen respondents answered yes. In their write-in responses, most students (eleven out of seventeen) expressed their belief that they would use all four interpretive strategies.

Throughout the student survey, there is a notable tension between responses to the more general questions and responses to the more specific ones. When considering the interpretive strategies collectively, students noticed a high degree of transfer (as indicated in the results above); however, when considering an individual interpretive strategy, students perceived a lower degree of transfer, especially when considering courses in fields other than English. When prompted to "rate the extent to which you believe the interpretive strategy 'surface/depth' is applicable to your reading in other classes," seven out of seventeen students felt it was "somewhat" or "barely" applicable, while the other ten answered that it was "very" applicable. One student wrote, "I think because I'm in engineering, it [surface/depth] is not very applicable, simply because academic writing in the sciences is meant to be as straightforward as possible." This sentiment was echoed in responses to identical questions regarding the genre and patterns interpretive strategies, with thirteen students rating genre and ten rating patterns as "somewhat applicable" or less. Responses to the same question regarding the context strategy are significantly different, though, in that thirteen students rated context "very applicable" and the remaining four students rated it "somewhat applicable."

The tension between student responses to general versus strategy-specific questions suggests that nearly every student believes that the interpretive strategies taught in this course were applicable to other academic and extracurricular contexts, but only if used in a process, often omitting one or two strategies depending on the situation or assignment. That is to say, students felt that each of these strategies could be used as tools for critical reading, with some tools being more or less applicable given a certain context. This could indicate that a large part of the knowledge transfer was not only how to use these literary strategies but also when to use them. Students even recognized this form of transfer, with one respondent claiming, "Patterns [isn't] really applicable in reading if I am reading the textbooks just for knowledge, however when reading a book, the usage of patterns is very applicable." These survey data suggest that students' perception of the transfer of reading practices from this course to other contexts lies in the process of literary interpretation—considering multiple tools to read a text or situation—rather than in the individual strategies themselves.

Reflective Essays

Students submitted a brief reflective essay (four to five hundred words) at the conclusion of each five-week unit of the course. The prompts for these reflective essays asked students to "reflect upon and demonstrate your learning from the past few weeks" (Unit 1), to "showcase the culmination of your development in writing and interpretation" (Unit 2), and to "describe one element of your learning in this course that you believe will transfer to other areas of your life" (Unit 3). These essays were analyzed through a combination of coding (Saldaña 2009) and close reading (Manarin 2018) to identify and categorize varying levels of student understanding and effective application of literary interpretive strategies. Evidence of transfer in Unit 2 and Unit 3 essays was identified not through simple reporting or summary (e.g., "In the first draft, I described the surface interpretation of the quote but then looked deeper") but rather through students' descriptions of their own reading and thinking processes.

Taken as a whole, the reflective essays from Unit 1 (which introduced literary interpretive strategies) suggest that eight of seventeen participating students demonstrated a firm grasp of these strategies, six demonstrated a tenuous grasp, and three demonstrated a weak grasp. A firm grasp of these strategies was characterized by (1) a recognition of multiple layers or possibilities of meaning (surface/depth), (2) specific location of those possibilities within (i.e., patterns) or outside (i.e., context or genre) the text, and (3) an attempt to construct increasingly complex interpretations through the synthesis of multiple interpretive strategies. For example, a senior pursuing a degree in civil engineering wrote the following about her several attempts to interpret Terrance Hayes's poem "Sonnet":

> Without thinking about the poem in a contextual setting, I could not find the drive behind the poem, or why someone would consider it so hostile. . . . As a result, I plopped in this background. Plopping, however, was a mistake in retrospect. I failed to relate the context to the structure. . . . So to address this mistake, I redrafted the assignment. Again, I believe it's important to discuss the structure of the poem: it's an overuse of these sonnet conventions that

make the poem feel insincere, it's the sounds in the opposing words about "slicing" and "smiling" that make the poem ominous. As a result, this uneasiness can be directly linked to the racism associated with the symbol of the watermelon in African American history.

This student locates layers of meaning in the poem's repetition of sounds ("slicing" and "smiling"), its "overuse" of sonnet conventions (the poem consists of the same line repeated fourteen times), and its author's identity as African American (the image of "watermelon" becomes associated with Jim Crow–era racism given this context). She not only locates these different layers through patterns, genre, and context (respectively) but also recognizes that simply "plopping" them side by side does not effectively capture the complexity of all three put together, and she subsequently attempts to synthesize them in a revised version of the assignment.

A tenuous grasp of literary studies interpretive strategies was characterized by (1) a recognition of multiple layers or possibilities of meaning, (2) generalized or inaccurate location of those possibilities within or outside the text at hand, and (3) an implausible or incomplete synthesis of layers of meaning. For example, a sophomore pursuing a degree in kinesiology wrote the following regarding his interpretation of Pixar's animated short film "Geri's Game," in which an elderly man plays himself at a game of chess: "The complex meaning that I derived from this short film was to never give up when faced with adversity. While the conservative Geri was a far worse chess player and outmatched during the whole game, he never gave up and was able to make the strategic move of faking a heart attack and flipping the chess board. . . . I chose to make this my complex interpretation of the text because overcoming adversity is a common theme in movies and books and I felt that this theme could be related to Geri's Game." This student does recognize multiple layers of meaning through patterns in the text (the demeanor and appearance of Geri change as he plays each side of the chess board—on one side he's more "aggressive" and on the other more "conservative") and the text's resonance with other, similarly themed texts. Ultimately, however, he flattens out what could become a complex interpretation by maintaining only a very generalized consideration of genre and a simple association of textual patterns to plot.

A weak grasp of literary interpretive strategies was characterized by (1) a disregard for multiple layers or possibilities of meaning, (2) generalized or inaccurate location of those possibilities within or outside the text, and (3) an attempt to eliminate plausible alternate meanings rather than to synthesize or reconcile those possibilities. A junior pursuing a degree in neuroscience, for example, wrote the following with regard to her interpretation of the final scene in the movie *The Truman Show*:

> I only used the ideas that were in my head at the time that I watched the movie, because I believed that those were my genuine thoughts on the film. For the depth interpretation of the film, I used what I gathered and what I already knew to draw conclusions from the surface depth part of the film.... When in class, I listened intently and wrote down the ideas that caught my attention.... Going through my head, I matched my analysis with my classmates' and found that there were similarities and differences to the theories. By comparing my analysis with others, I could use that standpoint and further my opinion and theories.

For this student, the other interpretive possibilities offered by her classmates presented counterpoints against which she could defend her predetermined interpretation of the scene—an interpretation grounded firmly in her personal reactions to the text. While attending to our personal experience of a text is certainly an important component of literary reading, relying solely on that personal dimension precludes our ability to further enrich and expound on that reading.

Unit 2 asked students to consider to what extent literary studies interpretive strategies were used or useful in public discourse. To pursue this question, we read J. D. Vance's memoir *Hillbilly Elegy*, which had been selected as the university's common read book that year, and students drafted and revised book reviews evaluating Vance's interpretation of the "hillbilly" culture he grew up in. Analysis of the Unit 2 reflective essays shows that a majority of students (eleven of seventeen) effectively used literary studies interpretive strategies while "reading the world" through their evaluations of Vance's memoir. This number includes all but one student who had previously demonstrated a solid grasp of the interpretive strategies in Unit 1 as well as four students who had previously demonstrated a tenuous grasp. Three students shared no explicit reflection on or demonstration of specific interpretive strategies in their reflective essays, instead focusing their reflections on rhetorical awareness (specifically, on their learning to tailor a piece of writing to a specific audience).

Common across all the effective applications was a consideration of the complexity of the texts at hand (i.e., the memoir itself as well as the social and cultural issues addressed in it). For example, a sophomore double-majoring in art and biology effectively applied the complexity-oriented surface/depth strategy by writing, simply, "If I would want my reader to take one thing away, it would be that there is more to a story and a situation than meets the eye." A junior gender and women's studies major shared this expectation that the ideas presented in the memoir are more complex than they seem, and she identified the patterns strategy as a particularly helpful one for starting to wrestle with that complexity: "By looking with a deeper analysis of his work [sic], I was able to consider patterns of contradiction throughout the memoir. This allowed me to further develop my critique, but also struggle with Vance's message. It was hard for me to distinguish whether his critique of welfare is a call for more aid or less aid. He continues to discuss how it does no good, and does not help his community, but what then does he want if he explains how he could not have succeeded with all the help he was given?" Most participating students, like the two quoted above, called attention specifically to patterns and surface/depth strategies in their Unit 2 reflective essays. Three discussed their use of the genre strategy in their evaluation of Vance's memoir, identifying the narrative conventions of the genre as both contributing to and detracting from the plausibility of some of Vance's interpretive claims.

The same three students who demonstrated a weak grasp of the interpretive strategies in Unit 1 ineffectively applied those strategies in Unit 2. A sophomore interested in pursuing mathematics, for instance, used the terminology of context, genre, and patterns in an effort to describe the effectiveness of Vance's writing style rather than to evaluate Vance's interpretive claims or to generate some of her own:

> Context is shown most throughout the book because it is a memoir and it is his story so the plot, or his words about his life hold much weight, and give much meaning to the book.... In Hillbilly Elegy, much of the context would not be as lively or brought to life without patterns. Much of the patterns employed in this memoir were imagery, and informal words and tone. Much of the colloquial words were a pattern that Vance could have chosen to take out, but he chose to keep in because it makes the book more engaging.

While this student successfully identifies some conventions of the memoir genre, her consideration of genre remains descriptive of the reading experience and does not extend into the province of meaning-making.

The third and final unit of this course asked students to consider to what extent literary studies interpretive strategies overlap with or are otherwise analogous to the interpretive strategies of their major disciplines. Students worked in groups to prepare an original research presentation on how their major disciplines "make or communicate meaning about the world in which we live." In conducting their research, students read scholarly publications in their fields as well as other disciplinary genres of writing, such as the business report.

In their Unit 3 reflective essays, instead of referencing individual strategies, students demonstrated transfer from Unit 1 by exhibiting a certain mindset that expects meaning to be constructed, to be complex, and to take shape in different ways depending on the context in which it is being constructed. Eleven out of seventeen students demonstrated this kind of transfer of mindset in their final reflective essays. Of these students, seven had demonstrated a firm grasp of the mindset in Unit 1 and effective application in Unit 2, and four had demonstrated a tenuous grasp in Unit 1 and effective application in Unit 2.

Students demonstrating this kind of transfer did so in consideration of both discipline-specific and nonspecific academic contexts. For example, the same gender and women's studies major quoted above reflected on how the case study as a research method reflected her field's attention to context as a significant factor in constructing meaning: "I learned that case studies in the GWS field explore specific cases in order to better understand and communicate broader concepts, which helped create political and social change within the GWS and social justice communities." Other students demonstrated transfer of the complexity mindset to more generalized academic contexts, such as coming to understand the central task of an assignment or narrowing a research question. For instance, the same student who crafted a complex interpretation of Hayes's "Sonnet" above reflects on how she and her fellow engineering majors needed to pause their research in order to reconcile their differing interpretations of the assignment: "The strength that I brought into this process [was that] I made the group communicate and agree on a single objective for this report. Because I was not sure of what the boys were trying to research, the questions I asked were valid and worth exploring. Through the discussion about my questions, the other two realized that their respective interpretations of our objective differed from each other. So even though the boys wanted to immediately start on creating the presentation, I forced them to stop and communicate what our objective was." The questions this student proposed to her research team helped them articulate the multiple possible avenues of meaning-making they could pursue in their research, which allowed them not only to foresee obstacles but to integrate research findings into a coherent and complex whole rather than present them as discrete parts with no central purpose. The recognition that meaning is complex and contingent on context presented a threshold at which effective transfer of literary interpretive strategies became possible.

Discussion

Our discussion of the study's findings takes the shape of a brief dialogue to capture the collaborative nature of our analysis.

ANGELA: Based on the survey results you presented, it looks like students largely felt that these literary reading practices are transferable to other contexts.

JAKOB: Yes, and what's interesting is that sixteen of seventeen students say they have consciously used these strategies since taking Intermediate Composition, but, in your analysis of the reflective essays, it looks like six of them weren't able to effectively use these strategies to extrapolate complex meaning from different texts. That indicates to me that there's a barrier in the process, or a barrier in knowing how or when to use these strategies. I think your third criterion for a "strong grasp" of interpretive strategies captures this element that is really transferable but also a barrier.

ANGELA: So, are you suggesting that this idea—that we need to actively engage in the construction of meaning by approaching a text from several angles—is the thing that is most transferable but also the thing that presents the biggest barrier to transfer?

JAKOB: Yes, that kind of difficulty illustrates for me an ability (or inability) to determine what combination of reading strategies to use when given a specific text or a specific course context. It's not like in certain STEM classes where you might have a set of conditions and you're able to use equations to get to where you need to go. Instead, there's something I want to describe as "play" or "discernment" in that process, where you need to be adept at using different tools at different times and at using these strategies in different combinations to create complex meaning—and it's all dependent on what the text requires.

In the survey responses, students talk a lot about the different kinds of texts they read, and I think that's why this is so important. Because, often, when you're in college, you're reading texts from a variety of different contexts that are written completely differently and require different types of engagement. For instance, I'm reading these really complex, jargon-filled research papers in zoology, but then I go to my philosophy class, and it's all logic and carefully sequenced arguments, and then I go to another class where we're reading subjective narratives. So, I think that when you're in college you're thrown into these different contexts, and this transferable process we're talking about is learning to discern to what extent strategies like surface/depth, genre, context, and patterns are going to help you do that.

ANGELA: That's exciting for me as a scholar of literary learning, to think that the grounding principle of literary interpretation—that meaning is complex and constructed through different kinds and layers of reading—is transferable to other contexts. Thinking about this process of discernment also helps me see where those individual strategies like attending to genre and patterns don't transfer universally or uniformly, though, too.

JAKOB: I think it's important for all instructors to be able to identify this process, because it will help them teach and assess reading for complex meaning in their disciplines. For instance, the professor and GTAs in my philosophy class did tell us that reading in philosophy is different from other classes, but they didn't provide explicit instruction in how to do it. This would have been really helpful because this skill can make or break a writing assignment, which is what you're graded on. It's important for instructors, too, because if they're not able to accurately assess what they're looking for—if it's just, "How good is this argument based on what I hoped it would be?"—they might not know whether their teaching strategies are effectively communicating the reading process that generates the kind of argument they're looking for.

The fact that a lot of instructors don't explicitly teach how to read and write in their discipline tells me that the work of teaching reading and writing probably falls to composition courses. In other courses, it's assumed that you already know how to do it.

ANGELA: That reminds me of this old-school idea about transfer: that college students will know everything they need to know about writing after taking First-Year Composition. Writing studies has pushed back against that idea for years. And it's important for us to remember that not all composition courses necessarily foreground reading as much as I did in Intermediate Composition, and not necessarily *literary* reading. I designed this course specifically to pursue the question of whether learning to read literature helps us "read the world."

So, perhaps literature instructors could also teach their disciplinary reading practices more explicitly *as* disciplinary, rather than assuming that they're teaching a kind of universally recognized "critical" reading that's applicable across disciplines. By doing so, they might also make explicit this process of discernment, or this approach to reading that says specific interpretive strategies will be more or less applicable from one situation to the next. And this may seem obvious to some people—*Of course how you read is going to be different in different contexts!*—but for a lot of instructors this idea may have become invisible precisely because it is so obvious.

JAKOB: Exactly. It's almost like when you've mastered this process of discernment, you don't notice that you're using all those different strategies. Does this make the idea that "college reading is a process of discernment" a threshold concept—that is, a "conceptual gateway" or "portal" that leads to a previously inaccessible and frequently troublesome way of thinking about something (Meyer and Land 2005, 373)?

ANGELA: I think that's a possibility worth exploring in future research. It does seem to be transformative and irreversible for those who "get it," and it presents a troublesome and liminal "stuck place" where about a third of the participants in this study weren't able to synthesize text- and context-appropriate interpretive strategies. The transferability of this process across contexts suggests that it is not bound to a single discipline, though, which seems to me to reinforce the idea that teaching reading in the university must be a multi- and interdisciplinary enterprise.

Before we close, I'm curious: Would you say these findings align with your personal experience of the course?

Jakob: I would. The survey results accurately describe what I perceive to be my transfer of knowledge to contexts outside of the course. But there is a notable difference. Coming out of a high school that really emphasized literature and composition, I feel that I already had a somewhat firm grasp on the specific interpretive strategies we learned. In that way, I often saw the applicability of these strategies in nearly every class I've taken since. Still, I never took the opportunity to use these types of reading strategies in nonacademic contexts. In my personal experience with the course, I started to discern when to use these strategies with things like film and even certain social situations. I found myself using these ideas as evidence in simple debates over the meaning of a particular movie or TV series. I believe there was a notable transfer of knowledge to other courses and to contexts within my life.

Conclusion

Ultimately, we propose that students can and do meaningfully transfer the interpretive strategies of literary study to other reading contexts, though most recognizably in their deployment of the strategies as part of a process of discernment. We understand this process of discernment to be a conscious sifting on the student's part of different reading strategies and approaches when encountering new texts and contexts, and an unconscious sifting among experts. Furthermore, we suggest that this process of discernment, while aligned with literary studies' grounding principle of complex and constructed meaning, does not seem bound to literary studies alone, whereas the specific interpretive strategies are. Rather, this process of discernment seems implicated in successful critical reading across disciplines, in that all disciplines employ multiple reading strategies in the construction, teaching, and learning of knowledge in their fields. This finding suggests that instructors across disciplines might better support student learning—and student learning transfer—by explicating disciplinary reading practices *as* disciplinary rather than universal.

References

Adler-Kassner, Linda, and Elizabeth Wardle, eds. 2015. *Naming What We Know: Threshold Concepts of Writing Studies.* Boulder: University Press of Colorado.

Anson, Chris M., and Jessie L. Moore. 2017. *Critical Transitions: Writing and the Question of Transfer.* Fort Collins, CO: WAC Clearinghouse.

Bass, Randy, and Sherry Lee Linkon. 2008. "On the Evidence of Theory: Close Reading as a Disciplinary Model for Writing about Teaching and Learning." *Arts and Humanities in Higher Education* 7 (3): 245–261. https://doi.org/10.1177/1474022208094410.

Bruns, Cristina Vischer. 2011. *Why Literature? The Value of Literary Reading and What It Means for Teaching.* New York: Continuum International Publishing Group.

Chick, Nancy. 2017. "Beginning Where the Students Are Beginning." *Pedagogy* 17 (3): 563–569. https://doi.org/10.1215/15314200-3975703.

Chick, Nancy, Holly Hassel, and Aeron Haynie. 2009. "Pressing an Ear against the Hive: Reading Literature for Complexity." *Pedagogy* 9 (3): 399–422. https://doi.org/10.1215/15314200-2009-003.

Corrigan, Paul T. 2017. "Teaching What We Do in Literary Studies." *Pedagogy* 17 (3): 549–556. https://www.muse.jhu.edu/article/671062.

Felski, Rita. 2015. *The Limits of Critique.* Chicago: University of Chicago Press.

Felten, Peter. 2013. "Principles of Good Practice in SOTL." *Teaching and Learning Inquiry: The ISSOTL Journal* 1:121–125.

Horning, Alice, Deborah-Lee Gollnitz, and Cynthia R. Haller, eds. 2017. *What Is College Reading?* Fort Collins, CO: WAC Clearinghouse.

Hutchings, Pat, ed. 2000. *Opening Lines: Approaches to the Scholarship of Teaching and Learning.* Menlo Park, CA: Carnegie Foundation for the Advancement of Teaching.

Linkon, Sherry Lee. 2011. *Literary Learning: Teaching the English Major.* Bloomington: Indiana University Press.

Manarin, Karen. 2018. "Close Reading: Paying Attention to Student Artifacts." In *SOTL in Action: Illuminating Critical Moments in Practice*, edited by Nancy Chick, 100–108. Sterling, VA: Stylus.

Meyer, Jan H. F., and Ray Land. 2005. "Threshold Concepts and Troublesome Knowledge: Epistemological Consideration and a Conceptual Framework for Teaching and Learning." *Higher Education* 49:373–388.

Rosenblatt, Louise M. 1994. *The Reader, the Text, the Poem: The Transactional Theory of the Literary Work.* Carbondale: Southern Illinois University Press.

———. 1995. *Literature as Exploration.* 5th ed. New York: Modern Language Association of America.

Saldaña, Johnny. 2009. *The Coding Manual for Qualitative Researchers.* Thousand Oaks, CA: Sage.

Salvatori, Mariolina R., and Patricia Donahue. 2005. *The Elements (and Pleasures) of Difficulty.* New York: Pearson.

Sullivan, Patrick, Howard Tinberg, and Sheridan Blau, eds. 2018. *Deep Reading: Teaching Reading in the Writing Classroom.* Urbana: National Council of Teachers of English.

Tinkle, Theresa, Daphne Atias, Ruth M. McAdams, and Cordelia Zukerman. 2013. "Teaching Close Reading Skills in a Large Lecture Course." *Pedagogy* 13 (3): 505–535. https://doi.org/10.1215/15314200-2266432.

Wardle, Elizabeth. 2009. "'Mutt Genres' and the Goal of FYC: Can We Help Students Write the Genres of the University?" *College Composition and Communication* 60 (4): 765–789.

Wilder, Laura. 2005. "'The Rhetoric of Literary Criticism' Revisited: Mistaken Critics, Complex Contexts, and Social Justice." *Written Communication* 22 (1): 76–119. https://doi.org/10.1177/0741088304272751.

———. 2012. *Rhetorical Strategies and Genre Conventions in Literary Studies.* Carbondale: Southern Illinois University Press.

Wilder, Laura, and Joanna Wolfe. 2009. "Sharing the Tacit Rhetorical Knowledge of the Literary Scholar: The Effects of Making Disciplinary Conventions Explicit in Undergraduate Writing about Literature Courses." *Research in the Teaching of English* 44 (2): 170–209. http://www.jstor.org/stable/27784356.

Wolfe, Joanna. 2003. "A Method for Teaching Invention in the Gateway Literature Class." *Pedagogy* 3 (3): 399–425. https://muse.jhu.edu/article/46557.

Wolfe, Joanna, Barrie Olson, and Laura Wilder. 2014. "Knowing What We Know about Writing in the Disciplines: A New Approach to Teaching for Transfer in FYC." *WAC Journal* 25:42–77.

Wolfe, Joanna, and Laura Wilder. 2016. *Digging into Literature: Strategies for Reading, Analysis, and Writing.* Boston: Bedford/St. Martin's.

Zito, Angela. 2019. "Broaching Threshold Concepts: The Trouble with 'Skills' Language in Defining Student Learning Goals." *To Improve the Academy* 38:67–81. https://doi.org/10.1002/tia2.20086.

Zunshine, Lisa. 2006. *Why We Read Fiction: Theory of Mind and the Novel.* Columbus: Ohio State University Press.

Angela J. Zito was a doctoral candidate in literary studies at the time this chapter was researched and written. She is now Faculty Associate in English at the University of Wisconsin–Madison.

Jakob T. Zehms was an undergraduate student at the University of Wisconsin–Madison as this chapter was researched and written. In 2020, he graduated with a degree in biochemistry and neuroscience.

12

CAPTURING CONFUSION

Multidisciplinary Reading as Productive Disruption

AIMEE KNUPSKY
M. SOLEDAD CABALLERO

Developing the skill to read within a single discipline is difficult for students making the transition to higher education (Horning 2013, 2007; Horning and Kraemer 2012). Asking students to read across multiple disciplines within the same course might then seem to be an unreasonable request. We contend that by asking students to think explicitly about how reading experiences differ across disciplinary texts, we create an experience of *defamiliarization* that helps to distinguish the process of reading from the content being read. By focusing on this process and fostering conversations about it, we have the chance to improve students' reading skills. In this chapter, we present an exploratory proposal for why interdisciplinary, team-taught courses with readings from multiple disciplines might improve students' reading skills.

We consider how affect and defamiliarization influence the development of reading strategies and skills. As a preliminary test of this idea, we used the Association of American Colleges and Universities (AAC&U, n.d.) Reading VALUE Rubric to assess change in reading skill as reflected in the blog entries written for our interdisciplinary, team-taught course, Cognitive Humanities: Exploring Emotion. As the authors of the rubric note, "readers . . . should be motivated to approach texts and respond to them with a reflective level of curiosity and the ability to apply aspects of the texts they approach to a variety of aspects in their lives." We suggest that the affect created through defamiliarization provides the motivation referenced by the rubric's authors. Furthermore, although a change in metacognition is not explicitly measured in the rubric, the authors note that it is an implicit requirement for growth on the individual rubric components. As they argue, "metacognition applied to reading refers to the awareness, deliberateness, and reflexivity defining the activities and strategies that readers must control in order to work their ways effectively through different sorts of texts." We think this metacognitive growth emerges through the defamiliarization that multidisciplinary reading engages.

Defamiliarizing Reading: Capturing Confusion

We propose that multidisciplinary reading provides a unique pedagogical opportunity to scaffold and enhance students' reading skills and motivation. Specifically, such a mix of reading provides an opportunity to place disciplines next to one another and to facilitate explicit integrative conversations across them. Placing disparate texts next to one another defamiliarizes reading and helps make students explicitly aware of the process of reading and not just its content. Defamiliarization is a concept from theater that suggests that sometimes narratives make common experiences feel strange and confusing. In line with the conception of defamiliarization developed by Russian formalists such as Viktor Shklovsky (1990) and Roman Jakobson (1987), defamiliarization serves to make the usual spectacular. So, when discussing how aspects of a poem can inform the results of an empirical article, a moment of discomfort is generated when an uneasy but important translation must take place across discourses and genres. Such discomfort makes the normal process of poetic analysis or empirical interpretation spectacular.

We distinguish between defamiliarization, a literary concept, and metacognition, a concept from cognitive psychology. Defamiliarization works through affect; metacognition relies on articulating hidden cognitive processes—for example, the "awareness, deliberateness, and reflexivity" referenced by the authors of the Reading VALUE Rubric. We suggest that defamiliarization is a process than can generate opportunities for metacognition. While both are important in conversations about improving student reading, we find unique value in exploring the idea of defamiliarization and its potential impact on reading.

In moments when common practices have become defamiliarized, the affect generated creates fertile ground for conversations about discomfort. This affect may be harnessed to have metacognitive conversations about reading. As Silvan Tomkins (1995) stressed in his early work, affect can serve as a motivational system that drives cognitive functioning so that the latter relies intimately on the activation of the former. Specifically, the confusion generated through the process of defamiliarization creates an opportunity to make explicit the requirements of successful reading across and within disciplines—allowing students to practice what Nancy Nelson Spivey (1996) calls *discourse synthesis* or what Alice S. Horning (2007, 2) calls *critical literacy*, defined as "the psycholinguistic processes of getting meaning from or putting meaning into print . . . used for the purposes of analysis, synthesis and evaluation." The practice of multidisciplinary reading juxtaposes multiple genres and time periods, placing disparate texts side by side and asking students to critically reflect on the similarities and differences and the connections that can be made among them. These are skill sets modeled in interdisciplinary courses, where instructors from different disciplines can serve as guides to model cross-disciplinary reading conversations.

We have had the opportunity to engage with this kind of reading with students as part of a team-taught interdisciplinary course in the cognitive humanities (Burke and Troscianko 2017; Zunshine 2010) focused on emotion at Allegheny College, a small liberal arts institution in rural, northwestern Pennsylvania with approximately nineteen hundred students. All students at Allegheny are required to major in one discipline (e.g., the humanities) and minor in a different discipline (e.g., the natural sciences). The main goal of the course was to model for students how to read, think, and integrate ideas across multiple disciplines, genres, and time periods. Teaching this course has allowed us to consider the benefits of asking students to read across disciplines within the context of the same course, with guidance from two instructors in different disciplines (i.e., British Romanticism and cognitive psychology). In our course, students read the treatise of Charles Bell (1824), a detailed examination of emotion expression written by an anatomist and surgeon for an audience of artists. With this text, students confronted the developmental nature of knowledge construction—recognizing that scientists did not always have a conception of the brain. Reading a scientific text outside of the modern era challenged students' assumptions about the truth of science and the evidence it uses. Students were then asked how this historical conversation informs current ones about the expression of emotion—for example, Paul Ekman's (2016) basic emotion approach versus Lisa Feldman Barrett's (2017) cultural construction approach. Putting old texts next to new texts, even within the same discipline, created a confusion that explicitly disrupted what students thought they knew and showed them how to engage with that disruption as active, critical readers.

The critical eye that multidisciplinary reading engages can also be turned toward recognizing the writing conventions of different genres. When students were asked to interpret an empirical article, they navigated debates over methodological paradigms and the use of statistical analyses to help them understand human behavior. For example, when critiquing James Gross's (1999) process model of emotion regulation, we learned that there is not one right strategy that works every time for everyone. In contrast, when asked to interpret a poem, students had to consider figures of speech and poetic structures and conventions used to portray human experience. For example, when reading Keats, students had to interpret the metaphors of coldness, paleness, and so on as signals of death, despair, and physical trauma. In a disciplinary course, their reading would, perhaps, stay within the bounds of each genre. In our course, when students engaged with the multiplicity of genres and conventions of texts simultaneously, they were able to see the approaches that are taken for granted and that are unconsciously shaping reading as a practice. These moments of defamiliarization reveal the assumptions, hierarchies, and conventions that we automatically employ when we wear our disciplinary hats (Minnich 2005), thus contributing to students' metacognition about reading.

At the heart of the defamiliarization experience is confusion. Multidisciplinary reading is not easy. Students may find the complexity and diversity of readings difficult to negotiate, slowing down and challenging their reading process, which is already vexed. In our course, the ongoing nature of the conversations and materials encountered required students to hold in mind, in a very present way, all the readings of the semester—rather than taking a one-and-done approach to reading. Students reported being overwhelmed and confused by having to hold so much material, simultaneously, in their mind—something they had to do in order to participate in class discussions and to complete course assignments. While some students found this difficulty invigorating and exciting, others reported feeling a sense of helplessness and were shaken by the inability to rely solely on their expert disciplinary knowledge.

Often, this confusion reveals itself through negative affect (e.g., anger, frustration, fear, anxiety, and boredom). Sarah E. Chinn (2012) describes how these structures of feeling impact both the student and instructor experiences in the classroom and makes the case for why we should not design the learning environment based solely on student comfort. Within the discomfort and negative affect lies learning. In fact, Megan Boler (1999, 176) builds her pedagogy of discomfort around the thesis that "a pedagogy of discomfort begins by inviting educators and students to engage in critical inquiry regarding values and cherished beliefs, and to examine constructed self-images in relation to how one has learned to perceive others. Within this culture of inquiry and flexibility, a central focus is to recognize how emotions define how and what one chooses to see, and conversely, not to see." Sometimes, this discomfort is driven by the complexity of the questions, topics, and assignments students are asked to engage in. In the context of an interdisciplinary course, this discomfort can also be driven by the questioning of cherished beliefs as students are confronted with the limitations of their discipline and recognize how their disciplinary lens has defined how and what they choose to see. We argue that the kind of defamiliarization we outlined previously is a part of a pedagogy of discomfort. We acknowledge that not all instructors will be able to negotiate productive student discomfort without engaging in some level of risk. For example, tenured instructors would be more able to weather unfavorable student course evaluations than untenured or contingent instructors. Also, power dynamics of gender, race, age, and so on produce the same uneven risk. In Boler's conception, a pedagogy of discomfort is not about perpetuating structural oppression or harm. Instead, by embracing the discomfort and negative affect generated through defamiliarization, instructors can push both themselves and their students to creative insights informed by unique synthesis that transverses the confines of disciplinary boundaries.

Course Motivations and Mechanics

To assess the idea that defamiliarization created by multidisciplinary reading will improve reading skill, we examined student performance in a team-taught interdisciplinary course called Cognitive Humanities: Exploring Emotion. Before outlining our specific assessment of student performance, we provide context for the course and what we asked students to do in it. This class integrated frameworks for how people express and regulate feeling and was grounded in texts from both British Romanticism and psychology. For example, students read Joanna Baillie's *De Monfort* ([1798] 2005), a play on the passions; John Keats's "Isabella, or the Pot of Basil" ([1819] 2009); Jane Austen's *Sense and Sensibility* ([1811] 2001); and a late eighteenth-century conduct book. In addition, students were asked to read medical treatises from the early nineteenth century; multidisciplinary texts by historians, philosophers, and scientists; and contemporary psychological and neuroscientific empirical papers.

Across the four modules of the course (Nature of Emotion, Emotion Expression, Emotion Regulation, and the Blush), these texts were juxtaposed such that students moved back and forth between different genres and time periods. So, in discussing emotion regulation, we applied the regulatory flexibility model (Bonanno and Burton 2013) to an analysis of sibling interrelational dynamics in *De Monfort*, or we discussed how the exchanges between the siblings suggested new avenues of exploration for the regulatory flexibility model. In other words, we fostered bidirectional exchanges between disciplines so that science informed literary analysis and close reading directed hypotheses for future empirical research. Our model of team teaching required both instructors to be in the room every day of class; to co-construct the syllabus, readings, and assignments; and to jointly evaluate student performance. We also had a common office hour so that students could consult with both of us simultaneously.

To evaluate learning across the semester, we used a variety of assessments including what we called synthesis papers, a collaborative final project proposal, and biweekly blog entries. For this chapter, we focus on how the writing of blog entries supported the development of students' reading skills. As previous research has illustrated, using writing as a way to evaluate reading comprehension is both appropriate and important, since we cannot otherwise see the process of reading (Odom 2013; Rhodes 2013; Graham and Hebert 2010; Scholes 2002). As Horning (2007, 2013) notes, reading and writing are inextricably linked, with the one helping improve the use of the other. In addition to helping us see students' reading growth, using blog entries allowed us to provide purpose for students in their reading assignments. As previous research has shown, blogging is a particularly effective way to increase student motivation and engagement with course materials (Robertson 2011; Halic et al. 2010; Churchill 2009; Kerawalla et al. 2009; Yang 2009).

However, its effectiveness depends on using it appropriately. For example, as Ifinedo (2017) argues, instructors should use blogging platforms that are user-friendly, incorporate some initial training on their use, encourage students to use visuals and to link to external resources, provide recognition or incentive for blog posts, and foster collaboration among students in the construction of the blog. If used appropriately, blogs can support critical reflection. In an early examination of blogging in the classroom, Nicole B. Ellison and Yuehua Wu (2008, 105) argue that blogging enhances learning because it relies on the critical skill of writing, enhances analytic and critical thinking skills, increases student investment in their writing, is part of an evolving, public discussion, and "disrupts the traditional communication and learning patterns in the classroom." As Ellison and Wu conclude, "blogging can potentially provide students with a window into peers' perspectives, a doorway to a global audience, and a mirror through which to reflect on their own thinking and writing" (119).

The use of blogging in our course incorporated these best practices. Students all contributed to a single course blog (constructed using Blogger), which was open to a public audience. Students were placed into four or five blog groups. On the day that their group was assigned to blog, each student contributed an individual post on the day's readings. During class discussion, students from the group took turns directing the conversation based on their analyses and discussion question for the day. Because it was important to give explicit guidelines for reading and writing purposes, we provided specific instructions for students to use. The syllabus stated that students should "make sure that your entries are thoughtful examinations of important aspects of the reading. For example, you might focus on a section of the reading that was difficult to process, identify important implications, or connect to a previous topic or theme from class. Each entry will require careful thought and should not simply indicate that you 'liked or didn't like' the reading or that the reading was 'interesting or not interesting.'" In the syllabus, students were also given a rubric they adhered to in order to earn full credit for their entry and contribution grade. There were six main components for a successful blog entry: (1) clear identification of the section or passage they were using for their analysis; (2) a critical reflection that prepared readers for a discussion; (3) a critical discussion question that was grounded in the reading and avoided dichotomous responses; (4) a link to an external resource that further explored the main topic of the entry; (5) the creativity of the blog including title construction, use of visual images, and so on; and (6) the success of the entry at generating class discussion. Students were also reminded that they were writing for a publicly available blog, and we discussed how in previous courses authors whose work we were reading had commented on student posts.

Our consistent and regular feedback to students was to find synthesis—to identify connections and conversations across the various texts we read. Our focus on synthesis was meant to foster a critical skill that Lynne A. Rhodes (2013, 3) explicitly characterizes as "woefully" underdeveloped in students. Students wrote approximately four or five blog entries during the semester (depending on the number of students in the course), which meant they practiced developing a successful entry. Each blog entry was posted to the shared course blog before the day of the class meeting. In their critical analyses, students were encouraged to reference previous readings and to focus on a synthesis of ideas across sources. They were also encouraged to consider how the topic of their entry might relate to other courses they had taken or how it might contribute to discussions of real-world challenges or debates.

For each day's class, one group of students was selected to contribute individual entries to the course blog. Students in the group writing entries for the day often consulted with one another to make sure coverage did not overlap; the students not writing entries for the day were encouraged to read the posted entries before class. The instructors read the entries before class and put them in an order that emphasized a logical flow among the questions raised. During class discussion, each blog entry author was introduced by an instructor, who asked, "Tell us about your entry and what your discussion question is for us." Student authors then briefly summarized their analysis with the goal of leading into their discussion question. Conversation for each entry was kept at approximately fifteen minutes so that all blog entries for the day could be addressed. Once the initial discussion question for a blog entry was considered, additional questions, comments, and insights were shared around the topic of the entry of focus. By prioritizing the presentation and discussion of student blog entries for the majority of class time, we heightened students' sense of responsibility and ownership of learning. Such prioritization is vital if students are going to be active readers.

Assessing Blog Writing to Evaluate Student Reading

Approval from the Allegheny College Institutional Review Board was obtained for the project. Three semesters of Cognitive Humanities: Exploring Emotion (spring 2014, fall 2015, and fall 2016) were included in the study. Each course was capped at fifteen students; a total of forty-two students enrolled in these sections. The present analysis assesses the first blog entry, written in the first three weeks of the semester, and the last blog entry, written in the final three weeks of the semester. Overall, eighty-four blog entries were reviewed. As instructors of the course, the authors saved copies of each blog entry to use for grading and then coding purposes. Student names were removed from the entries, and each was assigned a random number so the authors could link the first and last entry for each student.

Readings covered in these entries included a range of genres such as a literary analysis of theory of mind in literature (Zunshine 2010), the passion play *De Monfort* (Baillie [1798] 2005), the poem "Juana" (Hemans [1838] 1999), the novel *Sense and Sensibility* (Austen [1811] 2001), and contemporary psychological articles about the nature of emotion and emotion regulation (e.g., Bonanno and Burton 2013; LeDoux 2012; Barrett 2011; Ekman and Cordaro 2011). The average word count for the first set of blog entries was 549.64 (SD = 158.42); the average word count for the final blog entries was 605.51 (SD = 211.39).

To assess performance across entries, we used the AAC&U Reading VALUE Rubric (n.d.). Over a decade ago, the AAC&U developed a series of sixteen rubrics meant to help formalize the assessment of skills identified as crucial for a twenty-first-century education. These include critical thinking, creative thinking, written communication, and reading, among others. Since their development, they have been viewed by over fifty-six hundred institutions, and research using these rubrics has taken the form of case studies, experimental studies, multistate collaborations, and meta-analytic reports produced by the AAC&U (McConnell et al. 2019). As with the other VALUE Rubrics, the Reading VALUE Rubric was constructed through the work of teams of educational experts.

It should be noted that, as instruments, the VALUE Rubrics bridge the divide between quantitative and qualitative assessments. Specifically, although analyses based on scores from the rubrics are conducted with numerical designations, those designations are based on categorical identifications. For example, although when a student reaches the "milestone 2" level for Genres on the Reading VALUE Rubric, the number-two designation does not reflect a rating as with other Likert scale measures. The numbers assigned are not continuous, which would allow a linear assessment of change. Instead, milestone 2 for Genres means that the coder has recognized based on a close reading of a student's work that the student has produced work that "reflects on reading experiences across a variety of genres, reading both with and against the grain experimentally and intentionally." In a way, the VALUE Rubrics help coders conduct a kind of categorical, close reading broadly across large sets of student work, facilitating comparisons and assessments of growth and change.

In the framing of the Reading VALUE Rubric, the authors quote Catherine E. Snow (2002, 11), defining reading as "the process of simultaneously extracting and constructing meaning through interaction and involvement with written language." In its evaluation of reading, the rubric asks evaluators to consider six different components, including Comprehension, Genres, Relationship to Text, Analysis, Interpretation, and Reader's Voice. Each of these components is evaluated by scoring the written text as achieving one of four levels of performance: benchmark (1), milestones (2, 3), and capstone (4). To determine the performance level, evaluators examine the component of interest and use the guidelines provided for that component. For example, to assess the component Reader's Voice, benchmark would be achieved if evaluators saw "comments about texts in ways that preserve the author's meanings and link them to the assignment." In contrast, capstone would be achieved if evaluators saw that the student "discusses texts with an independent intellectual and ethical disposition so as to further or maintain disciplinary conversations."

We argue that the six components identified by the Reading VALUE Rubric can capture the kind of reading strategies that would be impacted through the process of defamiliarization that students experienced when engaged in multidisciplinary reading. This assumption seems appropriate given that the authors of the rubric argue that growth on many of the individual components requires the development of metacognition that we argue is facilitated through defamiliarization. We suggest that defamiliarization is the state created through the experience of multidisciplinary reading. This state of defamiliarization then influences growth in reading skill—as assessed through the individual components of the Reading VALUE Rubric.

To test whether students' experiences with multidisciplinary texts impacted their reading strategies and comprehension, we used the Reading VALUE Rubric to assess student blog entries. To ensure interrater reliability for coding for the present project, we first carefully read and discussed the Reading VALUE Rubric, considering its application for the specific context of the interdisciplinary team-taught course and the requirements of the blog entry assignment. Then, for training purposes, we selected an initial sample of blog entries for coding. We each separately coded these entries using the rubric. After coding, we compared performance and discussed any clarifications or questions raised. Upon reaching consensus about the use of the rubric, we separately coded each of the eighty-four blog entries. The first review of interrater agreement demonstrated that we either agreed or were one step away from each other (e.g., a milestone of 2 versus a 3) for most of the components scored (472 out of the total 504 observations; greater than 93 percent). For the remaining observations, we were more than one step away from each other. We discussed this small set of blog entries, resolving discrepancies in coding by revisiting the rubric.

After this process, the percentage of interrater agreement ranged from 81 to 92 percent, and Cohen's kappa ranged from 0.71 to 0.86. Because strong interrater reliability was obtained, we averaged blog entry scores for each component and submitted these scores to a within-subjects analysis of

Table 12.1 Change in average performance on the AAC&U Reading VALUE Rubric components across the semester. Standard deviations are given in parenthesis. Scores represent averages across the two raters for each component. The components could be rated as benchmark (1), milestone (2, 3), or capstone (4).

Reading component	First blog entry	Second blog entry
Comprehension	2.43 (0.68)	3.06 (0.63)
Genres	1.81 (0.78)	2.14 (0.73)
Relationship to Text	2.36 (0.69)	2.89 (0.63)
Analysis	2.33 (0.70)	2.98 (0.83)
Interpretation	2.26 (0.79)	2.77 (0.81)
Reader's Voice	2.42 (0.72)	3.05 (0.59)

variance with time of the entry (first entry versus last entry) as the within-subjects variable and component score as the dependent variable. These analyses showed that for each of the six components of the Reading VALUE Rubric, student performance significantly increased from the first blog entry to the last. The performance difference for the components of Comprehension, Relationship to Text, Analysis, Interpretation, and Reader's Voice were significantly different at $P < 0.001$ and partial eta squared at approximately 0.30 (ranging from 0.26 to 0.43). The performance difference for the component of Genres was significant at $P = 0.03$ and partial eta squared at 0.11. See table 12.1 for the change in performance across the semester for each of the six components of the Reading VALUE Rubric. For example, the scores for Comprehension significantly increased from an average of 2.43 (SD = 0.68) to an average of 3.06 (SD = 0.63). Similarly, Reader's Voice significantly increased from an average of 2.42 (SD = 0.72) to an average of 3.05 (SD = 0.59). Overall, scores increased by one step on average (e.g., from benchmark to milestone 2 or from milestone 2 to milestone 3).

READING TOGETHER: THE IMPACT OF INTERDISCIPLINARY COURSES

In this essay, we have put forward a proposal that the state of defamiliarization created through the experience of multidisciplinary reading can improve student reading skills. In the first part of the essay, we provided the rationale for why and how multidisciplinary reading generates feelings of defamiliarization and why that state might improve students' reading skills. To assess that potential change, we used the AAC&U Reading VALUE Rubric. The analysis demonstrated that students' performance improved on each of the components of the Reading VALUE Rubric. This outcome preliminarily supports the idea that defamiliarizing reading using multidisciplinary texts can change the way students approach the experience of reading.

Of course, it is important to keep in mind that these results are preliminary. In the present study, defamiliarization was not manipulated across different conditions. Therefore, defamiliarization is only one possible reason that our course influenced student reading. For example, it is not possible to separate the impact of multidisciplinary reading from the impact that blogging may have had on student reading outcomes. While we used student blogs as a way to see how students were engaging with multidisciplinary reading, blogging itself has been shown to be an effective pedagogical tool. To disentangle the impact of multidisciplinary reading from that of blogging, we would need to compare two different courses that use blogging, one with multidisciplinary reading and one without such reading. This possibility was not available to us when we taught the course and ran the study, reflecting the challenges often faced when engaging with the scholarship of teaching and learning.

Nevertheless, we think the findings of the present study are informative and can be used to inspire future conversations and research on multidisciplinary reading and about the impact of defamiliarization in particular. Moreover, we have some important additional evidence that reading skills are impacted by engaging with multidisciplinary reading. In an analysis of beginning- and end-of-the-semester synthesis assignments across ten interdisciplinary team-taught courses, Sarah L. Bunnell, Aimee Knupsky, and M. Soledad Caballero (2018) showed that students improved their critical and creative thinking skills across their time in these courses as measured by the AAC&U VALUE rubrics for these constructs. The fact that only one of these courses used blog entries provides some converging evidence that multidisciplinary reading itself can improve students' reading strategies and comprehension.

Although the changes may not seem substantial, they were consistent, and the effect sizes suggest they were strong. When the first blog entry was written, students were already demonstrating benchmark or first-level milestone reading performance. What we saw, then, was a shift to second-level milestone performance for almost all six components. When we consider our results in relation to previous research, we can highlight the importance of the reading changes observed. For example, we might think about research that illustrates students' struggles with synthesis. As Rhodes (2013, 3) has noted, "even when students are given explicit and enhanced instruction in reading, even when adjustments are made to curriculum to address demonstrated student weaknesses, we continue to see woefully low scores in synthesis skills in research writing."

The two components most relevant for an assessment of synthesis are the Analysis and Interpretation components of the AAC&U Reading VALUE Rubric. The milestone for Analysis requires students to "evaluate strategies for relating ideas, text structure, or other textual features in order to build knowledge or insight within and across texts and disciplines." The milestone for Interpretation requires students to "provide evidence not only that s/he can read by using an appropriate epistemological lens but that s/he can also engage in reading as a part of a continuing dialogue within and beyond a discipline or a community of readers." Clearly, both of these components required students to demonstrate synthesis. As such, the significant increase we saw on these two components (i.e., from milestone 2 to 3 on average) preliminarily suggests that multidisciplinary reading and writing is a powerful pedagogy.

We also saw strong improvement (i.e., milestone 2 to 3) in the components of Relationship to Text and Reader's Voice. We think this change may have been due to the nature of distributed expertise across students in the class—that is, some students had more experience reading neuroscientific texts, while others understood how to interpret a poem. Through their entries, these areas of expertise came through as they analyzed readings for the day and were essential in order for the class as a whole to understand the concepts presented. In this way, students were writing for each other and had an equal voice in the classroom. Therefore, their voice mattered and was given space and attention.

We think that our results suggest that students can care about reading despite the prevailing narrative that they are not motivated to read. One way to motivate students to care about reading is to not only give them a purpose for their reading but also take seriously what they write about and think about in their reading (Yeager et al. 2014; Ifinedo 2017; Kerr and Frese 2017). While small class sizes may more easily foster accountability, it is possible to acknowledge student expertise even in larger classes, perhaps through small-group conversation or think-pair-share activities (Yeager et al. 2014). The salient point is that students understand that their contributions can have an impact on the learning of their colleagues.

Even though performance on all six components (Comprehension, Genres, Relationship to Texts, Analysis, Interpretation, and Reader's Voice) significantly increased during the semester, it is important to note that performance on the Genres component looked different. Specifically, it started out at a lower level of performance and only hit milestone 2 performance by the end of the semester. Moreover, the magnitude of change for Genres across the semester averaged less than half of what we saw for the other five components. This smaller change suggests that we did not sufficiently scaffold for our students how to explicitly recognize how genre conventions shifted and changed. In her meta-analysis of undergraduate reading, Heather D. Porter (2018, 38) talks about how instructors can scaffold this skill through "explicit exposure to the ways of thinking unique to the community." For example, we might start a class (as do our colleagues at Ohio Wesleyan University) by having students read a poem through a literary and then through a scientific lens.

We hope to determine whether the mild growth we observed in Genres can be sustained or increased over time. It is likely that recognizing and incorporating genre conventions requires ongoing practice with and simultaneous exposure to multidisciplinary texts. We are inspired by the approach Jonathan Cisco (2016) took in observing how students negotiated differences across disciplinary reading. In particular, Cisco examined students' reading approaches in a humanities class and found differences in how students approached reading that emerged because he was using different types of texts and genres. In future iterations of our course, we plan to make explicit what genre is in each of our disciplinary fields as well as how those genres inform, challenge, and disrupt the creation of knowledge.

Compared to our previous experiences using the AAC&U VALUE Rubrics, using the Reading VALUE Rubric posed some challenges for us. We appreciated the holistic approach to assessing students' work using this rubric. Specifically, when considering each of the six components, it was necessary to consider the whole of each blog entry. At the same time, not always being able to pinpoint an explicit moment of, for example, Reader's Voice created some ambiguity and uncertainty. In order to identify if and how the component Reader's Voice emerged in an entry, we had to evaluate how the student engaged with text across the entirety of the entry (e.g., title, analysis, external link, and images) rather than look at one or two comments that students made about the content of the reading.

In addition, the guidelines offered to raters using the rubric are open to considerable interpretation and are less concrete than those of the other AAC&U VALUE Rubrics we have used. This ambiguity gives the rubric flexibility to be used in different courses and contexts. But using this rubric will require that the raters spend a considerable amount of time agreeing on and contextualizing those guidelines. We were not sure if the Reading VALUE Rubric would be appropriate for an interdisciplinary course, as it seemed that there might be aspects of students' reading experiences that were not quite captured in it. But overall, using the rubric generated important conversations and clarifications, helped us reconsider our grading practices, and gave us ideas about what to focus on for our team-taught course as well as other classes.

As with any scholarship of teaching and learning project, there are limitations to the current project, which suggest that we proceed with cautious optimism. As we have already suggested, it is difficult at this point to determine the separate impact that multidisciplinary reading may have over and above the influence of having students blog about their reading. In addition, using the Reading VALUE Rubric requires that the coders be familiar with what students have read, which increases the difficulty of having "naive" coders. Instructors will often be the most appropriate coders, but this increases the potential influence of researcher bias in the analysis. Another limitation is that the classes assessed took place at a small liberal arts college. The course itself was focused on emotion and was taught by two female, seasoned instructors. Any of these factors could impact our results, which is why our recommendations from this project are preliminary. There is still much work to be done.

That said, we think there are fruitful applications. First, most importantly, defamiliarizing reading demonstrates for students the unconscious or routine practices used when we read in different disciplines. Exposing these disciplinary preferences creates an opportunity for instructors to interrogate and discuss their own reading practices. Considering how we always read requires us to think about what that means, why that is, and how we came to read that way in the first place. Doing so will produce a disruption of disciplinary assumptions and common knowledge practices.

For example, in our case, the first author, an experimental psychologist, struggled with identifying the theme of emotion regulation in John Keats's "Isabella, or the Pot of Basil" ([1819] 2009). In other words, she was asking, What does a poem about decapitation have to do with the signal of blushing and how it informs emotion models? She had to set aside the literal interpretation of the text that she would normally use when reading an experiment. And the second author, a literary historian, was utterly mystified by methods and results sections but kept going to see what could be understood in order to find the relevance and connections of the experiment for literature. Finally, both authors had the opportunity to challenge disciplinary narratives that are taken for granted and difficult to disrupt on one's own. Such courses allow instructors to acknowledge disciplinary limitations and identify moments of synergy where the power of both disciplines can be brought to bear to reveal questions that are easy to miss when wearing disciplinary blinders.

In addition, students must be given purpose and voice in order to be motivated to read for synthesis. Therefore, instructors should make sure to integrate reading with assignments that heighten student responsibility and ownership for collaborative learning so that students become partners in shaping the course across the semester. Highlighting the unique contributions that students with different academic backgrounds can make requires dedicating classroom space to students' interpretations and not just the content we think is most important from the reading for any given day. When we give students the responsibility of building knowledge in the class, that content will eventually arise.

Finally, courses that aim to unmask disciplinary reading practices will inevitably create negative affect in both instructors and students. Instructors should consider how to talk about that discomfort productively with students in order to provide strategies for them to persevere. For example, we use a we're-all-in-it-together approach in which we are honest, vulnerable, and open about our own struggles with reading in disciplinary areas that are unfamiliar and, at times, intimidating to us. The role of affect in learning is a long-standing but still underrecognized pedagogical conundrum. Researchers have long examined or struggled with the role of affect in pedagogy (Boler 1999; Cavanagh 2016). When approaching difficult classroom readings, understanding how affect motivates, dissuades, or empowers student learning is all the more important. Cognition is a system that is fueled by affect; opportunities to learn are created by moments of affective disruption (Seigworth and Gregg 2010; Tomkins 1995). Engaging with multidisciplinary texts defamiliarizes the process of reading, thus creating a path for learning by generating affect that opens up metaconversations about why we read, how we read, and the power we can wield when we read.

Acknowledgments

This work was supported by an Expanding Collaboration Initiative grant from the Great Lakes Colleges Association funded through the Andrew W. Mellon Foundation. Thanks to the students in all three sections for this study.

References

Association of American Colleges and Universities (AAC&U). n.d. "Reading VALUE Rubric." Accessed June 1, 2020. https://www.aacu.org/value/rubrics/reading.

Austen, Jane. (1811) 2001. *Sense and Sensibility*. Edited by Claudia L. Johnson. New York: Norton.

Baillie, Joanna. (1798) 2005. "De Monfort." In *Plays on the Passions*, 301–387. Edited by Peter Duthie. Peterborough, ON: Broadview.

Barrett, Lisa Feldman. 2011. "Was Darwin Wrong about Emotional Expressions?" *Current Directions in Psychological Science* 20 (6): 400–406.

———. 2017. *How Emotions Are Made: The Secret Life of the Brain*. New York: Houghton Mifflin Harcourt.

Bell, Charles. 1824. *Essays on the Anatomy and Philosophy of Expression*. 2nd ed. London: Longman Hurst Rees and Orme.

Boler, Megan. 1999. *Feeling Power: Emotions and Education*. New York: Routledge.

Bonanno, George A., and Charles L. Burton. 2013. "Regulatory Flexibility: An Individual Differences Perspective on Coping and Emotion Regulation." *Perspectives on Psychological Science* 8 (6): 591–612.

Bunnell, Sarah L., Aimee Knupsky, and M. Soledad Caballero. 2018. "The Transformative Power of Interdisciplinary Team Teaching across the Arts/Humanities and Sciences." Paper presented at the International Society for the Scholarship of Teaching and Learning, Bergen, Norway.

Burke, Michael, and Emily C. Troscianko, eds. 2017. *Cognitive Literary Science: Dialogues between Literature and Cognition*. New York: Oxford University Press.

Cavanagh, Sarah Rose. 2016. *The Spark of Learning: Energizing the College Classroom with the Science of Emotion*. Morgantown: West Virginia University Press.

Chinn, Sarah E. 2012. "Once More with Feeling: Pedagogy, Affect, Transformation." *Transformations: The Journal of Inclusive Scholarship and Pedagogy* 22 (2): 15–20.

Churchill, Daniel. 2009. "Educational Applications of Web 2.0: Using Blogs to Support Teaching and Learning." *British Journal of Educational Technology* 40 (1): 179–183.

Cisco, Jonathan. 2016. "A Case Study of University Honors Students in Humanities through a Disciplinary Literacy Lens." *Literacy Research and Instruction* 55 (1): 1–23.

Ekman, Paul. 2016. "What Scientists Who Study Emotion Agree About." *Perspectives on Psychological Science* 11 (1): 31–34.

Ekman, Paul, and Daniel Cordaro. 2011. "What Is Meant by Calling Emotions Basic." *Emotion Review* 3 (4): 364–370.

Ellison, Nicole B., and Yuehua Wu. 2008. "Blogging in the Classroom: A Preliminary Exploration of Student Attitudes and Impact on Comprehension." *Journal of Educational Multimedia and Hypermedia* 17 (1): 99–122.

Graham, Steve, and Michael Hebert. 2010. *Writing to Read: Evidence for How Writing Can Improve Reading*. A Carnegie Time to Act Report. Washington, DC: Alliance for Excellence Education.

Gross, James J. 1999. "Emotion Regulation: Past, Present, Future." *Cognition and Emotion* 13 (5): 551–573. https://doi.org/10.1080/026999399379186.

Halic, Olivia, Debra Lee, Trena Paulus, and Marsha Spence. 2010. "To Blog or Not to Blog: Student Perceptions of Blog Effectiveness for Learning in a College-Level Course." *Internet and Higher Education* 13 (4): 206–213.

Hemans, Felica. (1838) 1999. "Juana." In *Records of Woman with Other Poems*, 67–69. Edited by Paula R. Feldman. Lexington: University Press of Kentucky.

Horning, Alice S. 2007. "Reading across the Curriculum as the Key to Student Success." *Across the Disciplines* 4:1–17.

———. 2013. "Elephants, Pornography and Safe Sex: Understanding and Addressing Students' Reading Problems across the Curriculum." *Across the Disciplines* 10 (4): 1–7.

Ifinedo, Princely. 2017. "Examining Students' Intention to Continue Using Blogs for Learning: Perspectives from Technology Acceptance, Motivational, and Social-Cognitive Frameworks." *Computers in Human Behavior* 72:189–199.

Jakobson, Roman. 1987. *Language in Literature*. Edited by Krystyna Pomorska and Stephen Rudy. Cambridge: Harvard University Press.

Keats, John. (1819) 2009. "Isabella, or the Pot of Basil." In *Keats's Poetry and Prose, Authoritative Texts Criticism*, 429–445. Edited by Jeffrey N. Cox. New York: Norton.

Kerawalla, Lucinda, Shailey Minosha, Gill Kirkup, and Graine Conole. 2009. "An Empirically Grounded Framework to Guide Blogging in Higher Education." *Journal of Computer Assisted Learning* 25 (1): 31–42.

Kerr, Mary Margaret, and Kristen M. Frese. 2017. "Reading to Learn or Learning to Read? Engaging College Students in Course Readings." *College Teaching* 65 (1): 28–31.

LeDoux, Joseph. 2012. "A Neuroscientist's Perspective on Debates about the Nature of Emotion." *Emotion Review* 4 (4): 375–379.

McConnell, Kathryne Drezek, Erin M. Horan, Bethany Zimmerman, and Terrel L. Rhodes. 2019. *We Have a Rubric for That: The VALUE Approach to Assessment*. Association for American Colleges and Universities. https://www.aacu.org/value/research.

Minnich, Elizabeth. 2005. *Transforming Knowledge*. Philadelphia: Temple University Press.

Odom, Mary Lou. 2013. "Not Just for Writing Anymore: What WAC Can Teach Us about Reading to Learn." *Across the Disciplines* 10 (4): 1–14.

Porter, Heather D. 2018. "Constructing an Understanding of Undergraduate Disciplinary Reading: An Analysis of Contemporary Scholarship." *Journal of College Reading and Learning* 48:24–46.

Rhodes, Lynne A. 2013. "When Is Writing Also Reading?" *Across the Disciplines* 10 (4): 1–9.

Robertson, Judy. 2011. "The Educational Affordances of Blogs for Self-Directed Learning." *Computers and Education* 57:1628–1644.

Scholes, Robert J. 2002. "The Transition to College Reading." *Pedagogy* 2 (2): 165–172.

Seigworth, Gregory J., and Melissa Gregg. 2010. "An Inventory of Shimmers." In *The Affect Theory Reader*, edited by Melissa Gregg and Gregory J. Seigworth, 1–25. Durham, NC: Duke University Press.

Shklovsky, Viktor. 1990. *Theory of Prose*. Translated by Benjamin Sher. Dallas, TX: Dalkey Archive Press.

Snow, Catherine E. 2002. *Reading for Understanding: Toward a Research and Development Program in Reading Comprehension*. Santa Monica, CA: RAND.

Spivey, Nancy Nelson. 1996. *The Constructivist Metaphor: Reading, Writing and the Making of Meaning*. San Diego: Academic Press.

Tomkins, Silvan. 1995. "Why Are Affects?" In *Shame and Its Sisters: A Silvan Tompkins Reader*, edited by Eve Kosofsky Sedgwick and Adam Frank, 33–74. Durham, NC: Duke University Press.

Yang, Shih-hsien. 2009. "Using Blogs to Enhance Critical Reflection and Community of Practice." *Journal of Educational Technology and Society* 12 (2): 11–21.

Yeager, David S., Marlone D. Henderson, David Paunesku, Gregory M. Walton, Sidney D'Mello, Brian J. Spitzer, and Angela Lee Duckworth. 2014. "Boring but Important: A Self-Transcendent Purpose for Learning Fosters Academic Self-Regulation." *Journal of Personality and Social Psychology* 107 (4): 559–580.

Zunshine, Lisa, ed. 2010. *Introduction to Cognitive Cultural Studies*. Baltimore: Johns Hopkins University Press.

Aimee Knupsky is Professor of Psychology and Director of Undergraduate Research, Scholarship, and Creative Activities at Allegheny College, Meadville, Pennsylvania. She teaches courses in cognitive psychology and the cognitive humanities and conducts interdisciplinary research on emotion and affect.

M. Soledad Caballero is Professor of English at Allegheny College, Meadville, Pennsylvania. She teaches courses in British Romanticism, women's gender and sexuality studies, and the cognitive humanities and conducts interdisciplinary research on emotion and affect. She is also a poet.

INDEX

Note: Page numbers in *italic* refer to images or illustrations.

abstract writing, 130–31, 133
accountability, 33, 40
accuracy, reading for, 32–33, 39, 40
acoustic bias, 32
acquisition-oriented readers, 73–75
"ACRL Visual Literacy Competency Standards for Higher Education," 83–84, 90, 93
active learning, reading as (threshold concept), 55–61
Advanced Research and Writing course
 abstract writing in, 130–31, 133
 and academic reading of DMA students, 124–26
 and agency of doctoral students, 128, 137–39
 and critical annotated bibliographies, 131–32, 133
 critique writing in, 131, 133
 and drafting literature reviews, 132–33
 literature review as focus of, 124
 and mapping fields of knowledge production, 132–33
 and metacognitive awareness, 134–35
 methodology, 128
 peer and instructor feedback used in, 129–30
 scaffolding principle in, 128, 130–32
 and shifts in reading practices, 135–37
 sources/übersources examined in, 133
 transparency principle in, 128, 129–30
aesthetic/efferent reading distinction, 7, 38, 39, 40, 221–22
affect, 34–35, 50–54, 66, 68, 92–93, 129, 137, 144, 200, 239, 240, 242–43, 254
Albers, Peggy, 9
Alderson-Day, Ben, 32
Alexander, Patricia, 68, 73, 74, 77

Allegheny College, 241
Allen, Ira James, 67, 69, 72, 74, 77, 184
Alverno College, 184. *See also* Analytical Reading in Psychology course
analysis of text, 11, 83, 84, 116, 147, 187, 219, 221–23, 241, 247, 249, 249, 251
Analytical Reading in Psychology course, 184–201
 and alignment of assignments with learning goals, 185–86, 189–90
 and cognitive skills in reading, 187–88, 192–94
 and grammar instruction, 186–87, 190–92, 197–98
 impacts of, 196–200, 201
 implementation of, 189–96
 and lack of readiness for academic reading, 184–85
 and meaning making, 188–89, 194–96, 199–200
 recommendations for instruction, 200
 and scholarly identity, 188–89, 195, 199–200
 and self-assessment, 189
 and vocabulary acquisition, 190, 192–93, 198–99
apprenticeship, cognitive, 10. *See also* Reading Apprenticeship (RA) framework
arguments, structure of, 198
Assembly for the Teaching of English Grammar (ATEG), 186
Association of American Colleges and Universities (AAC&U), 239, 247, 249, 250, 251
Association of College and Research Libraries, 83
audiobooks, 31
Austen, Jane, 243

259

Baillie, Joanna, 243–44
Barker, Angela, 127
Barrett, Lisa Feldman, 241
Barsalou, Lawrence W., 27
Bartholomae, David, 67, 74
Bass, Randy, 103, 205, 219
Bazerman, Charles, 67
Bean, Thomas William, 13
Bell, Charles, 241
Bernini, Marco, 32
Bernstein, Dan, 4
Bernstein, Jeffrey L., 103, 104, 105, 115, 117
Berry, Chad, 7
Bhattacharyya, Gautam, 166, 167, 179
bibliographies, annotated, 131–32, 133
big-world reading, 35, 39
Birkenstein, Cathy, 188, 193, 198
Black, Aaron E., 168, 176, 180
Blackmore, Heide, 25
Bloch-Schulman, Stephen, 26, 103, 104, 117
blogging, 244–46, 250, 252
Bodner, George, 166, 167, 179
Boler, Megan, 242, 243, 254
bottleneck to student learning, reading as, 76
Bower, Gordon H., 32
Boyer, Ernest, 3–4
Boyland, Joyce Tang, 13, 14, 16, 184–201
brain, 5, 6
    and "default" mode of reading, 27
    and reading for pleasure, 31
Braze, David, 187
Bridges, Laurie, 84
Brosch, Renate, 27
Brown, John Seely, 10
Brozo, William G., 13
Brumberger, Eva, 82, 84
Bunn, Michael, 130, 194, 195
Bunnell, Sarah L., 250
Burkholder, J. Peter, 125, 128

Caballero, M. Soledad, 13, 17, 239–57
Calder, Lendol, 103
California State University, Monterey Bay (CSUMB), 44, 49
Carillo, Ellen C.
    on learning transfer, 9
    "Mindful Reading" concept of, 69
    and reading pedagogy, 65, 66, 67
    on self-assessment, 189
    on spotlighting process, 73
    on student readers, 74, 134
charts, evaluation of, 85
chemistry, 4. *See also* organic chemistry, reading compliance in
Chick, Nancy L., 4, 10, 26, 28, 65, 66, 95, 221, 224
Chickering, Arthur, 179
child development course (case study), 205–15
    and exam preparation, 211
    just-in-time teaching and contingent teaching in, 207, 212–14
    low levels of reading compliance, 205–6, 207–8
    quizzes used to promote reading compliance, 206–7, 208–9, 210
    reading guides used to promote reading compliance, 207, 209, 210–12, 213
    student preparation for, 209–10, 212
Children of Men (film), 105, 107–9, 110–11, 112, 118n3. *See also* film reading in academic settings
Chinn, Sarah E., 242
Chittenden, Edward, 32–33
Choi, Youngok, 85–86, 91, 94
Christgau, Robert, 131
Ciccone, Anthony, 3
Cisco, Jonathan, 252
civic engagement, reading for, 82
close reading, 10, 219, 222, 223, 226, 229, 244, 247
cognition, 6–8, 28, 187–88, 192–94
collaborative faculty-student projects, 214–15, 220
collaborative learning, 55, 75, 147, 150, 154, 158, 160, 179, 254. *See also* online collaborative learning (OCL)
Collins, Allan, 10
compliance, reading, 57–58, 169–76, 205–18
comprehension, 2, 5–7, 46, 83, 97, 116, 179, 186–88, 197, 205, 210–11, 247–50
confidence of readers, 55
    of doctoral students, 138–39
    of first-year science students, 143–48, 152, 155, 156, 157, 158–60
    and online resources, 161
    of organic chemistry students, 178, 179
Conor, Erin, 134
content area reading, 12, 13
contingent teaching, 207, 212–14

Cook, Susan, 48
Corrigan, Paul T., 10
CRAAP Test, 86–87
cramming strategy, 208
critical literacy or reading, 82–84, 125, 241
critique, 103–8, 109–10, 129–31, 133
cross-disciplinary approaches, 4, 159, 162, 241. *See also* multidisciplinary reading in humanities course

Davila, Yvonne C., 10–11, 14, 16, 143–62
Deci, Edward L., 168, 176, 177
decoding meaning in reading, 6
Decoding the Disciplines, 76, 125
dedicated/situated reading, 37–38, 39
"deep" reading, 17, 72, 221–22
defamiliarization, 239, 240–43, 248, 249–50, 253, 254
De Monfort (Baillie), 243–44, 246
Digital Images Guide (DIG) Method, 95, 96, 97
digital natives, myth of, 84
discernment, reading as process of, 234–35, 236
disciplinary literacy, 9–11, 12–13, 26, 55–56, 61, 68, 73
diversity in readers and reading approaches, 25–41
  in accuracy/momentum distinction, 32–33, 39
  in efferent/aesthetic reading distinction, 38, 39, 40
  in flow/event readers, 36–37, 39
  in immersed/engaged relationship with text, 38–39
  in instinct for visual, acoustic, or emotion-based imagery, 31–32, 39, 40
  and knowledge from teaching reading, 28–29
  in optimal reading conditions, 31, 39
  and respecting readerly autonomy, 25, 41
  in risky/safe reading preferences, 34–35, 39
  and self-awareness of reading proclivities, 26, 40, 41
  in singular works/big-world reading preferences, 35, 39
  in situated/dedicated reading, 37–38, 39
  and value of free voluntary reading, 30
doctoral students
  as academic readers, 124–26
  agency of, 124, 137–39

critical importance of academic reading for, 123
  function of literature review for, 126–27
  and imposter syndrome, 138
  literature review requirements, 124, 125
  and metacognitive awareness, 134–35
  overwhelm experienced by, 123
  and parallels of reading music and prose, 134
  and shifts in reading practices, 135–37
  and time management, 135–36
  uncertainty and intimidation expressed by, 129, 137–38, 139
  See also Advanced Research and Writing course
documentaries, attitudes about, 114–15, 116, 117
domain learning, model of, 68, 73
Donovan, Jordan R., 16, 184–201
Douglas, J. Yellowlees, 38
Douglas, Kate, 10
Downs, Doug, 9
Dunkerly-Bean, Judith, 13

Easterling, Heather C., 11, 15, 64–78
Edmunson-Morton, Tiah, 84
efferent/aesthetic reading distinction, 7, 38, 39, 40, 221–22
Eisenberg, Michael B., 85, 90
Ekman, Paul, 241
Eliason, John, 11, 15, 64–78
Elliot, Norbert, 71
Ellison, Nicole B., 244
embedded reading instruction, 145–46, 147–48, 155–57, 159–60, 162
emotional risks assumed in reading, 34–35
English as an Additional Language students, 161
etymologies of words, 192, 199
evaluation of text, 2, 83, 84–86, 232, 241
event readers, 36–37
exam preparation, reading guides used in, 211
explicit approach to reading instruction, 52, 59, 116, 127, 145, 146, 147–48, 155, 159–60, 162, 184–204

faculty
  faculty development, 11, 75–76 (*see also* Reading Apprenticeship (RA) framework)
  self-awareness of reading proclivities, 40

Index 261

faculty reading practices, examining, 64–78
  focus groups used in, 69, 77
  gap in faculty awareness of, 66–67, 71, 73, 77
  implications and recommendations, 75–77
  literature review, 66–68
  meta-reading, 71–72
  methodology, 69–71, 70
  reading to produce versus to acquire, 73–75
  strategic reading, 72–73
Felten, Peter, 3, 7, 49, 81, 206, 225
Fernyhough, Charles, 32
film reading in academic settings, 102–18
  broad range of approaches to, 106–7, 116
  critiquing social and political implications, 108–10
  and general perceptions of film, 117
  implications of study, 116–17
  and making connections beyond the text, 111–13
  methodology, 104–5, 118n1
  passive/active interaction with text, 113–15, 117
  perceptions of documentaries versus fiction films, 114–15, 116, 117
  questioning and assessing the texts, 107–10
  questioning content, 107
  questioning focus and intent, 108, 116
  and strategies supporting questioning and assessment, 110–13
  and textual details, 110–11
  and think-aloud process, 104, 105, 106, 113, 115, 118n2
  and use of films to support learning, 102–3, 116
Fine, Gary Alan, 123, 124
First Year Curriculum Principles of Transition Pedagogy, 148
flow readers, 36–37, 39
Freer, Patrick K., 127
freshman composition classes, 8–9

Gee, James Paul, 5, 67, 125
genealogical perspective on academic literature, 133
genre, 2, 11, 48, 67, 94, 112, 124, 223, 226, 228, 229, 230, 232, 234, 242, 246, 249, 252
"Geri's Game" (short film), 230

Gernsbacher, Morton Ann, 186, 187
Global Challenges Inquiry course at McMaster University, 104, 105, 106, 109, 118
Gogan, Brian, 48, 57
Golde, Chris M., 126, 128, 132, 136
Gollnitz, Deborah-Lee, 14
Gonzaga University, 65
graduate students, 140, 161. *See also* doctoral students
Graff, Gerald, 188, 193
Graff, Nelson, 7, 11, 13, 15, 44–61
Graham, Steve, 8, 244
grammar instruction, 186–87, 190–92, 197–98
Green, Rosemary, 16, 123–40
Greenleaf, Cynthia, 44, 51, 55
Griffiths, Neela, 10–11, 14, 16, 143–62
Gross, James, 242
Guo, Ying, 186

Habraken, Clarisse, 166
Haller, Cynthia R., 14, 71, 127, 133, 139
Hand, Brian, 48
Hargadon, Andrew, 38
Harl, Allison L., 9, 67, 140, 144, 145
Hassel, Holly, 10, 221
Hattwig, Denise, 81
Haynie, Aeron, 10, 221
Head, Alison J., 85, 90
Hebert, Michael, 8, 244
Heidegger, Martin, 27
Henry, Rachel M., 16, 184–201
Hillbilly Elegy (Vance), 231–32
Hjortshoj, Keith, 72–73
Holschuh, Jodi Patrick, 2, 8
Horning, Alice S.
  on critical literacy, 2, 241
  and link between writing and reading, 244
  and meaning-making by disciplinary experts, 64
  on meta-readers, 71, 73
  on reading instruction across the curriculum, 14
  and reading pedagogy, 3, 65, 67, 210
  on student readers, 74, 77, 225, 239
Huber, Mary Taylor, 3, 4, 14, 69
Hughes, David, 82, 90
Human Flow (documentary), 105, 107, 108, 109, 110–11, 112, 114. *See also* film reading in academic settings

262 Index

humanities. *See* multidisciplinary reading in humanities course
Hutchings, Pat, 3, 4, 26, 44, 75, 95, 103, 220
Hutchins, Edwin, 28

identity, personal, 36–37, 112, 117
identity, scholarly, 13, 67, 74, 124, 167, 174, 188–89, 195, 199–200
Ifinedo, Princely, 244, 251
imagery, conjuring mental, 31–32, 39, 40
images, "reading." *See* visual literacy
immersed/engaged relationship with text, 38–39
Indiana University's Freshman Learning Project, 76
infographics, evaluation of, 86–87
instrumentalism by faculty readers, 72–73
intention, questioning, 108, 116
interdisciplinary learning, 13, 60, 236, 239, 241, 243. *See also* multidisciplinary reading in humanities course
interlanguage, 167, 169, 170, 173–74, 178
international relationships of students, 175–76
internet, images found on, 81, 85. *See also* online resources
intimidation, students' feelings of, 129, 137, 138, 144, 195
"Isabella, or the Pot of Basil" (Keats), 243, 253
Iser, Wolfgang, 7

Jakobson, Roman, 240
Johnson, Brittney, 48
Johnson, Tara, 48
"Juana" (Hemans), 246
just-in-time teaching (JiTT), 207, 212–13, 214

K-12, lessons from, 12–13
Kafka, Franz, 34
Kamler, Barbara, 126, 127, 130–32
Keats, John, 243, 253
Kędra, Joanna, 82
Kendeou, Panayiota, 2, 5
Kersnar, Rebecca, 15, 44–61
Kift, Sally, 148
Knupsky, Aimee, 13, 17, 239–57
Kozeracki, Carol A., 158, 159
Krashen, Stephen, 30–31

Kuh, George D., 13
Kuzmicova, Anezka, 30
Kwan, Becky S. C., 123, 125, 126

Lamott, Anne, 129
Land, Ray, 46, 47–48, 49
Lemke, Jay L., 167
letters, recognition of, 6
Leuzinger, Ryne, 15, 44–61
librarians
  integration of visual literacy instruction, 84
  professional responsibilities of, 25
Linderholm, Tracy, 2, 33, 39
Linkon, Sherry Lee, 10, 103
literacy, 1, 2, 27, 41
literature reviews, 123–40
  and critical annotated bibliographies, 131–32
  demands of, 125
  drafting of, 132–33
  function of, 126–27
  low levels of instruction on, 126–27
  value of, for academic reading, 139
  See also Advanced Research and Writing course
Little, Deandra, 7
logs, reading, 46, 53–54, 58, 59

Mackey, Margaret, 7, 15, 25–41
Manarin, Karen, 1–17, 69, 82–83, 87, 97, 143, 159, 161, 229
Mann, Sarah J., 125, 130, 140
Mannion, Greg, 3
mapping fields of knowledge production, 132–33
Marquis, Elizabeth, 8, 15, 102–18
"massed practice" study strategy, 208
Maurer, Trent W., 14, 16, 205–15
Mayer, Jennifer, 81–82
McAlpine, Lynn, 124, 125, 126, 129, 137
McClure, Hazel, 86
McCollum, Brett, 11, 14, 16, 166–80
McCracken, I. Moriah, 48
McKinney, Kathleen, 3, 4
McMaster University, 104
meaning in reading
  constructing, 6–7
  decoding, 6
  meaning making, 6, 188–89, 194–96, 199–200

Index   263

Messaris, Paul, 7
metacognitive awareness and tools
   and agency of doctoral students, 137
   and cognitive apprenticeship, 10
   and defamiliarization engaged by multidisciplinary reading, 239–40, 248
   of doctoral students, 134–35
   fostering, 77, 78
   Metacognitive Awareness of Reading Strategies Inventory (MARSI), 134–35
   and process of decoding a discipline, 76
   in Reading Apprenticeship framework, 46, 49, 51–52, 54, 55, 59, 60–61
   reading-to-write as site of, 133
   role of educators in developing, 3
   in support of meaning making, 188–89, 194–96
   as transdisciplinary, 11
   value of, 26, 39
meta-reading, 68, 71–72, 75, 78
Meyer, Jan, 46, 47–48, 49
Middendorf, Joan, 11
Mikulecky, Larry, 9
Miller, Carolyn, 67
modeling reading skills
   Carillo on need for, 67
   and coaching reading skills, 10, 51, 76, 191, 200
   and cognitive apprenticeship, 10
   in curriculum for first-year science students, 150, 158
   in interdisciplinary learning, 241
   in Reading Apprenticeship framework, 52
   and reading guides, 210
   value of, for students, 76
Moje, Elizabeth Birr, 12
momentum, reading for, 32–33, 39, 40
Moore, Jessie L., 48–49, 225
Morreale, Sherwyn P., 4, 14, 69
Morrow, Daniel G., 32
Morsch, Layne, 11, 14, 16, 166–80
motivation of students
   and blogging, 244
   and disciplinary literacy, 13
   identity tied to, 13
   impact of affect on, 239, 240, 254
   and multidisciplinary reading, 240
   and peer relationships, 169–70, 176, 177, 179–80
   and sense of purpose, 251, 254
   and taking students' efforts seriously, 251
Mount Royal University, 169
multiculturalism, 223
multidisciplinary reading in humanities course, 239–54
   assessing writing to evaluate reading, 246–49
   and blogging about reading, 244–46, 250, 252
   course mechanics, 243–46
   and defamiliarization, 239, 240–43, 248, 249–50, 253, 254
   discomfort generated in, 240, 242–43, 254
   impact of, 249–54, 249t
   and metacognitive growth, 239–40, 248
   and motivation of students, 239, 240, 244, 251, 254
   rubric used to assess, 239, 240, 247–49, 250–51, 252–53
   and students' sense of responsibility and ownership, 246, 254
   synthesis focus in, 245–46, 250–51, 254
Murphy, Lynn, 13, 44, 46, 49, 51, 55
Murray State University, 87
music studies. *See* Advanced Research and Writing course

naturally situated cognition, concept of, 28
Nilson, Linda B., 45, 56, 169, 208, 209
nonvisualizing readers, 40
normalization of difficulty and confusion in reading, 50–51, 53
Norton-Meier, Lori, 48
Novak, Gregor, 212

Odom, Mary Lou, 14, 67, 244
online collaborative learning (OCL)
   impact on local dialects, 177–79
   impact on reading compliance, 168–69, 170, 174–79, 180
   relationships forged during, 169, 175, 180
online resources
   and big-world reading, 35
   confidence building through, 161
   interactive modules, 149, 150, 151, 153, 157, 160–61
optimal reading conditions, 31, 39
oral language development, 6
organic chemistry, reading compliance in, 166–80

and confidence of students, 178, 179
influence of peer relationships in, 169–70, 176, 177, 179–80
and interlanguage, 167, 169, 170, 173–74, 178
and local dialects, 177–79
and low engagement with learning materials, 167–68
and study design, 171–72, 172
and study methodology, 172–74
and study participants, 170–71, 170
and symbolic language, 166, 167, 179

passive absorption of information, 113–14, 117
patterns interpretive strategy, 222, 226, 228, 229–30, 232, 234
Paulson, Eric J., 2, 8
pedagogical scholarship, 3–4
peer interaction
 and international relationships, 175–76
 and motivation of students, 169–70, 176, 177, 179–80
 and online collaborative learning, 169, 175, 180
 students' appreciation of, 161
 through writing, 131
 in workshop setting, 152, 158
Peers, Michelle, 9
Petrosky, Anthony, 74
podcasts, 31
Porter, Heather D., 8, 252
Prensky, Marc, 84
Prior, Paul, 67
problem solving
 of organic chemistry students, 168
 in Reading Apprenticeship framework, 52, 56, 61
productive readers, 73–75
pronunciations
 regional, 178, 179
 and vocabulary acquisition, 198, 199
psychology of domain learning, 68
psychology scholarship, student preparedness in. *See* Analytical Reading in Psychology course

quizzes
 contingent teaching in response to, 212, 214
 and metacognitive routines, 58
 promoting reading compliance with, 57–58, 206–7, 208–9, 210

and technology-enhanced learning, 160, 210

Ravas, Tammy, 86, 93, 94
reading aloud, 129
Reading Apprenticeship (RA) framework, 44–61
 development of self-regulated learners, 45
 literature review, 47–49
 metacognitive conversation/tools in, 46, 49, 51–52, 54, 55, 59, 60–61
 methodology, 49–50
 multiple dimensions addressed in, 46
 and reading logs, 46, 53–54, 58, 59
 and STEM educators, 55, 56–57, 59–60
 threshold concept: reading difficulties catalyze learning, 50–54, 61
 threshold concept: reading is active learning, 55–61
 and time constraints in classrooms, 55, 57
 and upper-division students, 58
reading guides, 207, 210–12, 213
reading logs, 46, 53–54, 58, 59
reading the world, 220, 223–25, 231. *See also* transferability of reading skills
reading-to-write, 123–40
 and abstract writing, 130–31, 133
 and agency of doctoral students, 137–39
 and critical annotated bibliographies, 131–32, 133
 and critical thinking, 137, 139
 and critique writing, 131, 133
 and drafting literature reviews, 133
 low levels of instruction on, 123
 and mapping fields of knowledge production, 132–33
 and metacognitive awareness, 133, 134–35
 and reader agency, 124
 and relationship of academic writing to reading, 125–26
 and scaffolding principle, 128, 133
 and shifts in reading practices, 135–37
 strategies required for literature reviews, 125
 and textual reengagements, 132
 and transparency principle, 128, 129–30
 See also Advanced Research and Writing course
Reading VALUE Rubric, 239, 240, 247–49, 250–51, 252–53
reasons for reading, 34–35

recall, 33, 40
recreational reading
　impact of academic reading on, 36
　and self-awareness of reading proclivities, 26, 40, 41
　value of, 30
Reeve, Johnmarshall, 168, 177
Reichard, David A., 4
Reisser, Linda, 179
rereading, 33, 34, 40, 208
respecting readerly autonomy, 25, 41
rhetorical awareness, 3, 48, 136, 188, 193, 194, 197, 198, 221–23, 231
Rhodes, Lynne A., 244, 245, 250–51
risky/safe reading preferences, 34–35, 39
Robinson, Rhonda, 81
Roehrig, Alysia D., 186
Rosenblatt, Louise, 7, 38, 39, 145, 221–22, 244
Russell, David, 67

safe/risky reading preferences, 34–35, 39
Salinger, Terry, 32–33
scaffolding
　and cognitive apprenticeship, 10
　and contingent teaching, 212–13
　in doctoral programs, 124, 127, 128, 130–32
　and first-year science students, 145–47, 159–60, 162
　and metacognitive awareness of faculty, 78
　and multidisciplinary reading, 240, 252
　in Reading Apprenticeship framework, 61
　and reading guides, 210
　and recommendations for instruction, 162
scanning techniques, instruction in, 150
Schoenbach, Ruth, 13, 44, 46, 49, 51, 55
scholarship of teaching and learning (SOTL)
　about, 3–5
　and Advanced Research and Writing course at Shenandoah Conservatory, 127–28
　and common language for trading ideas, 69
　and faculty development opportunities, 75, 77
　impact of, 4, 95, 205, 206
　and standards of evidence, 28
　student participation in, 77, 214, 225, 227
　as transdisciplinary opportunity, 15
　as transformational, 3, 95
　types of questions, 75, 103
Scholes, Robert, 65, 66, 73, 129, 133, 138, 244

science students, first-year, 143–62
　challenges faced by, 144–45
　confidence of, 144, 145, 155, 156, 157, 158
　description of curriculum design initiative, 147–52
　evaluation of curriculum design initiative, 152
　and exposure to primary literature, 146–47, 149, 157
　factors underpinning success of initiative, 159–61
　and flipped blended learning approach, 147, 160–61
　importance of reading instruction for, 143–44
　and lack of guidance, 144–45
　online modules and face-to-face workshop for, 150, 151, 152
　reactions of students to curriculum, 153–55
　recommendations for instruction, 162
　techniques for teaching reading to, 145–47
self-awareness of reading proclivities, 26, 40, 41
self-perception of readers, 36–37
self-regulated learners, 45, 168
Sense and Sensibility (Austen), 243, 246
sentence structure, understanding, 194, 197–98
series readers, 34
Shanahan, Cynthia, 12, 13
Shanahan, Timothy, 12, 13
Shapiro, Dan, 15, 44–61
Shemberger, Melony, 86
Shenandoah Conservatory, 124
Shipp, Catelyn, 14, 16, 205–15
Shklovsky, Viktor, 240
Shopkow, Leah, 11, 76
singular works/big-world reading preferences, 35, 39
situated/dedicated reading, 37–38, 39
skimming techniques, instruction in, 150
Smagorinsky, Peter, 48
Snow, Catherine E., 188, 192, 247
social comparison theory, 168, 175
"Sonnet" (Hayes), 229–30, 233
sounds, distinguishing between, 6
Spivey, Nancy Nelson, 241
Stark, Megan, 86, 93, 94
STEM (science, technology, engineering, and mathematics)
　and cognitive apprenticeship, 10–11

and Reading Apprenticeship (RA) framework, 55, 56–57, 59–60
symbolic language in, 166, 167, 179
See also organic chemistry, reading compliance in; science students, first-year
Sternberg, Robert J., 27
strategic reading performed by faculty, 72–73
structure of texts, 136, 150, 153–55, 158, 160, 188, 193, 194, 198, 251
student collaborators, 77, 214–15, 225, 227
surface/depth interpretive strategy, 221–22, 226, 228, 229, 231–32, 234
Swales, John M., 3
Sweeney, Susan, 82, 90
symbolic language in STEM fields, 166, 167, 179
synthesis, 2, 132, 229, 230, 241, 245–46, 250–51, 254

Takayama, Kathy, 4
Tarone, Elaine, 167
teaching commons, 4
teaching reading at university, 8–11
  developmental reading classes, 8
  disciplinary classes, 9–11
  faculty development opportunities, 11
  freshman composition classes, 8–9
  knowledge gained from, 29
textbooks, 34–35
texting, 37
They Say / I Say (Graff and Birkenstein), 188, 193, 198
Thompson, Dana Statton, 8, 15, 81–99
Thomson, Pat, 126, 127, 130–32
threshold concepts
  application of, 46–47
  characteristics of, 47, 235
  and faculty development, 11, 61
  liminal states in engagement of, 48, 235
time constraints in classrooms, 55, 57, 205
time required for academic reading/work, 135–36, 207, 212
Tomkins, Silvan, 240, 254
Toth, Christopher, 86
transferability of reading skills, 219–36
  barriers to, 234
  challenges associated with, 2–3, 9
  discussion of findings, 234–36
  and reading as process of discernment, 234–35, 236
  and reading the world, 220, 223–25, 231

students' applications of strategies, 229–33
students' perceptions of, 227–29
study design, 225–27
study results, 227–33
translation, reading as exercise in, 73–74
transparency, 57, 128, 129–30
The Truman Show (film), 231

undergraduate students, 8, 9, 158, 161, 252
University of Illinois Springfield (UIS), 170, 173
University of Wisconsin–Madison, 219
upper-division students, 58, 161
Urquhart, Sarah M., 127

Van Pletzen, Ermien, 125, 137
Vasquez, Kris, 16, 184–201
visual literacy, 81–99
  "checklist" approach to image evaluation, 85, 90
  and concept of critically reading images, 90
  and CRAAP Test, 86–87
  criteria used in image evaluation, 90–94
  critical importance of, 7–8, 81, 98
  and critical reading standards, 83–84
  definition of, 83–84
  and Digital Images Guide (DIG) Method, 95, 96, 97
  disciplines with instruction on, 94
  and future areas of study, 95
  and lack of criteria for evaluating images, 87
  limitations of study, 94–95
  limited instruction on, 82, 90, 94
  literature review, 82–87
  methodology, 87–88, 98–99
  recognition of alterations to images, 84–85
  recommendations for instruction, 84, 97
  and rise of visual culture, 83
  seven standards of, 83
  students' struggles with, 97–98
  study population, 88, 89t
  "Visual Literacy Competency Standards for Higher Education" (Association of College and Research Libraries), 83
vocabulary acquisition, 190, 192–93, 198–99, 210
Vygotsky, 48, 146, 168, 212

Walker, Clay, 137
Wardle, Elizabeth, 9, 48, 224
Wilder, Laura, 221–24
Williams, Rihana S., 186
Willingham, Daniel T., 5, 6, 208
Wohl, Hannah, 123, 124, 138, 140
Wolf, Maryanne, 17, 27
Wolfe, Joanna, 221–24
workshops, face-to-face, 150, *151*, 152, 153, 157, 158, 160, 161
Wright, Elizabeth, 86
writing
   blogging, 244–46, 250, 252
   evaluating reading through assessing, 246–49
   low levels of instruction on, 123
   and reading in composition classes, 9
   relationship between reading and, 48, 125–26, 129, 244
"Writing about Music Is Writing First" (Christgau), 131
writing across the curriculum (WAC), 13–14
writing in the disciplines (WID), 14, 221, 224
Wu, Yuehua, 244

Žakevičiūtė, Rasa, 82
Zehms, Jakob T., 9, 16–17, 219–36
Zito, Angela J., 9, 16–17, 219–36

KAREN MANARIN is Professor of English and Board of Governors Chair in Advanced Literacy at Mount Royal University. Lead author of *Critical Reading in Higher Education: Academic Goals and Social Engagement*, she has also published in a number of teaching and learning journals.

www.ingramcontent.com/pod-product-compliance
Lightning Source LLC
Chambersburg PA
CBHW030613230426
43661CB00053B/1963